Life in Victorian Era Ireland

Life in Victorian Era Ireland

Ian Maxwell

PEN & SWORD
HISTORY

AN IMPRINT OF PEN & SWORD BOOKS LTD.
YORKSHIRE – PHILADELPHIA

First published in Great Britain in 2023 by
Pen & Sword History
An imprint of
Pen & Sword Books Ltd
Yorkshire - Philadelphia

ISBN 978 1 39904 255 0

Typeset in INDIA by IMPEC eSolutions Printed and bound in the UK by
CPI Group (UK) Ltd, Croydon, CRO 4YY

Pen & Sword Books Limited incorporates the imprints of Atlas, Archaeology,
Aviation, Discovery, Family History, Fiction, History, Maritime, Military,
Military Classics, Politics, Select, Transport, True Crime, Air World,
Frontline Publishing, Leo Cooper, Remember When, Seaforth Publishing,
The Praetorian Press, Wharncliffe Local History, Wharncliffe Transport,
Wharncliffe True Crime and White Owl.

For a complete list of Pen & Sword titles please contact PEN & SWORD
BOOKS LIMITED 47 Church Street, Barnsley, South Yorkshire S70 2AS,
United Kingdom E-mail: enquiries@pen-and-sword.co.uk Website: www.pen-
and-sword.co.uk

or

PEN AND SWORD BOOKS 1950 Lawrence Rd, Havertown, PA 19083,
USA E-mail: Uspen-and-sword@casematepublishers.com Website: www.
penandswordbooks.com

Contents

Contents

Prelude

God Save the Queen!

The coronation of the eighteen-year-old princess Alexandrina Victoria took place on 28 June 1838. The new Queen's ministers were determined to put on a spectacle: the royal procession to Westminster Abbey was revived for the first time since the coronation of George III in 1761, and 400,000 of her loyal subjects journeyed to London to witness it. In Ireland, the coronation was greeted with almost universal enthusiasm in the popular press. It had been more than thirty-five years since Robert Emmet had been executed for leading a failed insurrection in Dublin. The country was largely peaceful in comparison with the social unrest in industrial England, where Chartism, a working-class movement for political and social change, attracted mass support, leading to fears of insurrection. The radical left in English cities, whose press complained of the expense in the run-up to the Coronation, had some success in dampening public enthusiasm in Manchester, where a campaign organised by trade unions and other groups reduced the attendance at the local procession organised by the city council to a third of the turnout of that for the previous coronation of William IV only seven years before.

In Dublin, on the other hand, the *Freeman's Journal* reported that 'there was an universal manifestation of loyalty and satisfaction at this happy advent among all classes of the citizens of Dublin'. The newspaper declared proudly, 'So general a demonstration of public feeling had been unexampled in the city: without compulsion or intimidation the whole town was illuminated; even the humblest abodes in the obscurest streets contributed upon this joyous occasion in the universal display of lights which were everywhere conspicuous.'

The Post Office in Sackville Street, 'was very tastefully lit with gas and oil. Across the pillars of this fine building was placed a large crown, on either side of which were the letters V.R. all displayed by gas burners. On the building itself, letters forming "God save the Queen" were exhibited by golden-coloured oil lamps – on the sides there were crowns and stars in variegated lamps.'[1] The multitude that filled the streets were in holiday mood: crowded trains plied backward and forward to the quays and pier of Kingstown harbour to attend the Dublin Bay Regatta organised by the Royal Irish Yacht Club in honour of the club's patroness, the new Queen.

In Cork, a review of troops stationed in the city was held in the exercise field near the barracks in the presence of an immense number of spectators: the correspondent of the *Southern Reporter and Cork Commercial Courier* gushed, 'A feeling of enthusiastic loyalty is everywhere observable towards the young and interesting Sovereign under whose auspicious, and, we trust, long and prosperous reign, every benefit may be expected for this country, and who is now presented to the contemplation of her admiring subjects at the outset of her career in every gracious and benign aspect, glittering like the morning star, full of life and splendour and joy.'[2] In Drogheda, 'All the houses were profusely decorated with branches and flowers, and several elegant triumphal arches in different parts of the streets added not a little to the picturesque and novel appearances of our crowded thoroughfares.'[3] Waterford Corporation had objected to such overt declarations of loyalty, but *The Chronicle* boasted that, 'the citizens were determined to exhibit the strength of their attachment to the Queen' and 'the morning was ushered by stirring peels from the Cathedral bells, and the firing of guns from the vessels in the river, which on this occasion, were decked out in their gayest colours. Throughout the day the city presented a scene of busy animation. In all directions preparations were making to giving éclat to the event. In the different streets, with the exception of a very few houses, it was apparent that there would be illuminations, and the preliminaries for that object were well-nigh completed in every quarter.'[4]

In the more overtly loyal North, the celebrations were even more enthusiastic. The factory bells were silent in Belfast and the smoky vapour that usually covered the city was notably absent. The clatter of steam engines, which was such a feature of the city, was hushed as crowds made their way from every street southward in the direction of the Botanic Gardens. The *Belfast Commercial Chronicle* reported with pride, 'In no other town in Ireland – the metropolis itself not excepted – has the Coronation of our young and interesting Queen been so enthusiastically celebrated, or given occasion to so evident a spirit of good natured enjoyment, as in the good old town of Belfast.' The article continued breathlessly, 'Early on Thursday morning the town was astir, and from its being a complete holiday, and the crowds of people arriving from the country, the streets had unusually crowded appearance. The shops and public establishments were closed – all were in holiday attire, and everything presented lots of gaiety and happiness.'[5]

The Queen's coronation marked a period of optimism in Anglo-Irish relations. It was popularly believed the young Queen had inherited the Liberal outlook of her father and mother the Duke and Duchess of Kent. Daniel O'Connell, founder of the Repeal Association that campaigned for legislative independence under the Crown, and known among his supporters as 'The Liberator', was optimistic that a long era of good government for Ireland under the Whig administration, had begun. 'There lives not a man,' he said, 'less desirous of a separation between the two countries; there lives not a man more deeply convinced that the connection between them, established on the basis of one Sovereign and separate Parliaments, would be of the utmost value to the happiness of both countries and the liberties of the civilised world.' His burly figure was conspicuous in the quadrangle at St James's Palace on 21 June 1837, the day after the death of William IV, when the young Queen appeared at a window of the Palace to be presented to her subjects.

At a meeting of the General Association, which he had founded to campaign for Catholic emancipation, O'Connell moved the following address to the Queen, which was unanimously adopted by members: 'We, the undersigned electors, and other inhabitants of the city of Dublin, beg leave to approach your Majesty with the tender of our most dutiful and unalterable allegiance to your Majesty's person and Government. We look forward, with confidence, to the cheering prospect which lies before us, of a long reign of prosperity to all parts of the empire, and of happiness and glory to our revered Sovereign.' She was assured that all the faithful people of Ireland wanted was 'a system of equal laws, privileges, and political institutions with the rest of the British empire; they wish for no more, and they would not deserve your Majesty's gracious protection, if they could be content with less.'[6]

For Ireland the future seemed full of hope: O'Connell wrote to the General Association on 28 June 1838: 'It being now certain that the young Queen – whom may God bless – places full confidence in that ministry which was the first during six centuries to desire honestly and faithfully to serve the people of Ireland – we must all, with one accord, rally round the throne of the Queen, and in support of her Majesty's government.' He considered it a propitious moment in the history of the two nations, 'This is the most happy period to work out the experiment. Ireland is now prepared to amalgamate with the entire empire. We are prepared for full and perpetual conciliation. Let Cork County and Yorkshire be put on a footing – let Ireland and England be identified. But for this purpose equality – of rights, laws and liberties – is essentially necessary. We desire no more, we will not take less. A real effectual union, or no union – such is the alternative.'[7]

The nineteenth century would indeed usher in a period of monumental change in Ireland. The railways, forged through the famine-stricken countryside, would transform the local economy, providing employment, developing towns across the country and provide the impetus for Ireland's first tourist boom. A succession of British governments would take an increasingly interventionist role in education and social reform: a national school system was established across the country that provided free elementary education for all children a full four decades before the establishment of a similar system in England. For those less fortunate, the Irish poor law system helped to eradicate the perennial problem of begging and vagrancy in the streets and would, in time, form the basis of a state-sponsored public health system. Local government was fundamentally overhauled and would introduce a significant amount of local democracy, providing opportunities for a growing number of Catholic professionals and politicians. Looking back over the century, the writer James Macaulay observed that Ireland had changed out of all recognition to that popularised by those such as Charles Lever and William Carleton and which enjoyed writers great success with English audiences in the early nineteenth century: 'The rollicking, reckless, fighting, fox-hunting squire or squireen; the half-pay captain of dragoons, professional duellist, gambler, and scamp; the punch-imbibing and humorous story-telling priest; the cringing tenantry and lawless peasantry; how unreal and unrepresentative all these characters seem now!'[8]

On the other hand, the early optimism felt by Daniel O'Connell would soon evaporate. By 1841 a more hostile Tory government had returned to power, persuading O'Connell to revive his campaign for the repeal of the Act of Union and the restoration of a parliament in Dublin. The mass movement he marshalled would, like the short-lived 1848 rising, be subsumed by the Great Famine, as a starving peasantry fought for survival. Those who emigrated to Britain and America in particular, developed a more physical-force nationalism, which would manifest itself in the Fenian Rising of 1867. Domestically Irish Home Rule would become the major force in Irish politics, prompting the opposition of the Unionist majority in the north-east of the island. Both sides were further entrenched by the second South Africa War at the end of the old Queen's reign, which ended with Ireland in a more reflective and uncertain mood than had greeted her accession more than sixty years earlier.

There are many books that tackle the political developments in the nineteenth century. The aim of this book is to show what life was like in Ireland during the last full century of British rule: to illustrate through contemporary sources the concerns and preoccupations of the majority of its people as they went about their ordinary lives. It covers a period of sixty-four years when the only thing that its disparate decades and generations had in common was the fact that the same head of state presided over them. It is a social history, in so far as politics can be divorced from everyday life in Ireland, which demonstrates the complexities of an age in which the vast majority lived in extreme poverty. It examines the impact of religion on the habits and customs of the people, the development of the towns and the countryside, changes in law and order and public health, the revolution in transport and the shattering impact of the Great Famine. On a lighter note, popular entertainment, superstitions, and marriage customs are explored through the eyes of the Victorians themselves.

With such a long period to cover and a wealth of contemporary material to explore, it is inevitable that in the process of selection much had to be trimmed or curtailed. However, I hope that this book will give the reader a better understanding of what Ireland was like during the period and encourage them to consider the complexities and paradoxes of an era that is still deeply embedded in many aspects of our culture today.

Chapter 1

A City of Lamentable Contrasts

At the beginning of the nineteenth century Dublin, with a population of over 230,000, could still claim for itself the title of "second city of the British Empire"; however, with the passing of the Act of Union in 1800, and the loss of its Parliament, it was largely bypassed by the industrial expansion of the Victorian era that transformed cities like Belfast, Manchester and Birmingham. It remained, nevertheless, the administrative, military, and cultural capital of Ireland, the headquarters of the medical profession and the superior courts of law, the banking and insurance business, the seat of two universities, and a busy port. With its grand public buildings, Dublin remained for most visitors the first port of call on their Irish odyssey, attracted by its faded grandeur that lingered on throughout the nineteenth century.

Situated on the western extremity of Dublin Bay and the River Liffey, the city itself extended in a 3-mile circumference from its centre and was surrounded on one side by the rich pastureland of Meath and on the other by the Wicklow mountains. Approached from the northern roads, the visitor in the 1830s was rewarded with some of Dublin's finest streets. Lewis' *Topographical Dictionary* (1837), enthused, 'In addition to the splendid line of communication afforded by the quays on both sides of the river, there are several noble avenues of fine streets, among which, that from the northern road is peculiarly striking, especially on entering Sackville-street, which is conspicuous for its great width, the magnificence and beauty of the public buildings which embellish it, and the lofty monument to Admiral Viscount Nelson, which stands in its centre.'[9]

On the southern side of the city, the road from Kingstown,[10] its port, into Dublin, was equally imposing. Novelist William Makepeace Thackeray thought that the southern entrance to the capital 'very handsome'. 'There is no bustle and throng of carriages, as in London', he mused, 'but you pass by numerous rows of neat houses, fronted with gardens and adorned with all sorts of gay-looking creepers. Pretty market-gardens, with trim beds of plants and shining glasshouses, give the suburbs a *riante* and cheerful look; and, passing under the arch of the railway, we are in the city itself. Hence you come upon several old-fashioned, well-built, airy, stately streets, and through Fitzwilliam Square, a noble place, the garden of which is full of flowers and foliage. The leaves are green, and not black as in similar places in London; the red brick houses tall and handsome.'[11]

The southern road met the north road at College Green, which had in its centre an equestrian statue of William III of cast metal, upon a pedestal of marble. It served as a focal point for annual Orange celebrations on 1 July, the anniversary of the Battle of the Boyne, and on 4 November, the king's birthday. On these dates the statue was painted white, the figure adorned with a yellow cloak, the horse garlanded with orange lilies and ribbons, and the surrounding railings painted orange and blue. Placing shamrock and green and white ribbons under the horse's uplifted foot was even more provocative to nationalists, who retaliated with stone throwing and rioting.[12]

Victorian Dublin was celebrated for its squares, which were enclosed with high iron railings and were the preserve of the wealthy inhabitants of the surrounding houses and a few subscribers who possessed a key to open the gate. German journalist Johann Kohl commented, 'As elegant clubs are, in London, more numerous than elegant houses of public resort, so in Dublin squares are more numerous than public gardens. The wealthy and privileged classes have entirely monopolized the enjoyment of these squares.' Kohl found that there was usually a painted board set up near the gate bearing the legend 'Any person imitating the keys of this square is liable to a fine of five pounds.'[13]

These fine squares, royal and military statuary and imposing public buildings gave Dublin an imperial aspect, as noted by a German visitor Johann Kohl, who considered Dublin uncharacteristic of the rest of the country, 'Dublin is, in its exterior, an entirely English city,' he reflected:

> the public buildings are just as rich in ornaments and columns, as full of rotundas, colonnades, and porticos, as the public buildings of English cities, like the houses of Pericles on the Acropolis of Athens ... Nelson's Pillar (a lofty, handsome column) stands in the middle of Sackville-street, the most splendid street in Dublin; whilst Wellington Testimonials and King George's Statues are as plentiful in the city as in English towns. Trinity College (the Dublin University) has its beautiful walled-in garden, like the Oxford colleges; and the Castle, the seat of the Viceroy, is a repetition of many similar castles to be found in England. You must not however imagine, because you are now in a Catholic country, that this its capital possesses anything peculiar in the way of old churches and cloisters, splendid Catholic cathedrals, or many-coloured chapels at the street corners. One remarks as little of Catholicism in Dublin as of Protestantism in Prague – just as little as in all the other towns of the British Empire.[14]

Dublin Castle embodied Dublin's position as an imperial city. The Castle had served as the seat of English government from the twelfth century. It was the office of the Lord Lieutenant or Viceroy, the senior member of the Irish executive, who with the Chief Secretary and the Under Secretary, was responsible for the implementation of Irish policy. Paschal Grousset paints a fairly stark picture of Dublin Castle, 'This is no Government office of the ordinary type, the dwelling of the Lord-Lieutenant of Ireland is a regular stronghold, encircled with ramparts, bristling with towers, shut up with portcullis, draw-bridge and iron bars.'[15] Highly sympathetic to Irish Home Rule, Grousset declared, 'The barracks of the English soldiers and of those giant constables whom you see about the town are also fortified with walls, and form a line of detached forts round the central stronghold. England is encamped at Dublin, with loaded guns and levelled rifles, even as she is encamped at Gibraltar, in Egypt, and in India.'

The British army regiments stationed in Dublin and around the country were a conspicuous reminder that Irish loyalty could not be taken for granted. As a London correspondent reminded the readers of the *Derby Daily Telegraph* in 1880, 'It worth bearing in mind that at the present moment Ireland is the most heavily garrisoned section of the empire – that is, in, proportion to its size. The troops stationed in Ireland are three to one of those quartered Scotland, and if we push the comparison according to the scale of population it far exceeds the strength of the Indian Army.'[16] The arch Imperialist Joseph Chamberlain MP put it more bluntly, 'The [English] system in Ireland, is founded on the bayonets of 30,000 soldiers, encamped permanently in a hostile country.'[17] For most of the Victorian period up to half this number were stationed in Dublin, based in eight barracks around the city. The predominance of army officers at social events was noted by many visitors to Dublin, including Henry Inglis, who observed, 'It has an undue proportion of the military classes. Few cities of its size have so big a garrison, so many officers and their connections, so extensive a social set associated with the army. That can easily be proved when a function of a military kind, such as a tournament or a ball, is held.'[18]

The function of the Lord Lieutenant was largely ceremonial, and his reputation often depended upon the generosity of his entertainment and successful dispensation of his patronage. The focal point of the social season was the move of the Lord Lieutenant from his out of season residence, the Viceregal Lodge in Phoenix Park, to live in state in the Viceregal Apartments in Dublin Castle, where he and his wife hosted a series of levees, drawing rooms, banquets and balls in the Castle from January to St Patrick's Day on 17 March each year. During this period, the major and minor nobility left their country residences and lived in Georgian mansions in places like Rutland Square, Mountjoy Square, Merrion Square and Fitzwilliam Square in Dublin.

The Viceregal court was the centre of Dublin society and to be asked to the Castle or to know people at the Castle ensured one of a certain social standing. Journalist and Irish Nationalist politician Justin McCarthy, who was not invited, recalled in his *Irish Recollections* (1912):

> The Viceroy and his Court still made their claims for supremacy very distinctly felt and effectively exercised them over the regions of rank and society and fashion. If in those days some ambitious head of an Irish family, not quite patrician in his origin, were filled with the desire to bring his wife and his sons and daughters into the inner circles of society, he knew well that there was little likelihood of his being able to accomplish such a feat unless he could first attract for them the favourable notice of the Lord-Lieutenant. Once introduced to the Castle the Dublin world might then be said to be all before him when he chose. Without that preliminary mark of recognition our aspirant must indeed have possessed some extraordinary charm of wealth and influence in order to prevail upon the world of Dublin fashion to acknowledge the existence of himself and his family. I need hardly tell my readers in general that among the qualities which won ready favour from Dublin Castle an avowed devotion to Ireland's national cause did not hold a place.[19]

Although Dublin was largely abandoned by the aristocracy with the closure of its Parliament in 1800, for those who attended Castle functions the maintenance of social divisions remained paramount.

The *Dublin Evening Telegraph* declared, 'Dublin is peculiarly, in proportion to its size, a city of the classes, that is, of the well-to do people.' At the top was a mainly Protestant professional class, although as the nineteenth century progressed the proportion of Catholics in the various professions rose steadily. Within the professional class the newspaper pointed out that there were more subtle divisions which it divided into six classes – the official, the military, the learned, the legal, the clerical, and the visiting.[20] This reflected the fact that much of the legal business of the country gravitated to Dublin, which also boasted numerous hospitals both state funded and private. Dublin provided the headquarters for major Irish banks, the largest military garrison in the country, had a Protestant and Catholic cathedral and many churches, two universities, and was the headquarters for the rapidly expanding civil service that administered education, public health, the police, prisons, hospitals, welfare institutions and local government. The Dublin-based *Irish Society* newspaper, which championed middle-class virtues on a weekly basis, observed, 'These are your people of the villas, the great houses, the squares, the crescents and terraces,' while the correspondent of the *Dublin Evening Telegraph* viewed them as 'the people of front seats at concerts and churches, the people of boxes and circles and stall at theatres, the people whom you will see in carriages and cabs or on cars, the people who find recreation and amusements in balls, bazaars, dinners, drives, clubs, and lectures'.[21] William Makepeace Thackeray, as was his habit, was not impressed, 'There is no aristocracy in Dublin. Its magnates are tradesman –Sir Fiat Haustus, Sir Blacker Dosy, Mr. Sergeant Bluebag, or Mr. Counsellor O'Fee. Brass plates are their titles of honour and they live by their boluses or their briefs. What call have these worthy people to be dangling and grinning at lord-Lieutenants' levees, and playing sham aristocracy before a sham sovereign? Oh, that old humbug of a Castle! It is the greatest sham of all the shams in Ireland.'[22]

Next in the social ladder came the respectable 'shopocracy', which was mixed in religious affiliations and competed with the upper and middle classes for prominence at social events. The *Irish Society* lampooned the rivalry between these groups. 'There are members of this middle-class who will not admit to their magic circle business people, that is, shopkeepers who sell over the counter, but they are pleased to run after and fawn on rich merchants whom they consider equal to professionals. These are the people who have a drawing room – flowerless, dusky, and fireless, except on one day in the week, or, perhaps, fortnight. A room such as that spoken of by one unfortunate lord of creation "as a 'curse'" in his house. He never was permitted to enter it before he had donned his house shoes, and even then he was forbidden to stand on the flossy hearthrug, or to poke the fire lest he should use the sacred brass implement instead of the pokerette so cunningly hidden inside the fender.'[23] *Irish Society* still hankered for the good old days when Dublin was the home of the elite. 'It makes one's teeth water to read the accounts of Dublin society in the last century, when our city was the home of so many brave men and fair woman. Hundreds of nobility, gentry, and famous men, both clerical and lay, who by their lavish expenditure combined with refined taste, wit, and elegance, made Dublin one of the most interesting as well as enjoyable cities in Europe.'[24]

At the beginning of Victoria's reign, the respectable classes could chiefly be found in the eastern parts of the city. The southeastern district, including St Stephen's Green, Merrion Square and Fitzwilliam Square, was chiefly inhabited by the remaining nobility, the gentry and members of the professions. The north-east, including Mountjoy and Rutland Squares, was principally inhabited by the mercantile and official classes. As the *Dublin Daily Express* pointed out, 'To live "on the other side of town," was to show that you did not belong to the "smart set". Every physician or barrister who wished to "rise" was ever struggling to get away from Mountjoy Square or

Gardiner's Place, and to cross Carlisle or O'Connell Bridge into the Promised Land of Fitzwilliam Place or Merrion Square.'[25]

To cater for the needs of this new elite, Lower Sackville Street (now O'Connell Street) became a highly successful commercial location; its terraces lined with purpose-designed shops including Delany's New Mart or 'Monster Store' (later to be purchased by the Clery family), which sold a wide variety of goods. The rise of the Monster Shop, the ancestor of the department store, excited great concern in the papers from the 1850s, 'The gradual diminution in the number of small shops in our metropolis, is a fact which admits of no dispute, and which is exciting a good deal of concern even among parties who have no immediate connexion with the sufferers,' warned the *Dublin Evening Mail*. It predicted that 'those extensive mercantile establishments, denominated Monster Houses, will eventually swallow up and absorb the business of the small traders, and thereby reduce a large number of our most respectable citizens to bankruptcy and ruin'.[26] This was seen to have a negative impact on the social ambitions of the humbler members of the middle classes. 'Until the monster houses were established,' complained the *Dublin Evening Packet*, 'a workman had the prospect before him, that if he could save a few pounds, he might be able to open a shop, and become the seller of articles which he, assisted with his children, could produce; that success might make him in time a small employer of others, and that he might transmit an independence to his children. The success of the monster shops cuts off all such hope from the industrial classes.'[27]

For many in Dublin the issue was academic. Scottish writer Leitch Ritchie, on visiting Sackville Street in 1837, was appalled at the contrast between wealth and poverty he encountered outside its principal hotel, 'in Sackville Street, near the door of Gresham's hotel, I saw lying upon the pavement entirely naked, two children of five or six years of age, shivering and moaning, and crouching close to each other for mutual warmth. This spectacle may, for aught I know, have been a mere charity trap; but the indifference with which it was glanced at by the passers-by proved their daily and hourly familiarity with scenes of misery and destitution.'[28]

By the accession of Queen Victoria the wealthy had vacated substantial townhouses in aristocratic districts such as Gardiner Street and Summer Hill on the north side and these one-family homes were rapidly subdivided to accommodate at least one family per room. Some mansions had been converted into hotels, public offices, charitable asylums, or schools. Charlotte Elizabeth commented ruefully, 'Sad enough it is, in passing on, to realize the fact that the stately abodes of Ireland's aristocracy know their former possessors no longer. Lines of noble houses, converted into hotels, shops, and public institutions, announce what Dublin has been, and too vividly declare what Ireland is.'[29] Dublin-born physician and Chief Medical Officer for the Dublin Corporation Sir Charles Cameron recalled:

> In my childhood days, many of the nobility and landed gentry still occupied houses on the north-east side of Dublin, Gloucester Street, Cumberland Street, Grenville Street, Summer Hill, Buckingham Street, Gardiner Street, and many others were residential localities. With few exceptions, each house was occupied by only one family. As the wealthy moved out poor families moved in to occupy rooms within the properties and outhouses. The coach houses and stables were occupied for the purpose they were designed for. Now, the vast proportion of them are occupied by cab owners, or are converted into dwellings or stores. The houses once tenanted each by a single family are now nearly all tenement houses. In many of them eight or ten families have replaced one family. Many fine houses in this part of Dublin have become dilapidated, and some are in ruins or have altogether disappeared, their sites being now waste places. In what were once private houses, shops, generally of a poor class, have been formed. Had I been absent from Dublin since the days

of my childhood until the present year, I would hardly have recognised a large part of North-East Dublin.[30]

This trend continued throughout the rest of the century as the middle class quit the city to live in the suburbs thanks to the expanding tram system. In 1899 T.W. Russell MP told the Select Committee of the House of Lords, which was considering extending the city boundaries, 'The exodus of rich people from the city had left behind the poor to people Dublin, and to bear the burdens of the high rates. He could mention whole streets on the north side of the city which when he first came to Dublin were occupied by the professional and mercantile classes who had since decamped.'[31]

In contrast to the more prosperous portions of the city, the south-western district, including the liberties of St Sepulchre and Thomas Court, formerly the seat of the woollen and silk manufacturers, was by the beginning of the Victorian period 'in a state of lamentable dilapidation bordering on ruin', while the north-western area presented 'striking indications of poverty'. English writer Jonathan Binns acknowledged that London was a city of contrasts but in Dublin the contrast between rich and poor was more immediately obvious: 'Dublin is indeed a fine city; but it is a city of lamentable contrasts. If the stranger be forcibly struck by the number and magnificence of the public buildings, and the general beauty of some of the streets, he is sure to be no less forcibly moved by the very different character of those parts which are term "the Liberties." Here, narrow streets, houses without windows or doors, and several families crowded together beneath the same roof, present a picture of ruin, disease, poverty, filth, and wretchedness, of which they who have not witnessed it are unable to form a competent idea.'[32]

Mr and Mrs Hall contrasted the architecture in the Liberties with the state of its inhabitants. 'In passing along its desolate streets, large houses of costly structure everywhere present themselves. Lofty facades adorned with architraves, and mouldings to windows, and door-cases of sculptured stone or marble; grand staircases with carved and gilded balustrades; panelled doors opening into specious suits of corniced and stuccoed apartments – all attest the opulence of its former times.' The magnificence of these surroundings did not hide the poverty within. 'They are now the abode only of the poor,' Mr and Mrs Hall observed, 'and as they decayed, they became the resort of the more abject, who could find no other shelter. So crowded were they at one time, that 108 persons were found in one house lying on the bare floor, and in one room seven out of twelve were labouring under typhus fever.'[33]

A seasoned traveller like Paschal Grousset was appalled by what he encountered in the Dublin sums of the mid-1880s, 'A sickening smell, recalling that of ill-ventilated hospitals, comes out of those lairs and suffocating you, almost throws you back. But it is too late. You have been caught sight of. From all sides visions of horror are emerging to light, spectres are starting up; old hags that would have surprised Shakespeare himself, swarm round you, holding out their hand for a copper.'[34] He was struck by poverty in Nicholas Street, which formed part of the great commercial artery of south Dublin on the way to the cathedral:

> From end to end it is lined with a row of disgusting shops or stalls, where the refuse of the new and the ancient world seems to have come for an exhibition. Imagine the most hideous, ragged, repulsive rubbish in the dust-bins of two capitals, and you will get an idea of that shop-window display; rank bacon, rotten fish, festering bones, potatoes in full germination, wormy fruit, dusty crusts, sheep's hearts, sausages which remind you of the Siege of Paris, and perhaps come from it; all that running in garlands or festoons in front of the stalls, or made into indescribable heaps, is doled out to the customers in diminutive half-pence morsels. At every turning of the street a public-house with its dim glass and sticky glutinous door. Now and then a pawnbroker with the

three symbolic brass balls, and every twenty yards a rag and
bone shop.

Newspapers like the *Freeman's Journal* and *Dublin Daily Nation*
campaigned against this destitution from the 1880s. One correspondent
explored deep into the poorest quarters to investigate the condition of
the destitute. In the warehouse district of Smithfield he found in one
ten-roomed tenement house 'one hundred people have been known
to reside, and the case is no exception at all of overcrowding.' In one
house he found a family of nine occupying a single room:

> The room was scantily furnished – in fact there was no
> room for furniture. One bed stood in the corner of the room,
> three beds occupied the floor. The wife's sister, and two
> little girls, her nieces, slept on one of these beds. A young
> fellow of seventeen, and his brother, aged fourteen, sleep in
> another; while the eldest girl of the family, aged eighteen,
> and her sister, nearly sixteen, slept in the third bed, on the
> floor. A few religious pictures hung on the walls, and the only
> other furniture to be found was comprised in a few broken
> chairs, which were once cane-bottomed, and a dresser, full of
> dilapidated china ware. As for bed covering, there was hardly
> any, and the beds themselves were of straw. The room was
> airy enough, for half a dozen broken panes of glass in the two
> windows provided ample ventilation. The floor had not been
> washed for months. It was an inch think with hardened dirt.
> The whole family could not muster between them a decent
> suit of clothes or a change of clean linen.[35]

In these streets it was a struggle to survive childhood. The
correspondent of the *Freeman's Journal* recounted meeting a child
who approached him begging him to buy matches. 'The child was only
eight years of age, and told me that she was fatherless and lived with

her mother. She dared not go home without at least sixpence or the affectionate mother would "hit" her and send her to bed supperless. "And what does your mother do, my child?" I asked. "She drinks, sir," was the simple reply.'[36]

Sir Charles Cameron was concerned for the sufferings of the children of the labouring poor and the impact it had on their future health. 'They rarely get new articles to wear, and are frequently clothed in the worn-out garments of their parents, ill-adjusted to the size of their new wearers. Thousands of children go with naked feet even in winter. The want of warm clothing in winter often lays the foundation of future delicacy, and renders them less liable to resist the attacks of disease. The want of good food and warm clothing often causes the fatal sequelae to attacks of the measles.'[37]

Life was a struggle for the labourers who came to Dublin from the surrounding countryside in search of work. When in work the labourer was paid on a weekly basis, and often by the day. For them, the only way to make ends meet was to pledge domestic items at the local pawnbrokers to raise some cash for the week ahead. The entrance to a pawnbroker's shop was usually up a side street to save its customers some embarrassment. This sensitivity was not misplaced because pawnbroker's customers were seldom those in abject poverty who had nothing of value to pledge, but those living close to the breadline who were in regular, yet poorly paid work. Clothing was often pledged on a Monday and redeemed on a Saturday after the breadwinner of the family had been paid. It was worn to chapel or church on a Sunday, and pledged again the next day. In the 1880s Paschal Grousset observed that, 'To a man Ireland dresses on the reach-me-down system, and wears out the cast-off garments which have passed on the backs of ten or twelve successive owners. Battered hats, dilapidated gowns, threadbare coats arrive here by shiploads.' He was amazed by the variety of costume he encountered in the streets. 'Knee-breeches, tail coats, white gowns, cocked hats, – Paddy and his spouse are ready for anything. So destitute are they of personal property, that they do not even possess an outline of their own. Their normal get-up resembles a travesty, and their distress a carnival!'[38]

The diet of the labourers, hawkers and those in similar precarious occupations was often meagre. The constant items were bread and tea, butter was not always obtainable, and bread was generally purchased from local bakers rather than baked at home. Baking was taught in very few city schools because the poor had no ovens to bake in. Beef and mutton were not often found on the tables of the poor and when they were they were generally saved for the breadwinner of the family. When they were obtained, they were fried or boiled, because there was no way of roasting them. Bacon was largely used, sometimes as rashers, but more frequently boiled with cabbage. Without the means of cooking, in the Dublin tenements, most food was bought prepared in the street from hawkers who frequently fell foul of the authorities for causing an obstruction on the street and of the Ratepayers' Association whose members had to pay rent and taxes for their shops. By the 1880s tea was drunk in prodigious amounts. It was usually consumed black with sugar and was 'boiled practically to extinction' on the hob or in the hot ashes of the fire. Dr John Lumsden, studying the diet of Irish brewery families, observed, 'The pot [was] replenished with water as long as any colouring matter [could] be produced. Thus all its tannin is extracted, and … Much of the … gastric derangement a doctor sees … chiefly amongst young women … is the result of this pernicious tea drinking habit.'[39]

Another problem for the Victorian digestive system was adulterated food and drinks. Ground bones, plaster, lime and pipe clay were often added to bread, and alum was widely used because it added both weight as well as whiteness. Even more alarming was the addition of potentially lethal salts of copper and lead to colour sweets. In his twelfth annual report, Sir Charles Cameron stated that having analysed 386 types of food and drink in the city, 'Of the adulterated specimens, the milk was adulterated with from 12 to 120 per cent, of water, but with no other adulterant; the bread was adulterated with alum, and in some instances it contained a large quantity of sandy matter. The flour was adulterated with alum, and six of the samples contained grit or sandy matter. The tea was composed of exhausted and decayed leaves, strengthened by the addition of some stringent gums. The coffee was adulterated with chicory and burnt sugar. The rum was wholly spurious, being new whiskey sweetened with treacle, and 25 per cent, under proof. The butter examined contained no foreign matter, but four species were rancid and unfit for use. The oatmeal was very middling, full of fungoid growths and unfit for use.'[40]

'No inconsiderable number of the poor,' as Sir Charles Cameron pointed out in his *Reminiscences*, 'get out of their beds, or substitutes for them, without knowing when they are to get their breakfast, for the simple reason that they have neither money nor credit. They must starve if they have got nothing which would be taken in pawn.' The alternative were the many charitable institutions in the city. One such was the free breakfast that could be obtained in the Christian Union Buildings, Lower Abbey Street. The correspondent from the *Dublin Daily Express* in 1888 witnessed a typical scene that could be replicated in many parts of the city. Their numbers included, not only the unemployed, but peddlers, costermongers, labourers, fiddlers, porters, and painters as well as professional beggars:

A crowd of 500 or 600 poor creatures had assembled in the neighbourhood of the Buildings when I arrived at half-past seven o'clock. This crowd gradually increases till eight o'clock. According as the crowd enters each person is supplied with a mug or tin and a package rolled in tissue paper of bread and butter quite large enough to supply the wants of a hungry individual. The seats in the building are so arranged that those arriving first are placed towards the front of a large platform at the upper end of the basement, seated for large choir, and the stewards so arrange them as they arrive in succession on the remaining seats, and by 8.15 the whole assembly has been seated and breakfast proper ready to start. A blessing is then asked, and about 30 stewards, each armed with one or two kettles of tea, fill up every mug and tin, beginning with those who had arrived first.'[41]

Diseases such as cholera, typhus and smallpox were endemic in Dublin, as they were in all major cities of the period. Once generated, disease spread from room to room and from floor to floor of the city's slums and was carried back to the houses of the rich by servants and employees. Inadequate sewerage systems, poor water supplies, slaughterhouses, and obnoxious activities such as soap-making and lime-burning right in the midst of the crowded population all contributed to the situation. A public meeting convened by a number of doctors in 1865 discussed means of dealing with the 'obnoxious and poisonous effluvia' that emanated from Dublin's chemical and manure works. A subsequent leader in the *Irish Times* about Dublin's air pollution stated that from the quays the observer 'sees a dense mass of heavy clouds ever thickening and slowing rolling onward to the West, if the East wind blows. A stranger would believe the heavens threatened a thunderstorm, the resident in Dublin feels that the atmosphere is in its normal states. Seven tall chimneys pour forth in volumes rolling pillars of smoke and round the tall chimneys are evolved gasses of every description, which unite in the air, and forming a horrible combination steal under doors and windows, and half suffocate people in their beds.'[42]

The city's high death rate remained a major scandal throughout the Victorian period and by the end of the century it was found to be equivalent to that found in London fifty years earlier. Sir Charles Cameron and eminent Dublin surgeon Edward Mapother's report into the high death rate in Dublin, published in February 1879, gives an interesting insight into the many causes of disease in the Irish capital. 'The average annual number of deaths in Dublin, from 1868 to 1877, inclusive, was 8,795, of which 2,589 were caused by phthisis and diseases of the breathing organs. We have no hesitation in asserting that a large proportion of these deaths were caused by damp in clothes, houses, and sites of dwellings. The thorough and frequent cleansing of the footpaths and streets would enable the roadways to dry more rapidly after rain, and would diminish the actual amount of damp in the streets.' This took its toll on the poorer population who, if they could afford boots or shoes, purchased lighter cheaper ones that were inadequate protection against the damp pavements of the city. 'Severe colds, leading to serious illness, are often the result of wearing thin-soled boots. We think that more attention should be given to the matter of allowing water from house-spouts to be discharged over the footpaths; they should be so arranged that the water would be discharged into the house sewer, or the street gutter, or channel communicating with the sewer. This is a matter for police supervision, and the attention of the police force might be called to it.'[43]

Action was taken to deal with the bad state of housing in the city, at first by bodies such as the Dublin Artisans' Dwellings Company, and from 1884 the Corporation took a more proactive role rehousing people in the poorer districts in newly constructed housing. The authorities were faced with enormous problems when clearing the unsanitary area of the city, as shown by an incident that took place in Temple Lane, off Britain Street, on Monday, 19 September 1898. The Public Health authorities had condemned as unsuitable for habitation a large number of houses and as a result seventeen families were thrown upon the streets. *Freeman's Journal* reported, 'The problem then presented itself to these poor people as to where they were to go. The relieving officer offered them the hospitality of the workhouse; but this was refused, and, unable to find other accommodation for the time being, they there and then literally encamped on the street.' The paper concluded, 'It is all very well to close up unsanitary dwellings; but where are the people to go unless they are to increase the congestion of other districts already overcrowded and unsanitary themselves?'[44]

Many diseases such as typhoid fever, sore throats, and diarrhoea were blamed on defective sewers. At the same time, there was a growing public recognition of the relationship between contaminated water and poor hygiene and the frequency of epidemics that proved fatal to large numbers of people, especially the elderly and children. The first priority, therefore, was the provision of a suitable sewerage network for the city. Cameron and Mapother commented, 'The domestic sewers in Dublin are, as a rule, very defective. In the houses of the best quarters there is commonly to be found a total disregard of the most obvious sanitary precautions. There are but few traps, and such as exist are more frequently out of order than otherwise. The water which is drank is often taken from the cistern which supplies the water closet, instead of from a tap on the water pipe. When a case of typhoid occurs in a house in which the water used is directly or indirectly obtained from a water-closet cistern, the disease is very likely to be spread throughout the household.'

Carrying water from a distance, especially in the more outlying districts, meant that they used it sparingly. Only the better class of house enjoyed the luxury of a direct connection to the water supply.

Contaminated water continued to be an issue for much of the century.

A Dublin Waterworks Commission meeting in 1860 heard that the water conveyed in the water pipes was not particularly clean. One report found that in addition to 'spongillae' the quantity of organic matter in the water was very considerable … and that there was a large quantity of fresh water algae. The pipes were encrusted with these growths, and there was a large quantity of maggots. The Very Rev Spratt gave evidence that the water supplied to the poor was very bad, 'there is nothing like a sufficient supply of water to the poor; very few of them are supplied with water in their own houses; pipes are very rare amongst them, and they are often inconveniently placed, sometimes in a "huckster's" shop for instance, the result of which is that the pipe is more or less used to create patronage.' He deplored the system of fountains in the city. 'At the fountain in Kevin Street large numbers of poor creatures may be seen collected at a late hour at night, waiting for their turn to get a supply of water, many of them having come from a distance, and with very little clothes on them.' 'I have often asked people,' he stated, 'why they lapse into drunkenness, and why they did not drink water at home, and they always say that the water was too bad to drink it.'[45]

Progress was made by Dublin Corporation over the years. In 1868, chiefly through the exertions of Sir John Gray, a pure and plentiful water supply from the Wicklow Hills was secured for every street where the poorer residents had to take their water from public fountains located along the leading thoroughfares. In 1878 the Public Health Act gave local authorities extensive powers that included the construction of drainage systems, regulation of buildings, enforcement of disinfection and sanitation where necessary to prevent infectious disease, the authority to supply water where none was available, regulate slaughterhouses, inspect meat offered for sale, and control lodging houses. Nevertheless, it was best to stay clear of the Liffey, as Captain Paul Boyton, the 'Fearless Frogman', demonstrated in 1890:

> Captain Boyton swam in that limpid stream to demonstrate the efficacy of his swimming costume, he was taken out exhausted, and lay for months in typhoid fever. ... Not a moment passes that we do not inhale the poisonous germs which continuously rise in invisible but fatal crowds from this hideous pool. If for one hour we could be gifted with microscopic eyes, we would see the foul clouds of disease germs spreading from the river, flooding the streets, attacking every person around, and stealthily borne to the remotest houses on the wings of the impalpable air. The entire atmosphere of the city and suburbs must be more or less

impregnated with these zymotic germs, and every person whose constitution is not braced above average health is in momentary danger of death. We may live in the suburbs, but the poison gets into the lungs, and clings in the clothes and – if such matters were patiently traced – many persons who die in Kingstown or Bray should be registered as having succumbed to the Liffey poison.[46]

Chapter 2

Magnificent Castles and Wretched Cabins

In the years before the Great Famine rural Ireland witnessed a rapid increase in population from about 5 million at the time of the Union to more than 8 million by 1841. With few opportunities for employment in local towns or cities, the majority of the rural population had no option but to live on the verge of destitution. Small holdings were divided again and again so that a son, on marriage, could have a scrap of ground on which to build a mud cabin and grow potatoes. Meanwhile, the countryside was dotted with the mansions of the great landowners replete with ballrooms, drawing rooms and libraries and maintained by a large retinue of servants. Traditionally referred to as 'big houses', their size and opulence reflected the often colossal scale of these great estates. Little wonder French radical politician Paschal Grousset condemned Ireland as a country of 'lords and serfs'.

Victorian visitors paint a bleak picture of the Irish countryside. To William Bilton, touring Ireland in the 1830s, the countryside had 'an unusually bare look in the eyes of an Englishman, and reminds him more of the interior of France than the smiling fields of England'. Irish-born lawyer Richard Lalor Sheil had to admit that, 'To those accustomed to English objects, the most fertile tracts look bare and barren. It is the country, but it has nothing rural about it; no luxuriant hedgerows, no shaded pathways, no cottages announcing by the neatness without, that cleanliness and comfort are to be found within; but one undiversified continuity of cheerless, stone-fences and roadside hovels, with their typhus-beds piled up in front, and volumes of murky smoke forth issuing from the interior, where men and women, pigs and children, are enjoying the blessings of our glorious constitution.'[47]

The scarcity of trees was noted by Grousset, 'The most striking thing on a first sight of the Irish landscape is the total absence of trees of any kind. They are only seen in private parks. As far as the eye can see the plains spread in gentle undulations, covered with grass and intersected with stone walls; no single oak, elm, or shrub ever comes to break its monotony. The tree has become a lordly ensign. Whenever one sees it one may be certain the landlord's mansion is not far.'[48]

These great mansions with huge households were often remote and required great organisational skills. The wealthier landlords ordered luxuries from the likes of the Army and Navy Stores in London which were conveyed by rail and steamer on a regular basis and trundled to the great estates by cart. The main household requirements were normally provided by the estate: peat or wood for heating, meat and game from the farm and woods, vegetables and fruit from the walled gardens.

J.M. Callwell recalled in her *Old Irish Life*:

> Our household allowance was a sheep every week and a bullock once a month, all that could not be eaten fresh being salted down in huge stone pickling-troughs. In addition the poultry-yard had its tribes of feathered fowl, farther afield rabbits multiplied in a manner devastating to the young plantations, trout abounded in the lake, so did game in its season. Fuel we had free, too, for we were surrounded by turf-bogs – a very important matter, indeed, in all Irish households in those days, for except in the towns near the coast coal was rarely burnt.[49]

Irish writer Edith Somerville remembered her grandmother's home, Drishane House in Co. Cork:

> Its rooms are lofty, and their proportions pleasant. Of these, the first that may be dealt with is the drawing-room, a place of great sanctity, wherein the foot of child never trod save

by special invitation (or command, which came to the same thing). Its wallpaper was white, spaced into large diamonds with a Greek pattern of gold and it shone like satin. It was less dashing in design than the paper of the inner hall and the staircase, whose pattern was of endless ladders of large blue and orange flowers (tropic, one believed them to be) that raged from the bottom of the house to the top, but the drawing-room was devoted to the ladies, and in it dash gave way to refinement. Portraits of ancestresses hung round it, close to the ceiling, according to the practice of those domestic picture-hangers who hold no brief for Art. Ancestors were relegated to the dinning-room, as being, I suppose, a more suitable environment for the thirstier sex.[50]

House parties formed the basis of landlord entertaining, most of them linked to hunting and shooting during the winter months. In summer there was tennis and cricket: these events were enlivened for the daughters of the house by a ready supply of young army officers from the local garrison. Great family events could also include the tenantry. The coming of age of the Hon. Hamilton Fitz Maurice Beane-Morgan, eldest son of Lord Muskerry, was celebrated by a brilliant ball attended by a large house party. A week later an immense bonfire illuminated the surrounding country as tenants and cottagers on the estate assembled in numbers around it, and 'gave hearty cheers for the popular heir and Lord Muskerry, the former's health being proposed on his birthday by the oldest resident in the neighbourhood, who alluded to the four generations of the Muskerry family he had known, and paid a well-deserved tribute to its present members. Needless to say the toast was drunk with enthusiasm by all present, and Mr Fitz Maurice Deane-Morgan returned thanks in suitable terms.'[51]

Landlords were the main source of local employment; estate works, servants, blacksmiths and stonemasons all looked to patronage from the great estates. At Powerscourt, employees, included gardeners, grooms, coachmen, agricultural labourers, herders, shepherds, gamekeepers, yardmen, blacksmiths, foresters, carpenters, masons and plasterers. At Castle Bellingham in Co. Lough, Sir Henry Bellingham employed a man to rake his gravel drive immediately after anybody had walked on it.[52] The larger the house, the greater the number of servants required to cope with the number of tasks involved. Recruitment of staff was usually through personal recommendations, particularly at the higher levels of housekeeper, governess and cook. Local women found opportunities for employment at the lower levels as maids in the house, kitchen, nursery or dairy. Most big houses imported their upper servants from England, Scotland or Northern Ireland, usually reliably Protestant.

Harriet Martineau, author of *Letters from Ireland* (1851), found that, 'On the whole, Catholic servants are preferred as far as the mere domestic work is concerned; that is, the female servants are Catholics. But it is not denied that the very safest – those who are living, and have lived for thirty years, on good terms with all their neighbours – do feel safer for having Protestant menservants. There is enough of distrust – not of individual neighbours, but of the tyranny of secret organizations – to make even the securest prefer for men-servants persons who are out of the reach of such organization.'[53] Those seeking employment often listed their religion in the newspaper classifieds as well as their accomplishments.

> Groom and coachman – Respectable young man desires situation as above; drives double and single: good rider: Protestant: native of North of Ireland; will be well recommended for strict sobriety and attention to business: desires house.[54]

The death of an employer could leave a servant without a home as well as unemployed. A servant who was discharged because of the break-up of an establishment, or death of an employer, was anxious to secure lodgings as much as employment.

Ladysmaid – Wanted, by a respectable young girl, a situation as above; had served three years to the dressmaking; no objection to travel; salary not so much an object as a comfortable home ...[55]

Local families provided servants over several generations in the same house and the more considerate estate owners rewarded this loyalty by providing a small pension or lodgings on the estate for long-term employees. These retainers were on the sort of familiar terms with their employers that Johann Kohl found disconcerting:

In England, where servants are kept at a proper distance, it is seldom that they venture on the familiar impertinence of which I saw frequent instances in Ireland. My worthy friend's coachman, a well-fed, merry-looking fellow, accompanied us through the stables and farm buildings, and pointed out every remarkable object to my attention, with a constant flow of eloquence, while his master followed modestly behind us. 'This stable you see, sir,' proceeded the coachman, '*we* finished last year. And a deal of trouble it cost us, for we had to begin by blowing away the whole of the rock there. But we shall have a beautiful prospect for our pains when the trees yonder have been cut down. And look down there, your honour, all them is his dominions (pointing to his master), and in two months he'll have finished the new building he has begun.' Now no English servant would have made equally free with his master, and yet the Irish servants are taken from a far more dependant class than the English peasants.

The more philanthropic landowners took an active role in the amelioration of poverty in the neighbouring area. William Makepeace Thackeray noted in the 1840s, after a visit to a gentleman's estate on his way between Carlow and Waterford:

Several men and women appeared sauntering in the grounds, and as the master came up, asked for work, or sixpence, or told a story of want. There are lodge-gates at both ends of the demesne; but it appears the good-natured practice of the country admits a beggar as well as any other visitor. To a couple our landlord gave money, to another a little job of work; another he sent roughly out of the premises: and I could judge thus what a continual tax upon the Irish gentleman these travelling paupers must be, of whom his ground is never free.

The major landowners managed great estates that were often distributed through two or three counties; the Marquess of Downshire had 115,000 acres in Antrim, Down, Kildare, King's County and Wicklow; Lord Landsdowne owned 120,000 acres in Counties Dublin, Kerry, Limerick, Meath and Queen's; and the Marquess of Conyngham owned more than 156,000 acres in Clare, Donegal and Meath. Condemned by Paschal Grousset as 'landowners of foreign origin' and portrayed in the radical press as Ascendancy or English, the landowners were in fact a diverse lot. A significant minority were descended from old Celtic-Irish or Anglo-Norman stock and regarded themselves as wholeheartedly Irish. This included the Duke of Leinster, Ireland's premier peer, and the Marquess of Ormonde, the FitzGeralds or Geraldines and the Butlers. Lord Inchiquin was descended from the 'O'Brien High Kings, Lord Carleton from the ancient kings of Ossory, and the Earl of Antrim from illustrious Celtic ancestors whose lands they still held.[56]

Absentee landlords were particularly vilified in the nineteenth-century press in both Ireland and England. Before 1845 an estimated 33 to 50 per cent of Irish landowners were absentees, although a substantial number of these owned more than one estate and when living on one were effectively absentee on all the others. Absenteeism did not necessarily mean estates were neglected or tenants exploited. Many estates were effectively run by land stewards or agents. The land agent on most estates was the landlord's representative, responsible for the day-to-day running of the estate. Their duties varied, but included collecting rents, setting leases and valuing property. As well as their duties on the estate, they were frequently justices of the peace, poor law guardians, and acting for the employer's candidate during elections. Paschal Grousset was impressed by the role of the agent:

> He is neither a notary, nor a steward, and yet he partakes of both, being the intermediary between the landlord and tenant. It is he that draws up the leases and settlements; he who receives the rents, who sends out summons, who signs every six months the cheque impatiently expected by the landlord; he who represents him at law, he who negotiates his loans, mortgages, cessions of income, and all other banking operations. In a word, he is the landlord's prime minister, the person who takes on his shoulders all the management of his affairs, and reduces his profession to the agreeable function of spending money.[57]

A lease granted by a landlord to a tenant gave him the right to occupy the property for a specific period of time. Two copies of the lease were usually prepared, the original lease was signed by the landlord and kept by the tenant. The counterpart was signed by the tenant and kept by the landlord. A lease was usually for a term of years – one, twenty-one, fifty or ninety-nine – but in Ulster, as in the western half of England, leases were usually for three lives: the lease expired when all the three persons named in the lease died.

S.M Hussey, in *The Reminiscences of an Irish Land Agent*, recalled his role as an agent on Lord Kenmare's estates in Kerry, Cork and Limerick, where he received the standard five per cent of the rents raised. 'Of course the agents as the outward and visible sign of the distant or absentee landlords obtained the greater share of the hatred felt for the later'.

Tenant farmers and their families accounted for half the rural population, numbering about 500,000 in the 1860s. As a group they were more varied than the landlords, their holdings ranging from a few acres to large graziers such as Edward Delany of Woodtown who held 500 acres in Co. Meath. They worked full-time on their farm with the help of their immediate family, hiring labourers to assist in the spring or harvest time. Sometimes they were also landlords to the smallholders and cottiers, subletting land that they rented on long leases from the landowner. Frequently referred to locally as 'respectable' when commentators wished to distinguish between them from the average tenant who held their land from year to year: one observer in the 1840s defined them as having 'very comfortable and independent circumstances ... they settle their sons well and give large portions [dowries] to their daughters on their marriage'. These better-off farmers also employed servants and the whitewashed cottage of the better-off farmer when encountered, was taken by visitors like Thomas Campbell Foster as a sign of 'progressing improvement' in the countryside.[58]

Most tenants had a yearly tenancy and could be evicted with only six months' notice to quit; rents could be increased annually and evicted tenants had no right to compensation for improvements. Gerald Fitzgibbon, one of the Masters in the Irish Chancery, was critical of these small farmers who were in no position to invest in their smallholdings, 'It is a fact, that the ability of the poor man to pay his rent entirely arises from diminution of expenditure in the cultivation of the land, and in the diminution also of expenditure in maintaining the wretched cultivator and his family, who consume but a small part of the produce, and sell the chief part, to provide for the rent, and avoid eviction.' The result, he declared, was:

Machinery is not used; therefore no demand is created for mechanical skill and labour. The farmer and his family are in rags; therefore, no market is created for manufacturers of home or foreign production. Hired labourers are employed but sparingly, and the small farmer can hardly be considered as a competitor amongst employers. His cattle are ill fed, and, if housed at all, are placed in dens, dark, filthy, and unwholesome, whereby the value of the cattle is proportionably lessened, and this part of the national wealth is, therefore, by so much diminished.[59]

In his report to the Poor Law Inspectors on conditions in Co. Donegal, published in 1870, Richard Hamilton, commented, 'Fencing and planting are done almost entirely by the tenants themselves. Iron gates are very uncommon. The tenant has no security for the value of his improvements, by guarantee or understanding; that he shall receive a fair proportion in the event of eviction or surrender; nor is any guarantee ever given that he shall be undisturbed in the enjoyment of the effects of his own improvements for a definite period.' He continued, 'So far as I could gather from the reports and answers made to me, I could arrive at no other conclusion than that it is the usual practice to raise the annual rents in consequence of the tenant's improvements, when the landlord thinks they have been enjoyed long enough to reimburse the tenant for the outlay.'[60] Tenants in the north were better off thanks to the 'Ulster Custom' which can be defined as the "three fs": free sale (the right of the outgoing tenant to sell his interest in the holding; fair rent (rent below market value as a reward for improvements; and fixity of tenure (no eviction provided rent was paid).

Throughout the Victorian period Ireland remained an overwhelmingly rural economy. An important source of employment in the countryside was spinning and weaving, in which women and children played an important role in bringing in extra money to the household. In many parts of Connaught and north Leinster a women's income from spinning was more regular than a man's earnings from agricultural labour, and women often provided the main cash income for a household. Weaving was a major source of employment, particularly among men, until the early twentieth century in both the towns and the countryside. It did not become mechanised as quickly as spinning but the change was taking place in the 1840s, as Kohl noted on his travels through Ireland, 'A very considerable quantity of the linen, I believe much more than one-half, is still made in the country by hand-looms; yet 'power-weaving' as the English call weaving by machinery, is increasing every day. The melancholy and much-felt battle between the hand-loom and the power-loom, which in some towns of England has been decided in favour of the latter, is going on in Belfast.'

Women were also a very visible presence in the fields, as noted by Harriet Martineau in 1852:

> We observe women working almost everywhere. In the flax-fields there are more women than men pulling and steeping. In the potato-fields it is often the women who are saving the remnant of the crop. In the harvest-fields there are as many women as men reaping and binding. In the bog, it is the women who, at half wages, set up, and turn, and help to stack the peat – not only for household use, but for sale, and in the service of the Irish Peat Company.

In big and small farms alike, women, of course, did all the housework.[61]

Further down the social scale was the cottier tenant, who worked for a landlord and lived in cabins provided by him on his estate in return for unpaid labour. Landlords and farmers used them to carry out manual labour such as drainage and land reclamation. The economic boom after the Napoleonic wars had contributed to a rapid rise in their numbers before the Great Famine. Leitch Ritchie considered the cottier as 'little better than a serf, being merely permitted to cultivate land for his own behoof [sic] as will afford him a bare efficiency of dry potatoes, on condition of his giving up the rest of his time to his mater'. Robert O'Brien, an agent in Limerick, told the Devon Commission that attempts had been made 'to introduce money wages amongst this class', but these had been unsuccessful as the cottiers preferred to take the land, grow potatoes and pay off the rent in labour.

The largest group found in the countryside, and at the bottom of the social scale, were agricultural labourers, who walked the roads in search of work. In 1841 the one-room mud cabins they lived in accounted for 40 per cent of the houses in Ireland. Furniture in these mud cabins usually consisted of a bed of straw, a crude table and stool and a few cooking utensils. Henry David Inglis left an account of the mud cabins he visited in the Wicklow Mountains in his *Ireland in 1834*, 'It was neither air nor water tight; and the floor was extremely damp. The furniture consisted of a small bedstead, with very scanty bedding, a wooden bench, and one iron pot; the embers of some furze burnt on the floor; and there was neither chimney nor window.'[62] Thomas Campbell Foster, in his *Letters on the condition of the people of Ireland* (1846), recalled:

> The chief features of the country which strike a stranger entering the county of Mayo from Sligo, are the wretched and filthy cottages of the peasantry, denoting a state of great debasement and poverty; and the vast tracts of level unreclaimed bog-land, capable of producing wealth, and giving the means of comfort to the wretched-looking and squalid peasantry that live on its borders. Each cottage has its dunghill and filthy cesspool close to the door, rendering cleanliness impossible, and generating fever and disease. The pig routs up the dunghill, and the ducks dabble in the cesspool, and run in and out of the cottage at pleasure. The children roll about on the mud floor, made damp and filthy by the feet of the ducks and pigs, and nothing can exceed their

ragged, dirty, and lost appearance, unless it be the forlorn aspect of their bare-footed mother.

According to the *Royal Commission for inquiring into the condition of the poorer classes in Ireland*, which conducted an extensive survey from 1833 to 1836, rural Ireland in the 1830s was characterised by unemployment. In their third report they estimated that the number of people 'out of work and in distress for thirty weeks of the year would amount to 585,000 people.' Jonathan Binns found at Philipstown, Co. Offay, 'Between potato time and harvest the distress is general, and very great; and in consequence of it fevers are prevalent. Many of the witnesses expressed a willingness to work and declared that it was not the amount of wages they cared so much about, but employment.' In terms of diet, a local sergeant informed him, 'Milk is a luxury here. Sergeant Malone informed us, that many a man sends his milk to the town, eats his potatoes without any; and he knew one man who had only three pints of milk in the year.'[63]

The poor labourer walking the roads in search of work was a common sight in Ireland until the late nineteenth century. The first of these migrants made their appearance in the spring, when the ground was being broken up for tillage. At the end of the season he took his pay and set off again to his own place, to dig potatoes or save his own little crop. In their absence their families frequently lived by begging, especially during the 'hungry months' or 'meal months' of June and July after the year's stock of potatoes had been used up and before the new ones became available. A good harvest of potatoes could mean the difference between starvation and survival during the hard winter months.

The Irish labourers flocked to Britain during the harvesting period, where they followed the harvests round – haymaking in June, turnip hoeing in July, corn harvesting in August, hop or fruit picking in September. The passenger steamers from Ireland were packed between June and October with those seeking work in England

and Scotland. Upon leaving Ireland from Londonderry, Charlotte Elizabeth recorded:

> A little beyond, we overtook and passed the St. Columb, a small steamer bound for Glasgow, so densely crowded with passengers that her bulwarks were fringed by their legs hanging over the sides. These were all poor Irishmen going to seek a precarious employment in the harvest fields, to earn the rent of their miserable cabin, and the dues of their grasping priest. What a monstrous anomaly, that the labouring class of Ireland should thus be compelled to migrate for a few weeks' employ while her rich bog-lands are unreclaimed, her fine soil half cultivated, and her abundant mines almost altogether unworked! Certainly the spirit of blindness is poured out upon our rulers; and is leading all classes equally or at least similarly astray.[64]

Seasonal migrants were a regular feature of Irish towns and countryside as they trudged their way to and from the ports. While staying in Edgeworthstown, Co. Longford, German visitor Johann Kohl noted:

> Numerous parties of poor Irish reapers and labourers passed through Edgeworthstown during my sojourn there, and excited compassion by their miserable appearance. On my way from Dublin I had already met with vast swarms of them, who all complained of the little they had earned in England. They were mostly of that class of labourers who wander every year chiefly from the western parts of Ireland, and principally from Connaught, in order to assist the rich English farmers in their harvest. The last year's harvest was very good, but there were so many unemployed hands to be hired at low wages in England, that the Irish emigrants found themselves badly off: hungry and in rags, they crossed over to England;

and in the very same plight they came back, since they had scarcely earned enough to pay the expenses of the journey.[65]

It was also tough on those they left behind. With a substantial number of rural labourers absent for long periods of time, it was the women who supplemented the family income through cleaning, mending, dressmaking, piecework, washing and taking in boarders. The *Illustrated London News* noted the number of beggar women and children in the Irish countryside:

> Where is the husband of that wretched, houseless wanderer from door to door – the father of those 'young barbarians' – where is he? He is in England, reaping and mowing to earn you seven times the value of his little patch of ground that he may keep the hovel of a homestead which is upon it over his family during the hard winter. This must be given up, if whilst away his wife and children cannot get enough to support life, and should present themselves at the gates of the union workhouse. Not a penny of outdoor relief![66]

Visitors to the Irish countryside were struck by the varieties and eccentricities of dress they encountered. The better-off farmer wore knee britches, waistcoat, shirt and cravat, tailcoat and sturdy boots, while his wife wore a cloak that covered a bodice, 'midi'-skirt and shift. The lower grades had generally the same cut of clothes, but they were more ragged and patched. Few of the labourers had overcoats and the women and children generally went barefoot. Among the very poor clothing was little better than rags. Dr John Forbes condemned men in the 1850s for their:

> abominable habit, so long prevalent among the poor in Ireland, of wearing the cast-off clothes of others. This habit, originating, no doubt, in poverty, has, I think, been carried

much further than was absolutely necessary, merely because it had become a habit. I think it must be beginning to wear out, as I observe that a fair proportion of the boys and young men show themselves, as least on Sundays, in jackets and short coats, evidently originals ... Nothing could convey to a stranger a stronger impression of wretchedness and untidiness, than this vicarious costume of the Irish, disfiguring at once to the person of the wearers, and calling forth in the mind of the observer the most disagreeable associations. Even when not in holes, as they too often are, those long-tailed coats almost touching the ground, and those shapeless breeches with their gaping knee-bands sagging below the calf of the leg, are the very emblems and ensigns of beggary and degradation.[67]

Chapter 3

Poverty, Poor Law and Famine

The first thing that struck many visitors to Ireland in the first half of the nineteenth century was the multiplicity of beggars. The stranger waiting for a coach would swiftly become the centre of attention. Mr and Mrs Hall, when they arrived in Ireland in 1841, found, 'Their wit and wisdom are as proverbial as their rags and wretchedness, and both too frequently excite a laugh at the cost of serious reflection upon their misery and the means by which it might be lessened. Age, decrepitude, imbecility and disease surround the car the moment it stops.'[68]

Asenath Nicholson, author of the *Bible in Ireland*, wrote of her visit to Tullamore in the mid-1840s:

> The chief centre of attraction was now where we stood, as I was a stranger. They attacked me with, 'God bless you,' 'a penny, if you plase, lady,' 'a ha'penny for a poor woman and child, whose father is dead this twelvemonth,' 'one ha'p'orth for an old man,' and 'the price of bread for a poor boy'; the boy grasping my clothes, and holding fast, in spite of my efforts to disengage myself the cries and importunities redoubling, while, like swarming bees, they sallied out from every quarter, till the crowd was immense.[69]

To deal with this perennial problem, the government introduced the English workhouse system to Ireland in 1838. Destitute poor who were previously granted relief at parish level were to be accommodated in new workhouses, where conditions were to be as unpleasant as was consistent with health. For the next century the shadow of the workhouse hung over most members of the working class and even some of the middle class. Orphaned families and foundling children, women with large families who were suddenly widowed, the old and infirm all dreaded incarceration within the forbidding walls of the workhouse. In England the units on which the poor law was administered were civil parishes, but in Ireland, where the parishes had become outdated due to changes in population and settlement, the poor law unions were devised. The unions ignored traditional divisions, such as the county, barony and parish, and were centred on market towns where workhouses were built. In all 137 unions were created, varying considerably in size: the largest ones being in the west of Ireland and the small ones in the eastern part of Ulster where the population was most dense.

The new workhouse-building project began in January 1839 with the arrival in Dublin of architect George Wilkinson. His brief from the Poor Law Commissioners stated that, 'The style of building is intended to be of the cheapest description compatible with durability; and effect is aimed at by harmony of proportion and simplicity of arrangement, all mere decoration being studiously excluded.' The same design was used for all but a tiny minority of the new workhouses and their stark appearance was a menacing feature of towns across the country. Construction proceeded with amazing speed, and by April 1843 Wilkinson was able to report that 112 of the new workhouses were finished, and eighteen others were almost complete.

As the workhouses replaced local charity, beggars swarmed to those parts of the country where these forbidding structures had not yet been erected. Johann Kohl noted this phenomenon when travelling through Ireland in the early 1840s, 'They [workhouses] command an extensive prospect over the country, and are the terror of the beggars, who prefer the independence of a mendicant's life to confinement in one of these houses. Some places, in which workhouses have not yet been erected, are at this moment swarming with beggars, who have retreated to escape from these dreaded buildings'. He noted as he travelled into Co. Wicklow, 'In all the little towns through which we passed the people complained that they were now inundated with beggars, who had migrated from the larger towns where workhouses are erected, and where a stricter watch is kept over them.[70]

The poor law system was designed to discourage all but the most needy paupers from applying to the workhouse for assistance. The prescribed clothing for adult males was a coat and trousers 'of barragan', cap, shirt, brogues and stockings, and for females a striped jerkin, a petticoat of 'linsey-woolsey' and another of stout cotton, a cap, a shift, shoes and stockings. It was a crime to abscond from the workhouse wearing these clothes: William Dunne was brought before the magistrate in April 1854 for absconding from the Parsonstown workhouse 'with clothes, the property of the guardians'. The prisoner admitted the charge and was sentenced to be imprisoned for one month with hard labour.[71]

Children were not provided with shoes and stockings on the grounds that they were unused to footwear. It was a fundamental rule of the workhouse system that 'no individual capable of exertion must ever be permitted to be idle in a workhouse and to allow none who are capable of employment to be idle at any time'. The men were employed breaking stones, grinding corn, working on the land attached to the workhouse or at other manual work about the house; the women at house duties, mending clothes, washing, attending the children and the sick, as well as manual work including breaking stones. The average day in the workhouse started at 7 a.m., when the inmates had to rise, dress in their workhouse clothes and then attend the central dining hall, where they waited for prayers to be read. The roll was called and they were inspected for cleanliness. They then lined up for their stirabout (porridge) and milk. After breakfast the inmates were allocated work until late in the afternoon, when they had dinner of either potatoes or brown bread and soup. Inmates could not go to the dormitories until bedtime at eight o'clock.[72]

Such leisure time as they were allowed was strictly monitored: playing cards or any game of chance, smoking or drinking any 'spirituous or fermented drink' was forbidden. Inmates could see visitors only when accompanied by the master, matron or other duly authorised officer. Punishment for infraction of the rules was severe, as can be seen in the punishment books kept by the masters of the workhouse. Punishments authorised for Armagh workhouse for 8 November 1845 included 'Maria McQuaid; disturbing the ward and swearing; to break stones for a week' and 'John Brown, Robert Minday, Thomas Martin and John Hamilton; abusing their new shoes; to go without shoes for a week and to be flogged'. The Master of Ballymoney workhouse reported that:

> Thomas Smyth, James Brown and John McCord were caught pulling turnips and throwing them into the cess pools ... the schoolmaster found Robert Quigley endeavouring to hang himself with a boy's belt tied to the front of one of the desks; he is a bad boy and tries to frighten the children by various means. Ordered that Smyth, Brown, McCord and Quigley be each flogged and put on the dietary of children for two weeks.[73]

Horror of the workhouse was soon ingrained in the Irish peasant, who would frequently endure any hardship rather than enter. Kohl put it down to the Irish love of freedom:

> The Irish are thoroughly by nature as well as by habit, a migratory people, and fond of change. The Irishman would rather wander through the entire world seeking employment, than endure the discipline of a workhouse, so long as he is in possession of his health and strength. Imprisonment, and confinement of every kind, is to the Irishman more irksome than to the Englishman. Consequently, even though he were

much better off in a workhouse than he could be at home, he would never enter one except in case of the most extreme distress; and he will be sure to remain in it not a single moment longer than this distress continues.[74]

Thomas Campbell Foster was less charitable, and put down the paupers' reluctance to go into the workhouse as being due to their unwillingness to wash:

The chief objection, however, of the paupers against going into the workhouse, or remaining in it, is that they are compelled to wash themselves and keep themselves clean. When a three months' coating of dirt has been removed from their limbs, they go shivering about as if they had lost half their clothing, and no doubt do feel cold from the want of their accustomed covering. They are also forbidden to smoke, which is the greatest hardship to them.[75]

While the guardians were legally responsible for the management of the workhouse and the collection and expenditure of money, the day-to-day running of the workhouse was carried out by a number of salaried officials. The staff consisted of a master, matron, clerk, chaplain, schoolmaster, medical officer, porter and additional assistants and servants that the guardians deemed necessary. The guardians were under pressure from the Poor Law Commissioners in London to discourage all but the neediest of paupers from applying to the workhouse for assistance. They therefore frequently hired officials who were chosen for their ability to discipline and regiment the paupers rather than for their pastoral qualities.

In addition to the attentions of staff and the board of guardians, the inmates had to put up with visitors interested in seeing the workings of the poor law system. One such was Sir Francis Head, author of

A Fortnight in Ireland (1852), who after arriving in Clifden in the evening lost no time in visiting the local workhouse:

> I only wanted to see its inmates, I requested the master to assemble them, at once, in their respective yards. The girls below fifteen, who were dressed in blue, without hats or shoes, appeared healthy, but very small; many of them had been in the house three or four years. The little boys below fifteen were – as I have before observed – fearfully diminutive. The women and girls above fifteen I found all standing in the yards, in a row, with their backs against the wall. Almost everyone had an honest countenance, was clean, but all were barefooted. The men and boys over fifteen, who generally speaking looked weak, were dressed in clothes so old that they appeared to be on the confines of turning into rags.

It was with relief that Sir Francis returned to the free air again.[76]

The management of the workhouses was the responsibility of the boards of guardians composed of elected representatives of the ratepayers in each union, together with ex-officio members including justices of the peace. The guardians were answerable to local ratepayers and were expected to account for all monies spent in the administration of the workhouse. Sidney Godolphin Osborne pointed out in his *Gleanings in the West of Ireland* (1850):

> It may easily be conceived that the office of a Guardian is not a bed of roses in these Unions. A small body of police, I was told, are here regularly in attendance on the Board on admission days; applicants are very apt to be violent when refused altogether, or relieved in a way not according to their own views. It has happened that a Guardian has been severely wounded as he sat, by a stone thrown by one of these unruly spirits.[77]

Landlords managed to maintain a large measure of control on boards of guardians during the early years. They served as ex-officio guardians and were able to assert a deal of influence over their tenants during elections. For much of the workhouses' history elections were fought along party lines, with many contests reduced to power struggles between local priests and landlords with both national and local political issues a crucial factor. This was important because the boards of guardians were the only administrative body in rural areas with directly elected representatives. Throughout much of the country the Catholic middle classes came to dominate the boards as the century progressed and were later to use it as a stepping stone to greater political ambitions: many went on to serve as MPs.

To prevent the religious issue dominating the administration of the Irish Poor Law no person in Holy Orders or a regular minister of any religious denomination could serve on the boards of guardians. Chaplains were to celebrate divine service and to preach to the paupers every Sunday. They were to 'examine and catechise the children at least every month', and to record in a special book the progress of the children as well as the dates of their attendance at the workhouse. The clergy in many workhouses regarded each other with considerable hostility and a constant watch was kept to ensure that members of their flock were not poached by their opposite number.

The workhouse remained substantially empty until the arrival of the potato famine. Before the mid-1840s between 30 per cent and 35 per cent of the population depended upon the potato: the average agricultural labourer in the south and west of the country consumed between 10 and 14lb of potatoes a day. Typically, they were boiled in an iron pot or roasted on the open fire. Theresa Cornwallis West, who visited Ireland in 1846, commented, 'The general system of "boiling them with the bones in them", alias with the heart as hard as a flint, goes much against an English stomach and grinders.'[78] The more fortunate agricultural labourer could make them taste better with some salt, pepper or, if on the cost, dulse or herring. The potato when taken with buttermilk provided all the vitamins and nutrients required by a labourer. It also had the considerable advantage of being the only crop that could be grown in sufficient quantity on a small plot of land for most of the year.

Labourer and cottier shared a potato diet and by the early nineteenth century over 2 million acres of land were under potatoes. When the stock of potatoes was used up in June and before new ones could be planted in August, the labourer and cottier frequently went hungry. The Poor Law Commissioners found in Co. Longford that during lean times, 'They go through the fields and gather the wild weeds; they boil them with salt, and they live on them, without even a potato to eat along with them,' and the Rev. O'Brien told the Commissioners that he knew of two families of labourers who remained in bed all day, as they said 'to stifle the hunger'. They told him several of their neighbours did the same. In Tipperary the Commissioners found that, 'There is not much work for the labouring classes from May to August – as this time labourers and even tradesmen can scarcely get one full meal in the day, besides this they will often collect cornkail, and rape, and nettles, and eat them.'[79]

Sidney Godolphin Osborne, who visited Ireland at the height of the Famine, condemned landlords for their support for this dependence on the potato. In his *Gleanings from the West of Ireland*, he declared:

If Providence had not blighted the potato, I do not believe the West of Ireland would have seen the landlords so bent on the destruction of the small holding class. So long as 'Pat's' lazy bed of potatoes enabled him to pay the Rack-rent, which kept up the old style of Irish living, of the agents at home, and of the absent landlord; a style notorious for its extravagance; Pat might have slept and bred as much as he liked; the more mouths, the more potatoes would be wanted – the more competition for potato land; such competition was the very soul of rack-rent [an excessively high rent; especially one whose annual amount was equal, or almost equal, to the value of the property.]

The first region to be affected by the potato blight was Belgium in June 1845 before word came of a strange disease attacking the potato crop in the south of England in August. The first sign of blight in Waterford and Wexford occurred in September 1845 and then spread rapidly until about half the country was affected. In November, Prime Minister Sir Robert Peel spent £100,000 on Indian corn and meal in order to prevent soaring food prices in Ireland. Unlike potatoes, Indian corn required considerable preparation, and initial difficulties in grinding produced poorly refined meal that caused digestive discomfort, earning it the epithet 'Peel's brimstone'.

The potato crop had failed before, and people hoped that the next harvest would be all right. However, the blight returned in 1846 and this time the failure was complete. The speed with which the blight struck added to the horror. In December 1846, a local magistrate in west Cork visited Skibbereen with bread to feed the starving population. Nothing prepared him for the horrors he witnessed. In the first hovel he entered he found 'six famished and ghastly skeletons, to all appearances dead' huddled in a corner on some filthy straw. He was soon surrounded by more than two hundred destitute and hungry people 'such phantoms, such frightful spectres as no words can describe, either from famine or from fever. Their demoniac yells are still ringing in my ears, and their horrible images are fixed upon my brain.'[80]

In July 1846, Lord John Russell headed a new Whig government that resolved there would be no government buying; the supply of food was to be left exclusively to private enterprise, thereby obliging landlords to contribute to the cost through the rates and charitable donations. Relief was limited to public works and this time the government refused to meet half the cost, which was to be borne entirely by the rates. The idea was to force the Irish landlords to subsidize famine relief. During the bitter winter of 1846–47, a great deal of work was done by various voluntary groups. Societies, committees and individuals and many landlords raised funds for the establishment of soup kitchens, which for many months provided a large section of the population with their only means of subsistence.

The Religious Society of Friends, better known as the Quakers, took a proactive approach to famine relief by setting up soup kitchens in towns such as Waterford, Enniscorthy, Limerick, Clonmel and Youghal, where they had a strong presence. In Dublin Joseph Bewley, a prominent and wealthy Quaker, financed his own soup kitchen. Asenath Nicholson, American missionary, philanthropist and traveller, visited the soup kitchen, as recounted in her book *Annals of the Famine in Ireland*:

> The regulation of this soup establishment was a pattern worthy of imitation. The neatness and order of the shop; the comely attired Quaker matrons and their daughters, with their white sleeves drawn over their tidy-clad arms – their white aprons and caps, all moving in that quiet harmony so peculiar to that people; and there, too, at seven in the morning, and again at midday. All this beauty and finish, contrasted with the woe-begone, emaciated, filthy, ragged beings that stood in their turn before them, was a sight at which angels, if they could weep, might weep, and might rejoice too. Often have I stood, in painful admiration, to see the two extremes of degradation and elevation, comfort and misery, cleanliness and filth, in these two classes, made alike in God's image, but thrown into different circumstances, developing two such wide and strange opposites.[81]

In January 1847, during the worst winter of the Famine, Nicholson began her one-woman relief operation in Dublin by establishing a soup kitchen in Cook Street for the relief of the poor in the Liberties.

She painted a Dickensian picture of the poverty in Dublin for her supporters in America, 'The reader may be informed that in the wealthy, beautiful city of Dublin, which can boast some of the finest architecture on earth, there are in retired streets and dark alleys, some of the most forbidding, most uncomfortable abodes that can be found in the wildest bogs of that wretched country.'

Nicholson also took food to those in need distributing bread in the streets, 'The distribution of the bread in the street was continued, not even Sabbaths excepted; my basket was often taken near the chapel door, and left in some house till I came out. So pressing at last was the crowd, that I dare not go into a shop to take out my purse to buy the most trifling article, and a bread-shop above all was avoided.'

She condemned the better off in Dublin society who considered the many charities and poor law in the city as adequate to deal with the growing crises, 'The people of Dublin, among the comfortable classes, whatever hospitality they might manifest toward guests and visitors, had never troubled themselves by looking into the real home wants of the suffering poor. Enough they thought that societies of all kinds abounded, and a poorhouse besides, were claims upon their purses to a full equivalent for all their consciences required, and to visit them was quite unlady-like, if not dangerous.'

The situation reached its worst by February 1847 when great gales blew and the country was blanketed in thick snow. A fever epidemic spread throughout the country. Dubbed 'Famine Fever', it was in fact two separate diseases, typhus and relapsing fever. Bodies lay for days in cabins that the survivors had deserted. Many others were found on the roadside, often with no means of identification.

By the beginning of 1847 the Cabinet at last began to realise that a radical change of policy was needed. A temporary act was passed in February 1847 in order that soup kitchens should be established that would help bridge the gap until the harvest of the following autumn. The provision and distribution of food was to be a charge on the local rates; though the government would where necessary advance funds to start the new scheme. Throughout Ireland those workhouses in operation began to fill up for the first time. The board of guardians in many parts of Ireland were soon overwhelmed by this cataclysm. The workhouse hospitals, designed to deal with a very limited number of sick or injured inmates, were unable to cope with the level of distress as fever followed in the wake of famine. By 1847 almost every person admitted into workhouses was suffering from either dysentery, fever or were in the early stages of disease, and with separation impossible, disease spread, infecting not only the inmates but also the staff. During the first four months of 1847, more than 150 of the workhouse officers were attacked with disease, of whom fifty-four died, including seven clerks, nine masters, seven medical officers and six chaplains. There were casualties among the boards of guardians, including the chairman of Lurgan board of guardians, Lord Lurgan, who died from the fever in 1847.

As a direct result of the extraordinary circumstances brought about by the Famine, exceptional measures were introduced in Ireland in order to prevent the complete breakdown of the workhouse system. In June 1847 a separate Irish Poor Law Commission was set up and put in charge of further assistance under the Poor Relief (Ireland) Act. This also permitted the board of guardians to grant outdoor relief to the aged, infirm and sick poor, and to poor widows with two or more dependent children. The Enniskillen boards of guardians welcomed that fact that the Poor Law Commissioners had declared that able-bodied paupers were still to go to the workhouse, which they felt sure would 'prevent imposition from idle able-bodied persons'.

The blight was not as severe during autumn 1847, bringing with it a glimmer of hope. Having come to the decision that the worst of the crisis was over by the end of the summer, the government brought the system to an end and the last of the soup kitchens were wound up at the end of September 1847. However, the blight returned with greater force.

While travelling along the southern side of the mountains near Bantry Bay, the Reverend John East was horrified to hear stories of packs of dogs feeding on the dead, who were often laid to rest uncoffined and covered with a little earth;

> Half-starved dogs, having tasted human carrion, are becoming insatiably eager for the horrid food. In another part of the country, they were lately discovered preying upon seven human bodies that had been deserted in a hedge. In vain did I hear a clergyman, in another place, apply to a police-officer to render aid in the destruction of the dogs. His reply was – 'The law is against us.' A clergyman told me that he had recently seen one of these animals with part of the body of a child in his mouth.

The towns were filled with ragged and destitute people. On visiting Clifden in 1849, Sidney Godolphin Osborne, in his *Gleanings from the West of Ireland*, confessed himself hardened to the poverty of the people, unlike his travelling companion:

> My friend here again indulged himself in large investments in bread, to feed the poor wretches he found in the street, and with the customary result; he soon being forced from the pressure, to make a retreat at the rear of the shop. I cannot wonder at the perseverance he displayed, he was new to Ireland; less hardened than myself. From a window we got an opportunity of seeing, ourselves unseen, some of the bread he had given consumed; there was no deceit in the way it was devoured; more voracious reality, it would be hardly possible to conceive; to see the fleshless arms grasping one part of a loaf, whilst the fingers – bone handled forks – dug into the other, to supply the mouth – such mouths too! With an eagerness, as if the bread was stolen, the thief starving, and the steps of the owner heard; was a picture, I think neither of us will easily forget.

That was not an end to their tribulations caused by his friend's benevolence. On their way out of town they were followed and 'a pack of famished creatures of all descriptions and sexes, set off in full chase after us; the taste of fresh bread, still inflamed the spirit of some; the report put others in hot hungry pursuit'. Their driver did his best but the road was up a very steep hill and they gained on the worried English passengers. 'No two luckless human brings were ever so hunted; no ravening wolves ever gave more open expression of their object – food. A little coaxing – my friend's; a little violence – my own; a little distribution of copper coin from both if us, at last rid us of the inconvenient, but natural result of an Englishman, with money in his pocket, and a baker's shop near, wishing in Ireland to feed some starving people.'[82]

Travelling through Ireland at the time, the Reverend East was struck by fact that:

> There were towns in which the entire population seemed in motion, either to administer or to obtain relief; while one might see a pile of coffins, lodged against a carpenter's wall, exposed for sale, ready-made. In fact, I elsewhere passed through towns where this was the only mechanic trade carried on to advantage, and where the timber-merchant was heard to say that he might close his yard and dismiss his sawyers, but for the demand for coffins.

In Cork, which he dubbed 'The City of Destruction', he saw, 'Children, wan and livid, were dying or actually dead, in the arms of fathers and mothers, who had scarcely strength to carry them; or, if they lived, their cries, especially at night, were terrible to hear. Here and there one might observe young men, not long since athletic and fit for any labour, now scarcely able to move one limb before another.'[83]

The workhouses proved for many their only chance for survival. In their *Annual Report* of May 1848 the Irish Poor Law Commissioners underlined the importance of the workhouses in preventing a greater number of deaths during the Famine years:

> Including the large number of inmates maintained in the workhouses, we may state that more than 800,000 persons are daily relieved at the charge of the poor-rates, consisting chiefly of the most helpless part of the most indigent classes in Ireland; and we cannot doubt that of this number a very large proportion are by this means, and this means alone, daily preserved from death through want of food … Including the relief contributed by our Inspectors from the funds of the British Association, in certain distressed Unions, the entire number of persons provided with daily sustenance in Ireland, may be stated, in round numbers, to be 1,000,000, or about one eighth part of the whole population.

Although they were a refuge for many, life inside the walls of the workhouse was often brutal. Sidney Godolphin Osborne left a vivid description of a visit to the Limerick workhouse in his book *Gleanings in the West of Ireland*, published in 1850. He had visited the workhouse a year earlier and had found it clean and in good order, so this visit was something of a shock:

> In the parent and auxiliary houses there was no less a number than 8,000 paupers; every department, except the fever hospital, shewed evident symptoms of gross neglect. I have no words with which I can give any real idea of the sad condition of the inmates of two large yards at the parent house, in which were a very large number of young female children; many of them clothed in the merest dirty rags, and of these they wore a very scanty allowance; they were in the dirt collected on their persons for many weeks; there was not about them the slightest evidence of any the least care being

taken of them; as they filed before me, two and two, they were a spectacle to fill any humane heart with indignation: sore feet, sore hands, sore heads; ophthalmia evident in the case of the great proportion of them; some of them were suffering from it in its very worst stage; they were evidently eat up with vermin – very many were mere skeletons ...[84]

It was the plight of the children that moved him most. He found on his visits to various infirmary wards in Ireland that he never heard one single child, suffering from famine or dysentery, utter a moan of pain. 'I have never heard one ask for food, for water – for anything,' he recalled; 'two, three, or four in a bed, there they lie and die, if suffering, still ever silent, unmoved.'

In the midst of the suffering, a group of idealists had become estranged from Daniel O'Connell's constitutional politics in favour of revolution preached by Newry lawyer and journalist John Mitchel and powerful Waterford orator Thomas Francis Meaghan. The rising, when it came, took place at the height of the famine but failed to attract widespread support from the starving, dispirited and destitute who roamed the country in search of food or employment. It was led by the most unlikely of revolutionaries: William Smith O'Brien was the second son of Sir Edward O'Brien, who had entered Parliament as a Conservative in 1826. The horrors of the famine and the French Revolution of 1848 combined to urge O'Brien to insurrection. He gathered a band of 500 peasants at Boylagh Common in Co. Tipperary on 29 July 1848 and these attacked a body of policemen and drove them into the farmhouse of Mrs Margaret McCormick, taking the widow and her five children hostage. Shots were exchanged before rumours of police reinforcements caused the insurgents to flee. The newspapers subsequently dubbed the rising the 'Battle of Widow McCormick's Cabbage Patch', reflecting as much a sense of relief as of contempt.

In the midst of the Great Famine, and rebellion having been suppressed, Queen Victoria paid her first visit to Ireland. Alarmed by reports from Ireland, she had contributed £2,000 to the British Relief Association and was determined to visit the country to see for herself. The Irish Viceroy, Lord Clarendon, was eager to support the visit, although he worried about the reception she would receive in Ireland, 'Everything tends to secure for the Queen an enthusiastic reception, and the one drawback, which is the general distress of all classes, has its advantages, for it will enable the Queen to do what is kind and considerate to those who are suffering.'[85]

The Royal party arrived at Cobh, Co. Cork, which was renamed Queenstown in her honour. She recalled in her diary, 'I stepped on shore amidst the roar of cannon (for the artillery were placed so close as quite to shake the temporary room which we entered); and the enthusiastic shouts of the people.'[86] In Cork preparations for the royal visit were only half completed because the Queen had arrived a day earlier than anticipated, which caused a great deal of discontent among local traders. According to the *Cork Examiner*:

> Decorations were only half completed, painters were in full operation, carpenters hammering and sawing, proprietors of stands commencing to hide the naked planks with verdant boughs and flowers, triumphal arches half in skeleton, members of the corporation taking a river excursion preparatory to the grand day of exhibition – when, like a thunder clap, came the announcement that the Queen was in Cove, and would come up to Cork this day.

The potential loss to local businesses of the crowds that were expected the following day prompted the *Cork Examiner* to complain that 'her Majesty had not exhibited that degree of consideration for the people of the south, upon whom devolved the duty of first welcoming her to the shores of Ireland, which might have been expected even from royalty, and which the people of Cork well merited by their elaborate preparations and liberal expenditure'. Although the crowds in the city were sufficient to impress the visiting royals, and 'although there was given to the Queen a greeting sufficiently warm and general, it was not of that intense and universal nature – far from it – which we remember to have seen manifested in this city when Daniel O'Connell passed through its streets'.[87]

After travelling by yacht to Kingstown, the Queen spent four days at the Vice-Regal Lodge in Phoenix Park. The Queen was enthusiastically received on her arrival in Dublin, 'It was a wonderful and striking scene, such masses of human beings, so enthusiastic, so excited, yet such perfect order maintained; then the numbers of troops, the different bands stationed at certain distances, the waving of hats and handkerchiefs, the bursts of welcome which rent the air, – all made it a never-to-be- forgotten scene; when one reflected how lately the country had been in open revolt and under martial law.' Before moving to Belfast, Victoria created Edward the Prince of Wales Earl of Dublin.[88]

For Queen Victoria's one and only visit to Belfast the streets were thronged by immense crowds despite wet and windy weather. Many thousands had arrived by the railway and any conveyance that could be begged or borrowed from the surrounding countryside, so that one reporter calculated the population of the city more than doubled. The Queen recalled, 'Hundreds of banners and flags decorated the leading thoroughfares, while whole plantations of laurel and other evergreens were transferred to the fronts of the houses. Expensive draperies, of every hue, festooned the balconies. The town was beautifully decorated with flowers, hangings, and very fine triumphal arches, the galleries full of people; and the reception very hearty. The people are a mixture of nations, and the female beauty had almost disappeared.'[89] According to the *Belfast News-Letter*, 'The Queen was rather plainly dressed in a robe of light blue flounced tabinet'. She wore no ornaments of any kind. Prince Albert was considered to be in his appearance 'of a decidedly foreign cast' but was 'universally admired for the noble bearing of his manner and the perfect grace of his movements'.[90]

At North Queen Street the Queen finally encountered some of those who had been directly impacted by the Famine. 'On entering this street, a most pleasing display presented itself to the illustrious visitors', wrote the *Belfast News-Letter* correspondent:

> On the advance of the procession to the Belfast Charitable Society's noble institution, the poor boys who constitute the band of the poorhouse, 24 in number, their ages being from seven to fourteen years, and who sat, amidst the other children, 100 in number, on an elevated platform, handsomely covered with crimson cloth, struck up the National Anthem. Prince Albert most graciously saluted the little musicians, and the Queen appeared most deeply interested with the spectacle. Almost everyone in the Royal train rose up and bowed to the children. These poor boys have been but a few months under musical tuition, and yet they played most correctly, though only those who were nearest to them could hear their performance, from the vociferous huzzas which arose in all directions.

Overall Lord Clarendon was pleased with the visit. He thought it was 'a turn in the tide of their affairs after four years of suffering, with an unprecedented influx of strangers and expenditure of money, and as they will contrast this year with the last, their conclusion must be unfavourable to political agitation'. The militant revolutionary leader John Mitchel had to concede that 'the debased nation set its neck under her feet in a paroxysm of fictitious "loyalty". It is painful to relate, but it is the disgraceful fact.'[91]

Chapter 4

Spectator to a Revolution

To visitors like William Stevens Balch, Ireland was a bleak place as it emerged from the worst vestiges of the Famine. 'The darkness thickens in her skies, corruption festers at her heart, poverty and crime mark her career, and distraction and ruin are in reserve for her future,' he wrote in 1850. 'Not a ray of hope or comfort gleams from any point of heaven, upon the masses of her sons and daughters. Oppression, starvation, or emigration are inscribed everywhere – on every hill and valley, in every town, village, and hamlet. Peace, justice, and competence are nowhere to be found.'[92] As the impact of the famine lingered landlords and tenants turned to two long-established methods of survival: eviction and emigration.

Many landlords were ruined by the Famine: in debt before the potato blight, they were faced with tenants who could not pay them rent but who had to be provided with food or relief work in order to alleviate the distress. In a county like Mayo, where 75 per cent of all occupiers had holdings valued at £4 or less, landlords faced difficult choices. With little rent coming in and having had to borrow £1,500 to pay his rates, the Marquess of Sligo saw himself in October 1848 as being 'under the necessity of ejecting or being ejected'.

Home Rule journalist and politician A.M. Sullivan paid tribute to those landlords 'who at every sacrifice sustained and retained their tenantry' during the Famine years. The Encumbered Estates Act of 1849, which superseded a similar act of 1848, was designed to facilitate the sale of insolvent landed estates and inject new capital into the country. Between 1849 and 1857 over 3,000 estates were sold but it did not bring into the country new landlords from Scotland and

England, which the government had predicated, but a new breed of speculators whose objective was to increase and evict to get a quick return from their investment.

Both old landlords and the new breed of speculators took the opportunity presented by the Famine and emigration to clear the smallholders from the land and to consolidate their estates into larger and potentially more profitable concerns. The tenants on short-term leases had no defence and were driven from the land in vast numbers. In Mayo the Earl of Lucan evicted some 2,000 people and destroyed 300 houses in Ballinrobe parish alone between 1846 and 1849. The cleared lands he converted to pasture and then either retained them in his own hands, or, more usually, transferred them into those of large graziers, some of whom were Protestants from Scotland. Lucan boasted that he 'would not breed paupers to pay priests'.

A series of merciless evictions in Kilrush, Co. Clare, where some 4,000 people were evicted in about seven months, were so shocking that the Lord Lieutenant the 4th Earl of Clarendon warned the Home Secretary that, 'The case is too shocking for publication if it can be avoided.' Sidney Godolphin Osborne visited Kilrush shortly after the evictions and was shocked:

> I know not how a country looks, after the passage of an enemy through it, bent on desolating its people's homes; but I am quite certain, the work of destruction could not be done more effectively, though perhaps it would be done less methodically, by such an army, than it is done in these western counties of Ireland, by the proprietors of the land. Roofless gables meet your eye on every side; one ceases to wonder that the Union Houses are so full, when there is this evidence of the fact that no other home is left to so many thousands.[93]

James Hack Tuke, an English Quaker who observed a number of official evictions, was shocked by what he saw and described the process in detail in a series of letters. In Erris, in a remote part of Connaught, for example, 140 families were evicted. After the notice to quit had been read, Tuke described how:

> The policemen are commanded to do their duty. Reluctantly they proceed, armed with bayonet and muskets, to throw out the miserable furniture … But the tenants make some show of resistance – for these hovels have been built by themselves or their forefathers who have resided in them for generations past – seem inclined to dispute with the bayonets of the police, for they know truly that, when their hovels are demolished, the nearest ditch much be their dwelling, and that thus exposed, death could not fail to be the lot of their wives and little ones.[94]

Clarendon viewed the increase in lawlessness at the end of 1847, especially attacks on landlords, as having roots in the wholescale evictions and demanded more powers to deal with the situation. At the end of 1847, a Crime and Outrage Bill was rushed through parliament and 15,000 additional troops were sent to Ireland.

Eviction was carried out assisted if necessary by the constabulary. Many landlords and their agents also used physical force or heavy-handed pressure to bring about evictions. It was the practice to level or burn the affected dwellings there and then, as soon as the tenants' effects had been removed. This was frequently carried out in front of a large number of spectators and, as the century progressed, ladies and gentlemen of the press. 'Last year I passed the scene of a small eviction operation,' Osborne recalled. 'The wretched creatures were most of them sitting in two or three groups by the side of their furniture, such as it was; the only voice of lamentation I heard was that of a little child about six years old, who was crying most lustily, as it kept running round the flattened, fallen roof of one of the cabins; I made my driver ask, what made the little thing so miserable? the answer was, "that the cat was supposed to be under the thatch". Osborne had the satisfaction of seeing the cat emerge from the debris and left the child the richer with a four penny piece.

Many voices of opposition to clearances were raised in Ireland and contemporary newspaper accounts of evictions are harrowing. *The Limerick and Clare Examiner*, whose special correspondent was chronicling the depopulation, protested in May 1848 that 'nothing, absolutely nothing, is done to save the lives of the people – they are swept out of their holdings, swept out of life, without an effort on the part of our rulers to stay the violent progress of human destruction'. Those evicted had little choice but to seek outdoor relief or the workhouse. The *Galway Vindicator* devoted two whole columns to a list of 187 families whom Lord Lucan had dispossessed in the previous eighteen months, stating that of the 913 individuals evicted, 478 persons were receiving public relief and another 170 had emigrated, while as many as 265 were 'dead or left to shift about from place to place'.

It is impossible to be certain about how many people were evicted during this period because the police only began to keep an official tally in 1849. They record a total of nearly 250,000 persons as formally and permanently evicted from their holdings between 1849 and 1854 but this figure does not take into account illegal evictions and voluntary surrender of land. Some landlords or their agents eased their consciences with the distribution of a few shillings to the evicted tenants. Joseph Kincaid, one of the most extensive land agents in Ireland, explained to a House of Lords committee in 1848 how he had removed 150 families (probably 800 or 900 people) in the Kilglass district of Roscommon. To induce them to leave for England or Scotland, he gave these tenants £3 or £5 per family, or as little as 10s to 18s per head. Kincaid claimed that 'the people were in that state of destitution that they entreated to have a few pounds to take them anywhere'.

Violence was uncommon and the whole country was remarkably calm throughout the Famine period. A rare exception was the murder of

Thomas Bateson, agent for the Templetown estate in Co. Monaghan, who was battered to death by three men as he walked down the Keady Road leading out of Castleblayney, Co. Monaghan, on the afternoon of 4 December 1851. He was loathed because he had refused rent reductions during the Famine, had struck a farmer during an ejectment (for which he was fined) and had evicted thirty-four families totalling 222 people to create a model farm.

Some landlords were prepared to finance their own programmes of emigration in an effort to find a permanent solution to the burden caused by surplus tenants. Lord Lansdowne in Co. Kerry financed such a scheme, which his agent calculated was a cheaper alternative to tenants becoming a burden on the local poor rates. The vast majority of those who fled the Famine, however, had to raise the money for their passage through the sale of their stock or their interest in the farm. The *Westmeath Guardian* deplored the impact of the emigration of the more prosperous small farmers, 'The number of emigrants conveyed to the metropolis by the Midland Great Western Railway during one week in March, averaged 100 daily; and of these the majority were young and healthy – the flower of the peasantry. The public conveyances from Longford and Cavan arrive here every day loaded with the more respectable class of emigrants, while every station of the line of railway to Galway contributes its numbers to swell the tide of emigration now flowing from the land.' It warned that, 'We are, in fact, daily losing the better portion of our peasantry; the frugal and industrious small farmers and their loss will, ere long, be felt.'[95]

After about 1850, it became increasingly common for a son or daughter to go out first and then send money home to enable another member of the family to follow. An article published in the *Anglo-Celt* on 24 April 1851, show that impact of emigration was clearly being felt:

> Never before in the recollection of the oldest inhabitants, have so many persons left this neighbourhood for the land of the Stars and Stripes. Travel on any road through the county,

and crowds of Ireland's stalwart sons are to be met, wending their way, (accompanied by their families) to the seaports, and with few exceptions they are comfortable farmers, leaving behind them the home of their birth and the lands which they tilled, to be turned into grazing lands, thus saving the landlords' pockets in the payment of poor rates.

Henry Coulter found when he travelled through the west of Ireland in the early 1860s:

There is scarcely a family in Clare which has not some member or members in America or Australia, and remittances are constantly being sent by these exiles to their relatives at home. Sometimes the old couple receive five or six pounds from their son, whose horny hand need never lie idle in his bosom in the new world. Sometimes, as in a case which was lately mentioned to me, a young girl earning good wages in America, sends several pounds to her brother, who is willing to work, but can find no employment in his own country. The large sums thus sent home by Irish emigrants have often excited surprise and elicited the warmest admiration, as proofs of the deep-seated feelings of family affection which characterise our people.[96]

The *Northern Standard* of 4 June 1864 was alarmed by the domestic impact of emigration on such a massive scale:

The results of the emigration drain will soon be sensibly felt in nearly every locality throughout the South and West; nor is the exodus confined to those parts of the country alone. We learn that a large number of emigrants have left Ulster for America, as well as Australia. If we stop to consider the rate at which the people are leaving this country at present, we must come to the conclusion that the land will soon revert into pasturage, and that in a short time Ireland will have to depend on foreign countries for breadstuffs. A large number of the peasant class from the counties of Roscommon and Galway left this neighbourhood during the last week, seemingly in excellent spirits, and rejoicing at their good fortune to get off. Instead of the lamentable wailings which formerly characterised the scenes of separation, we are informed that on some late occasions the parting salute was a ringing cheer, those left behind looking forward to being able soon to cross the Atlantic after their friends. So many passengers have been booked by one Liverpool firm that it has written to its agents to engage no passengers for any vessel before the 23rd June.

Others saw emigration as a positive sign. James Macaulay wrote in 1872: 'It is sad to see everywhere the deserted villages, and ruined homesteads, and roofless cabins. But these ruined houses are in reality marks of the country's progress, as much as the ruined castles and fortresses are marks of the bad old times, which have passed away. In the times when "every rood of ground maintained its man" it was a poor and precarious maintenance at the best, and always on the verge of starvation by famine, which did come at last. The emigration, which then began to flow in earnest, saved the country.'[97]

Harriet Martineau agreed:

The clearance of the land by a method which secures the maintenance of the inhabitants seems to us a very great good. The aged are more safe and comfortable in workhouses than they could have been amidst the chances of Irish cabin life in these times, and as for the children, the orphans and the deserted, they are the hope of the country. From the workhouse schools, a large body of young people will be coming forth, very soon, with new ideas, good habits, and qualifications which will make of them a higher order of peasantry than Ireland has ever yet known.

With this mass exodus of the Great Famine, emigration was to become an important element in Irish society during the next one hundred years. Many travellers to Ireland commented on it. Dr John Forbes, who travelled around Ireland during the autumn of 1852, arrived at Killaloe, 12 miles from Limerick, to join the steamer for a pleasure cruise to Athlone, where he came across a party of emigrants. They were all making their way to Liverpool via Dublin. Most of them were going to the United States, but several, particularly the young women, were bound for Australia. Forbes was moved by the distressful scenes he witnessed at the quayside:

> With the utter unconsciousness and disregard of being the observed of all observers, which characterises authentic sorrow, these warm-hearted and simple-minded people demeaned themselves entirely as if they had been shrouded in all the privacy of home, clinging to and kissing and embracing each other with the utmost ardour, calling out aloud, in broken tones, the endeared names of brother, sister, mother, sobbing and crying as if the very heart would burst, while the unheeded tears ran down from the red and swollen eyes literally in streams.[98]

A notable trend was the number of women who left the country during the second half of the nineteenth century. It has been estimated that women formed about half the numbers of those who emigrated and by the end of the century more than half of them were unmarried, leaving by choice, hoping for better prospects in America or the colonies. Most ended up in domestic service; in America it was estimated that as many as 43 per cent of domestic servants were Irish.[99] The potential to better oneself attracted many emigrants from the 1850s. As French politician and writer Jules de Lasteyrie reported in his *L'Irlande et lest causes de sa misere* (1860), 'It is no longer the destitution of Ireland, but the wealth of Canada, of the United States, and of Australia, which now promotes Irish emigration.'[100] William Stevens Balch, a celebrated American Universalist preacher and politician, agreed, 'They know no better, and too few seem disposed to teach them. There is nothing systematic in their emigration. They have no matured plan; no distinct object, farther than to get "till Amiriky." They speak of it as dying men speak of going to heaven – believing the battle will be fought and the victory won when they get there, and a feast of fat things in preparation for them. They are directed by instinct, more like birds of passage than by well-informed judgment, like men of reason.'[101]

For those tenants, cottiers and agricultural labourers who remained in Ireland and had difficulty paying their rents, the fear of famine and eviction remained a very present concern. Famine returned in parts of the west of Ireland in the 1860s, 1880s and 1890s, however, although it caused much suffering, the impact of these famines was less severe partly due to the mass exodus of the Great Famine and subsequent emigration, which was one of its most enduring legacies. The Famine evictions remained long in the public memory and the uncertainty they created contributed to the particularly violent agrarian unrest of the second half of the nineteenth century. By the 1860s thousands of small farmers and labourers had joined a radical group, the Irish Republican Brotherhood, or the Fenian movement as they were more popularly known, which was founded simultaneously at Dublin and New York in 1858. Many of its leaders, such as James Stephens and John O'Mahony, had been involved in the 1848 rising and they prepared a secret military force dedicated to the ideal of armed insurrection. Although many among the Catholic clergy, including Archbishop Cullen of Dublin, considered them to be socialists and agnostics, their objective of Irish independence secured them a great many recruits. James Stephens declared in the *Irish People*, a newspaper he had founded, that a free Ireland would not be achieved by 'amiable and enlightened young men', imagining that 'they are surely regenerating their country, when they are pushing about in drawing room society ... creating an Irish national literature, schools of Irish art, and things of this sort'. Such people were 'dilettante patriots, perhaps the greatest fools of all'.[102]

The Fenian movement differed from earlier national movements in that it drew much of its support from those who had emigrated to the U.S.A. or who had migrated to Britain in search of work. Rumours of insurrection were rife, fuelled by accounts of arms seizures in the newspapers. The *Cork Examiner* of 2 November 1865 reported:

> ANOTHER SEIZURE OF ARMS – In Belfast, on Wednesday, a further seizure of arms was made on board the Fleetwood steamer by the Customs' officers. A large cask, consigned to a merchant in town, was opened, and, on being searched, was found to contain a number of rifles and several bullet-moulds. Several cases containing arms, which were seized during last week, were forwarded last evening on board the Fleetwood steamer to the manufacturers in Manchester.

Much was made of the presence of former soldiers returning from the American Civil War. According to the *Cork Examiner* for 27 December 1865: 'The *Morning Herald* anticipates an outbreak in Ireland during the present winter. It grounds its belief on two reasons – one, that Ireland is now full of returned emigrants from America, who are reckless, but first-rate soldiers; the other, that it is generally supposed that there are at present at sea, on their way from America, steamers laden with arms and ammunition, and considerable numbers of fighting men.'

The Fenian rising of 1867 when it came was quickly crushed. The government had been kept extremely well informed by John Corydon, a man who had infiltrated the highest ranks of the Brotherhood, ensuring that most of the Fenian leaders were already in prison. In Co. Cork insurgents took Knockadoon coastguard station and captured the police barracks in Ballyknockane, where they derailed the Dublin express. Throughout the rest of the country any signs of discontent were swiftly dealt with: the constabulary dispersed groups of rebels in Drogheda's Potato Market, at Drumcliffe churchyard in Co. Sligo; and at Ballyhurst in Co. Tipperary the constabulary repelled attacks on barracks at Ardagh and Kilmallock in Co. Limerick. Dublin produced the largest Fenian turnout, with several hundred men marching out of the city to Tallaght, were, after a brief exchange of gunfire, the insurgents which signaled the collapse of armed insurrection. The Irish Constabulary had been able to suppress the Fenian rising without seeking the assistance of the military. Queen Victoria was so pleased that she renamed the force the Royal Irish Constabulary.

The rising may have been a failure but a groundswell of support for the Fenian movement remained, as noted by the *Irish Catholic Chronicle and People's News of the Week* on Saturday, 12 October 1867:

A Fenian funeral which took place in Limerick last Sunday, gave occasion for a demonstration which seems to have startled the authorities not a little. A gasfitter named Kelly had been arrested last year as a Fenian suspect and only released, like young Stowell, when in a dying state. It was resolved to bury him with honours of a patriot and a martyr to the cause; and in the teeth of the Habeas Corpus suspension the resolve was boldly and fully carried out. There was nothing secret in the movement – it was carried out in broad day, and united in by hundreds at the outset, but by the time the procession reached the graveyard it had been increased to thousands. The heads and trappings of the horses which drew the hearse, as well as the vehicle itself, were decorated with laurels and evergreens; behind came the coffin, containing the remains, borne on the shoulders of six men who each carried green boughs, the coffin itself being also strewn over with wreaths of laurel and other emblematic symbols of nationality. Then followed over 300 young and old men in regular military order, four abreast, nearly everyone having beard clips on the chin, such as is worn by 'Irish-Americans.' The flagways at both sides of the street were thronged.

James Macaulay, who travelled through Ireland a few years afterwards, noted the undercurrent of sympathy that remained for those Fenian prisoners who were serving penal servitude, 'The general feeling throughout Ireland is that these are political prisoners; and though this feeling is erroneous, it is not the less powerful in keeping up disaffection towards England. To treat political prisoners with the same severity as common felons is against the usage of civilized nations, and is regarded, in the case of these prisoners, as a wrong to Ireland. These prisoners have apparently been treated with exceptional harshness.'[103] Macaulay urged the government to be as magnanimous as the American government, which had given amnesty to confederacy troops.

In rural areas as the century progressed opposition to evictions grew. To galvanise this discontent the Land League was founded in October 1879 by Michael Davitt, a Fenian activist who had spent many years in British prisons, to press for a national reduction in rents, an end to evictions and ultimately for a transfer of the ownership of the land from landlord to tenant. Davitt persuaded the MP for Co. Meath, Charles Stewart Parnell, to become its president. Parnell was himself a landlord, owning some 5,000 acres in Co. Wicklow. In the summer of 1879, Parnell addressed a meeting of tenant farmers at Westport and outlined the future campaign against the landlord class:

A fair rent is a rent the tenant can reasonably afford to pay according to the times, but in bad times a tenant cannot be

expected to pay as much as he did in good times … Now what
must we do in order to induce the landlords to see the position?
You must show them that you intend to hold a firm grip on
your homesteads and lands. You must not allow yourselves
to be dispossessed as your fathers were dispossessed in 1847
… I hope that on those properties where the rents are out of
all proportion to the times a reduction may be made and that
immediately. If not, you must help yourselves, and the public
opinion of the world will stand by you and support you in
your struggle to defend your homesteads.

The campaign was fought with increasing bitterness and violence
– against the landlords and their agents and also against those who
disobeyed the Land League, and particularly those who took land
from which others had been evicted.

Process serving and evictions became the occasion for mass
demonstrations; families evicted for the non-payment of rent were
assisted; and those who bid for farms from which their neighbour had
been evicted were ostracised by the local community. Parnell outlined
the latter policy at a big outdoor meeting held at Ennis in 1880:

What are you to do with a tenant who bids for a farm from
which his neighbour has been convicted? Now I think I heard
somebody say 'Shoot him' – but I wish to point out a very
much better way, a more Christian and more charitable way.
You must show what you think of him on the roadside when
you meet him, you must show him in the streets of the town,
you must show him at the shop counter … even in the house
of worship, by leaving him severely alone, by putting him into
a sort of moral Coventry, by isolating him from the rest of
his kind as if he were a leper of old, you must show him your
detestation of the crime he has committed.

Paschal Grousset noted the form that social exclusion took:

> Let a farmer, small or great, decline to enter the organisation, or check it by paying his rent to the landlord without the reduction agreed to by the tenantry, or take the succession of an evicted tenant on his holding, or commit any other serious offence against the law of land war, he is at once boycotted. That is to say, he will no longer be able to sell his goods, to buy the necessaries of life, to have his horses shod, his corn milled, or even to exchange one word with a living soul, within a circuit of fifteen to twenty miles round his house. His servants are tampered with and induced to leave him, his trades people are made to shut their door in his face, his neighbours compelled to cut him. It is a kind of excommunication, social, political and commercial; an interdict sometimes aggravated with direct vexations. People come and play football on his oat fields, his potatoes are rooted out, his fish or cattle poisoned, his game destroyed.[104]

As the nineteenth century progressed rural violence became increasingly marked as the rural population began to resist eviction. Among the landlords killed was Lord Mountmorris, who was murdered in September 1880 near his residence, Ebor Hall in Co. Galway. He had a small estate with fifteen tenants with whom he had a poor relationship, having shortly before his death obtained ejectment decrees against two of them. Even more unpopular was William Clements, 3rd Lord Leitrim, who owned property amounting to 94,535 acres, including an estate of 54,352 acres in North Donegal, who was murdered on 2 April 1878. His arrogance and brutality had become a byword that alienated him even from members of his own class. He had, for example, removed all the tenants of Rawros to build his castle at Manorvaughan and those at Cratlagh to plant a vista of trees; he had a chapel pulled down with the aid of crowbar men and forced a farmer keeping goats against the rules to kill them on the spot before his eyes. The *Manchester Guardian* of 4 April 1878, in condemning the murder had to concede:

> It is unfortunately impossible to deny that Lord Leitrim was accustomed to think far more of his own rights than of what was due to his tenants. He was in a state of constant warfare with the people on his extensive property and he drew upon himself increased odium from the personal part he took in the work of eviction. We are told, for example, that he 'usually appeared as his own counsel and witness in ejectment cases' – a practice which could hardly fail to intensify the popular resentment against him. Whatever may be said of him, he was certainly unfortunate in his relations to tenantry; but it is only in Ireland that this circumstance would be pleaded as an extenuation of the dreadful crime which has been committed.

Marie Anne de Bovet, a French journalist who came to Ireland in the 1870s to report on the Land War, was fascinated by the excitement an eviction could create in the locality:

> Ordinary evictions are commonplace affairs, but those which are carried out at the price of a regular battle are worth going to see. The whole apparatus of the law is brought into play – police, infantry, and cavalry. Barricading themselves in their houses, the inhabitants launch from the windows stones, broken pots, hot oil, and boiling water. To break in the doors a sort of battering ram is employed, the walls are demolished stone by stone, men, women and children are dragged forth by main force, the movables are turned out, the doors and

windows closed with planks, and sometimes the roof itself taken off to render the tenement uninhabitable. All this goes on amid the execrations of a yelling crowd, which an agitator or the priest of the parish inflames with well understood exhortations to abstain from violence.[105]

Evictions caused dramatic changes in many parts of the Irish countryside. Bernard H. Becker noted in the early 1880s while travelling through Connaught:

Not only that professional 'deludher,' the car-driver, but tradesmen, farmers, and all the less wealthy part of the community still speak sorely of the evictions of thirty and forty years ago, and point out the graveyards which alone mark the sites of thickly populated hamlets abolished by the crowbar. All over this part of the country people complain bitterly of loneliness. According to their view, their friends have been swept away and the country reduced to a desert in order that it might be let in blocks of several square miles each to Englishmen and Scotchmen, who employ the land for grazing purposes only, and perhaps a score or two of people where once a thousand lived – after a fashion.[106]

In *My Visit to Distressed Ireland* (1883) Richard F. Clarke found a country denuded of large tracts of its population, 'No one who lives in a country likes to see it depopulated. What more mournful sight than ruined houses, empty cottages, towns falling into decay? The traveller through Ireland has to encounter this painful sight. If it is painful to him, how much more to those who dwell there! Not only painful, but a source of a thousand miseries. Trade decays, shopkeepers depart, the country markets are deserted, there is no life, no activity, no demand for the work of the carpenter or the mason or the smith.'

Shortly after Lord Leitrim's murder, Margaret Dixon McDougall, author of *The Letters of 'Norah' on her Tour Through Ireland* (1882), was driven over his estate and found:

> The murdered Earl has left a woeful memory of himself all over the countryside. He must have had as many curses breathed against him as there are leaves on the trees, if what respectable people who dare speak of his doings say of him be true, which it undoubtedly is. Godly people of Scottish descent, Covenanters and Presbyterians, who would not have harmed a hair of his head for worlds, have again and again lifted their hands to heaven and cried. 'How long, Lord, are we to endure the cruelty of this man?'

Dixon McDougall attended a Land League meeting while stopping in Omagh, where she witnessed a speech by one of its most influential leaders, politician John Dillon. 'There was a great force of constabulary in town, and military also.' She had a prominent seat at the meeting and watched proceedings with a great deal of interest:

> The first speakers, not accustomed to pitch their voices so as to be heard by a crowd, were quite inaudible where I sat. On the contrary, every word Mr. Dillon said was distinct and clearly audible. He has a clear voice, pleasant to listen to after those who preceded him. He is tall, slim, rather good-looking, very black hair, which he wears long, and which was so smooth and shining that it made him look like an Indian, and truly he is as well made, lithe and nervous-looking as one.[107]

McDougall found the atmosphere in the country frightening:

> It must be borne in mind that there was a famine in the land but a short time ago, that these thousands and thousands

of people who are under eviction now have no money and no place to go to but the ditch-back, or the workhouse. The workhouse means the parting with wife and children. These things must be taken into consideration, to understand the exasperation of mind which is seething through the whole country.

McDougall deplored the fact that the newspapers' coverage of the land war was entirely one-sided. She was particularly struck by the fact that no mention was made of the suffering of the tenantry, while paragraph after paragraph was given over to the prevention of cruelty to animals. In her opinion, 'One great trouble among the people is, they cannot read much, and they feel intensely; reading matter is too dear, and they are too poor to educate themselves by reading. What they read is passed from hand to hand; it is all one-sided, and "who peppers the highest is surest to please."'

In April 1880 Benjamin Disraeli's Conservative administration was defeated in the general election and William Gladstone's Liberal Party was returned to power. Gladstone was determined to address the land issue; in February 1870 he introduced a bill to bring about a radical reform of the Irish land system. Its leading feature was a Land Commission to adjudicate rents, and therefore to establish the principle of dual ownership of land, by both owners and tenants, into the law. The new Act also guaranteed the tenant fixity of tenure provided he paid the rent and gave him the right to sell his holding, together with any improvements he had made to it, to an incoming tenant. Although it did not go far enough for many, it worked well. The rents fixed by the land courts were reasonable and the return of better potato harvests meant that the crisis on the land was temporary easing. On the other hand, landlords experienced reductions in rent that averaged out at around 20 per cent. As one contemporary observer noted, there was an unpleasant irony to this, 'The landlords who have suffered least have probably been those who simplified their properties by wholesale evictions.'

A series of Land Acts followed, culminating in the 1903 Act, popularly known as the Wyndham Act, which offered the landlords a 12 per cent bonus in addition to the agreed price if they agreed to sell out their entire estate. The act introduced the principle of sale of the whole estate, with tenants agreeing to common terms, rather than the piecemeal sale of holdings. Provision was also made for the purchase of estates by the Land Commission and the resale of untenanted lands to uneconomic holders or evicted tenants. The act was popular with tenants because it guaranteed annual repayments lower than existing rents. Therefore by the beginning of the twentieth century, government legislation had brought about in Ireland a complete revolution in land ownership. Within a generation the position of the landlords in Ireland had been altered as the land passed into the hands of the former tenants. In the words of the Nationalist MP Tim Healy, 'The Act undid the confiscations of James I, Cromwell, and William III.'[108]

Chapter 5

Small and Invariably Shabby

Ireland remained a predominately rural society throughout the nineteenth century. Only five centres, Dublin, Cork, Belfast, Limerick and Waterford, had more than 20,000 inhabitants. What did change was the physical fabric of nineteenth-century towns as new public and commercial buildings multiplied, while public libraries, theatres, railway stations, banks and shops gave the high streets a more prosperous look. In his book *Ireland in 1839 and 1869*, H.S. Thompson noted with approval:

> In all the principal towns public buildings of a substantial and handsome appearance have been erected since 1839. New churches, banks, asylums, are everywhere to be met with, and English magistrates and guardians of the poor might with advantage visit the Irish court-houses and union workhouses. The ornamental character of these buildings is doubtless partly due to the beauty of the blue limestone of which they are for the most part built, but their designs show good taste, as well as fitness for their purpose, and the sites have in general been selected with great judgment, so that they contrast very favourably with the barrack-like appearance of many public buildings in England.[109]

It reminded English tourists of home. James Macaulay observed in his book *Ireland in 1872*:

> At the remotest towns and villages the post arrives with laudable regularity, and the electric-telegraph wires reach to

every corner where there are English-speaking inhabitants. At the railway stations there are bookstalls, with newspapers and miscellaneous literature; and the traveller, whether commercial or non-commercial, will notice no great differences from what he has been accustomed to in provincial journeys in England.[110]

Until the beginning of the Victorian reign military barracks were often the finest and most substantial buildings in many towns. The fact that town rents were often higher in Ireland than in England was put down to the need for accommodation for officers and this was a contributory factor to their unpopularity with those locals who were not renting property or selling merchandise. The soldiers were often the chief support of the local tradesmen, the officers generally dinning at taverns, while the common soldiers bought meat and other provisions in the shops. While visiting Limerick, Thackeray was struck by the presence of army officers 'with very tight waists and absurd brass shell-epaulettes to their little absurd frockcoats, walking the pavement – the dandies of the street'. An avid admirer of the beauty of Irish women, he continued, 'the street is full and gay, carriages and cars in plenty go jingling by – dragoons in red are every now and then clattering up the street, and as upon every car which passes with ladies in it you are sure (I don't know how it is) to see a pretty one, the great street of Limerick is altogether a very brilliant and animated sight'.[111]

By the mid-nineteenth century Irish towns were lit by gas, as noted by Kohl on his journey between Newry and Belfast in the 1840s, 'Nearly all the little towns through which we passed that evening were lighted with gas. It is remarkable how this important new invention has already penetrated all through this country.'[112] Early gasworks in Ireland were generally stationed in low-lying areas of cities and towns to take advantage of the tendency of gas to rise. They were generally sited close to navigable waterways to facilitate the cheap transport of coal and limestone. In the second half of the century it also became common for textile mills and large institutional buildings like hospitals to build their own private gasworks, particularly if they lay outside the existing supply networks.[113] The by-products of coal gas production ensured that gas works were also the first large-scale sources of ammonia, sulphur and sulphuric acid as well as tar for caulking roads, creosote for wood preservation and naphthalene for moth balls.[114]

The second half of the nineteenth century saw increased numbers of small entrepreneurs such as shopkeepers and merchants in the larger towns and villages. William Makepeace Thackery observed:

> Besides the bookshops, I observed in the long, best street of Limerick a half-dozen of what are called French shops, with knick-knacks, German-silver chimney-ornaments, and paltry finery. In the windows of these you saw a card with 'Cigars': in the book-shop, 'Cigars'; at the grocer's, the whiskey-shop, 'Cigars': everybody sells the noxious weed, or makes believe to sell it, and I know no surer indication of a struggling, uncertain trade than that same placard of 'Cigars'.

Harriet Martineau was unimpressed by the relaxed approach to opening hours adopted by traders, 'The shops in the Irish towns open late, and close very early – at 6 or 7 o'clock,' she complained and, as Thackeray found in Waterford, even when they were open you could not always guarantee service:

> We went into one, a jeweller's, to make a purchase – it might have been of a gold watch for anything the owner knew; but he was talking with a friend in his back-parlor, gave us a look as we entered, allowed us to stand some minutes in the empty shop, and at length to walk out without being served. In another shop a boy was lolling behind a counter, but could not say whether the articles we wanted were to be had; turned

out a heap of drawers, and could not find them; and finally
went for the master, who could not come. True commercial
independence, and an easy enough way of life.[115]

The development of the banking sector helped facilitate the growing
number of shops and businesses. Although there had been banks in
Dublin since the seventeenth century, it was not until the 1820s that
parliamentary legislation allowed banks to be established outside a radius
of 50 Irish miles (longer than an English mile) from Dublin. A series
of joint-stock banks were subsequently established: the Northern
(1824), the Provincial and the Hibernian (1825), the Belfast (1827), the
Agricultural and Commercial (1834) the National (1835) the Ulster and
the Royal (1836) and the Munster Bank (1862). Leitch Ritchie, in his
book *Ireland Picturesque and Romantic*, found on a visit to Sligo that,
'four banks were now established in the town: the first bank established
here, a branch of the Provincial Bank of Ireland, has done much good.
The Scottish plan of lending money on good security, or opening what
are technically called cash credit accounts, was exactly what Ireland
wanted. It did not introduce proximately new capital into the country,
but it put into activity the dormant capital already existing.'[116]

Ritchie welcomed the prosperity the new banks brought to provincial
towns no longer dependent upon Dublin financial institutions:

The effects of this are strikingly visible in the rising fortunes
of more than one country gentleman in the neighbourhood
whom I could name. The establishment of these banks
throughout the country, I look upon as the greatest step
that has been taken in my time towards the advancement of
Ireland in wealth and civilization. Dublin is no longer the
centre and reservoir of everything valuable. People are able
to look at home even for loans of money; and the advantages
of a metropolis are distributed over the whole kingdom.[117]

The new banks also liberated many farmers and businesses from the hands of lenders who set exorbitant interest rates. Henry Coulter, when travelling through the west of Ireland in 1862, found that:

> The extortions of the usurers, who are to be found in almost every country town, also press very severely on the unfortunate people whose necessities force them to have recourse to those harpies, for the mass of the people are absolutely ignorant of the commercial value of money, and though they feel the burden, and sometimes sink under it, they do not really know how atrociously they have been 'fleeced'. Fifty, sixty, seventy, eighty, and one hundred per cent, are frequently charged by these money-lenders. If the debtor appeared to be in embarrassed circumstances before the half-year's rent becomes payable, the usurer lost no time in taking out a decree at the quarter sessions ensuring that he anticipated the landlord in demanding payment of his rent.[118]

Coulter found that the only establishments flourishing in Kilrush were the pawn offices.

The shortage of ready cash remained a perennial problem for much of the Victorian period. In the 1880s a French visitor to Dublin found, 'Money is so scarce that if you want to exchange a five pound note, in nine cases out of ten you do not get your right amount of change in specie. They give you back a quantity of small Irish banknotes, plus the change in half-crowns and shillings, and that not without having caused you to wait a long time while the important transaction was entered in and brought to a termination, and then only by the united energies of half the neighbourhood.'[119]

The proliferation of licensed premises in Irish towns was the source of displeasure to those Victorians with a temperance outlook. 'Everywhere in this county we see the fearful words emblazoned, prophetic of misery and crime – "Licensed to sell beer and spirits";

to which are frequently added "wine and tobacco," which are apt to keep close company,' complained American preacher William Stevens Balch in 1850. 'Here is another prolific cause of the wretchedness of this country. Intemperance is the parent of innumerable vices, half the world's misery; and tippling is the immediate cause of intemperance. Jails and poor-houses are always needed where dram-shops are common; and, if governments will license one, they must support the others, and the people, who consent to both, must be the sufferers.'

Margaret Dixon McDougall, active in the American Baptist Home Missionary Society, condemned the inhabitants of Ballymena, Co. Antrim for the easy availability of alcohol in the town, 'Notwithstanding the depression in the linen trade, this town presents a thriving, bustling appearance as it has always done. The number of whiskey shops is something dreadful. The consumption of that article must be steady and enormous to support them. There is squalor enough to be seen in the small streets of this town, but that is in every town.'[120]

Contemporaries frequently blamed workmen for squandering what money they had in public houses. Sir Charles Cameron noted sympathetically that:

> it is to him what the club is to the rich man. His home is rarely a comfortable one, and in winter the bright light, the warm fire, and the gaiety of the public-house are attractions which he finds it difficult to resist. If he spends a reasonable proportion of his earnings in the public-house, is he more to be condemned than the prosperous shopkeeper or professional man who drinks expensive wines at the club or the restaurant, spends hours playing billiards or cards, and amuses himself in other expensive ways?[121]

Although visitors noted with approval the public buildings that adorned many towns, those streets that radiated off the main street were generally shabby. Henry Coulter visited Tuam in 1862, finding it, 'remarkable for the extent of its suburbs, which are larger in proportion than those of any other place that I have visited; and I regret to say that much poverty exists among the people who inhabit them. Rows of mud cabins extend in various directions, some to a distance of fully one mile from the town, and the aspect which they represent is miserable in the extreme.'[122]

Dr John Forbes, during a visit to Cork in the early 1850s, found similar conditions of wealth and poverty that he had encountered in Dublin:

Like all large towns, and more especially the large towns of Ireland, Cork contains masses of hidden streets of the most squalid description, inhabited by a ragged and seemingly wretched population. In passing through such streets, however, it is but just to the inhabitants to state that we saw no riotous or indecorous behaviour, and were but rarely solicited for charity. In going along the better streets, on Sunday, we observed many wretched-looking women, most of them with ragged children on their laps or by their side, squatted in the recesses of the doors of the shut shops, obviously beggars, yet not begging, except with that speaking look of misery more emphatic than words. Even the children were as silent as their mothers.[123]

Limerick, lying south of the great grazing counties, carried on a good trade in corn and provisions, for, although the city was more than 60 miles from the sea, ships of 500 tons were able to sail up the Shannon and unloaded their cargoes at the quays. Walking through the district of Newtown Pery in the 1840s, William Makepeace Thackeray commented:

You are at first led to believe that you are arrived in a second Liverpool, so tall are the warehouses and broad the quays; so neat and trim a street of near a mile which stretches before you. But even this mile-long street does not, in a few minutes, appear to be so wealthy and prosperous as it shows at first glance; for of the population that throng the streets, two-fifths are barefooted women, and two-fifths more ragged men: and the most part of the shops which have a grand show with them appear, when looked into, to be no better than they should be, being empty makeshift-looking places with their best goods outside.

Henry Inglis took a remarkably similar view, 'A person arriving in Limerick by one of the best approaches, and driving to an hotel in George Street, will probably say, "What a very handsome city this is!" while, on the other hand, a person entering the city by the old town, and taking up his quarters there – a thing, indeed, not likely to happen – would infallibly set down Limerick as the very vilest town he had ever entered.'[124]

The fictional heroes of Emily Taylor's *The Irish Tourist* were impressed by the thriving appearance of Cork, once considered the 'Bristol of Ireland':

The people of business, appeared to me highly respectable; the shops, about on a level with those of Bristol; and though I certainly met with beggars, I can say, that I have seen quite as many in Islington or Hampstead as I saw this day in Cork. The numbers of poor, but decently clad people, going to and fro on their day's work, showed that there was no lack of employment. 'If this be a fair specimen of Ireland,' thought I, 'I shall go back and contradict all our reports of Irish wretchedness, especially I might say this, when, in answer to my enquiries about wages, I was told that many of these men earned sixteen-pence per day, at the mills and breweries and distilleries, which are the leading manufactories of the place. These flourmills are magnificent establishments: I have never seen any equal to them in England. The city, also, exports in large quantities, bacon and butter and livestock.

Cork was for many visitors their first port of call in Ireland. The introduction of steam had dramatically reduced the journey time between Cork, Bristol and Liverpool from the days and sometimes weeks spent on uncomfortable sailing boats, dependent as they were upon the tide and weather, to less than twenty-four hours. Mr and Mrs Hall felt sure that, 'Under such circumstances it is not surprising that comparatively little intercourse existed between the two countries and that they were as much strangers to each other as if the channel that divided them had actually been impassable.' The new luxurious steam ships tempted an increasing number of tourists to Ireland, as Mr and Mrs put it, 'as much as a bridge across St George's Channel would have done'. Cork was also an important port for emigrants. Mr and Mrs Hall stood on the quay to watch some emigrants embark in one of the steamers for Falmouth on their way to Australia. 'The band of exiles amounted to two hundred and an immense crowd had assembled to bid them a long and last adieu. The scene was very touching, and it was impossible to witness it without heart-pain and tears.'[125]

The streets of Irish towns frequently thronged with country people selling their wares or in search of work. American visitor Asenath Nicholson observed in the mid-1840s when visiting Galway:

On my return to my lodgings, I saw a company of men assembled in a square, and found it was a collection of poor countrymen from distant parts, who had come hoping on the morrow to find a little work. Each man had his spade, and all were standing in a waiting posture, in silence, hungry and weary; for many had walked fifteen or twenty miles without eating, nor did they expect to eat that day. Sixpence a day was all they could get, and they could not afford food on the Sabbath, when they could not work. The countenance of one

near me was a finished picture of despair, which said clearly,
'It is done: I can do no more.'[126]

Hardship in the surrounding countryside could have a major impact
on the market towns, as noted by Sir Francis Head in his *Fortnight in
Ireland*, published in 1852. He asked the waiter at his hotel in Westport
what impact recent evictions had had locally: 'They have ruined it,' he
replied, 'the poor used to support the rich; now that the poor are gone
the rich shopkeepers are all failing. Our town is full of empty shops,
and, after all, the landlord himself is now being ruined!'

Most towns had regular fairs that attracted retailers of hats, stockings,
shoes, cloth and wool and pedlars who specialised in women's ware
and hardware, and who travelled from one market or fair to another
throughout the year. Author William Makepeace Thackeray described
a fair he encountered at Nass in the 1840s:

> the town, as we drove into it, was thronged with frieze-coats,
> the market-place bright with a great number of apple-stalls,
> and the street filled with carts and vans of numerous small
> tradesmen, vending cheeses, or cheap crockeries, or ready-
> made clothes and such goods. A clothier, with a great crowd
> round him, had arrayed himself in a staring new waistcoat
> of his stock, and was turning slowly round to exhibit the
> garment, spouting all the while to his audience, and informing
> them that he could fit out any person, in one minute, 'in a
> complete new suit from head to fut.' There seemed to be a
> crowd of gossips at every shop-door, and, of course, a number
> of gentlemen waiting at the inn-steps, criticising the cars and
> carriages as they drove up.

The Great Famine contributed to the rapid expansion of many
towns across Ireland. On 25 February 1847, the editor of *The Newry
Telegraph* drew attention to the fact that the soup kitchen that had

been established in Newry was encouraging the destitute poor from the outlying regions to come into the town:

> For weeks past, there have been observable in our streets numbers of mendicants with whose faces frequency of their appearance had not rendered the community familiar ... they travel into the town in quest of food, not obtainable in their own localities. Squalid objects they generally are. Their appearance sufficiently attests that their plea of Want is no deceptive subterfuge. In nine cases out of every ten, moreover, in reply to your questioning, you have from these evidently distressed supplicants for alms the statement, that they had patiently endured privations rather than beg, but that, disease having been superinduced by insufficiency of the necessaries of life, and innutritiousness of the food scantily partaken of, they had had no alternative but either to allow sufferers from 'the complaint' to perish of hunger or come into Newry and seek for bread, no relief being obtainable in their part of the country.[127]

The influx of these starving and destitute multitudes into the towns and cities excited more than pity – there was the general fear of fever, which provoked even greater inhumanity in the fearful townsfolk. John East, who witnessed this phenomenon in Cork commented:

> Now and then might be seen a number of persons running to a particular spot; and, on inquiry, you would hear of one having sunk to the earth in the sudden crisis of fever, or in death itself. From ten to fifteen bodies would be found in the streets, at the dawn of every returning day. A labouring man told his clergyman, that, in going direct from his own door to his work, he saw, in a single morning, five corpses in the way. So great was the alarm of fever, that numbers were daily

expelled from the low lodging-houses into the streets, as soon as the malady appeared. I myself saw and conversed with a family, consisting of a mother and three children, who had been discarded from a brother's house; and all their shelter in cold, stormy, and drenching weather, was a broken dresser, placed against a wall, in a vacant space, between two houses. There lay a boy in fever; while his mother and two sisters were sitting on the ground beside him!

In the north vast numbers fled to Belfast, already heralded as the great Victorian success story which the cotton and linen industries helped transform from a small town into a major industrial city. By the middle of the nineteenth century, Belfast, with its thirty-two linen mills and over half a million spindles, was well on its way to replacing Leeds and Dundee as the major linen manufacturer in the country. Mr and Mrs Hall were impressed by the industrial character of the city, which set it apart from the others they had visited in Ireland, 'It is something new to perceive rising above the houses numerous tall and thin chimneys which are indicative of industry, occupation, commerce and prosperity, with the volumes of smoke that issued from them giving unquestionable tokens of full employment, while its vicinity to the ocean removed at once all idea that the labour was unwholesome or the labourers unhealthy.' They went on to declare that, 'The clean and bustling appearance of Belfast is decidedly unnational. That it is in Ireland, but not of it, is a remark often on the lips of visitors from the south or west.'

Samuel Smiles, a Victorian celebrity whose book *Self Help* (1859) promoted thrift and claimed that poverty was caused largely by irresponsible habits, saw Belfast as an example of where men of drive and ambition could achieve greatness:

To show what energy and industry can do in Ireland, it is only necessary to point to Belfast, one of the most prosperous

and enterprising towns in the British Islands. The land is
the same, the climate is the same, and the laws are the same,
as those which prevail in other parts of Ireland. Belfast is
the great centre of Irish manufactures and commerce, and
what she has been able to do might be done elsewhere, with
the same amount of energy and enterprise. But it is not the
land, the climate, and the laws that we want. It is the men
to lead and direct, and the men to follow with anxious and
persevering industry. It is always the Man society wants.[128]

The rapid growth of Belfast had a profound impact on the people who
arrived in the town from the surrounding countryside, as noted by
the author of *Ireland Picturesque and Romantic* (1838). Leitch Ritchie
visited the town at the very beginning of the Victorian age and was
impressed by what he saw:

The streets, generally speaking, are wide and well aired, and the
houses by which they are lined, clean and respectable, although
built of unstuccoed brick as plain as a bandbox. The suburbs,
inhabited by the hewers of wood and drawers of water to the
easier classes, having nothing of that filth and misery which are
almost an unfailing characteristic of an Irish town. Everything
in and around Belfast proclaims that it is the abiding place
of a shrewd and intelligent population devoted to worldly
gain and far from being unsuccessful in its pursuits. This of
course is a general picture; for a town which has more than
doubled its numbers three times within the last seventy years
must draw constant supplies from the country; and to correct
the habitual imprudence and want of neatness observable
in the Irish peasant must be a work of time. A considerable
number of the masters, however, now provide their workmen
with lodgings; and some of these establishments are clean and
wholesome, and extremely neat ...[129]

The growth of Belfast impacted on life in the surrounding towns, which saw a decline in local industries such as soap boiling and tobacco spinning. Its prosperity was founded on three major industries, textile, engineering and shipbuilding. During the second half of the nineteenth century the population of Belfast rose from 90,000 to 350,000. Only by constantly redrawing the city's boundary could Dublin keep its coveted position as the largest city in Ireland. In 1888 Queen Victoria granted Belfast City status, and four years later another charter conferred on the Mayor the title of 'Lord Mayor'. This charter declared that Belfast was the capital of the province of Ulster and that in commercial and manufacturing it was the first town in Ireland.[130]

A *Times* special correspondent who visited Ireland in 1886 was impressed by Belfast's industrial prosperity, having visited the great linen factories, iron foundries, distilleries, mineral water manufactories and various other industries. However, what impressed him most was the shipbuilding yard of Harland and Wolff on the Queen's Island:

> There every trade connected with shipbuilding is carried on, down to sail-making, joinery, and upholstery. The smiths' department has a weird effect, with a hundred fires blazing and a hundred anvils at work, and the engine-making department is on a gigantic scale. In another department there are huge iron masts, between two and three hundred feet long; in another, sheets twenty-seven feet in length, ready to be fitted to the side of the vessel, and in another immense boilers that look as if they would sink any ship in which they were placed.[131]

In common with other industrial cities of the time, Belfast had its share of slum housing to which the poor were forced to live in the most desperate conditions. Periodic slumps in the textile or cotton industries left many unemployed and forced to depend on charity. Those in work were often on the breadline when hard seasons raised the price of food. With widespread destitution came diseases such as cholera and typhus. And it was not only the agent and middleman in the country who extracted rents; the same held true in the tenements of the cities. According to the Reverend W.M. O'Hanlon, Congregationalist minister for Upper Donegall Street Church in the city, writing in the 1850s:

> plunging into the alleys and entries of this neighbourhood, what indescribable scenes of poverty, filth, and wretchedness everywhere meet the eye! Barrack-lane was surely built when it was imagined the world would soon prove too strait for the number of its inhabitants. About five or six feet is the space here allotted for the passage of the dwellers, and for the pure breath of heaven to find access to their miserable abodes. But, in truth, no pure breath of heaven ever enters here; it is tainted and loaded by the most noisome, reeking feculence, as it struggles to reach these loathsome hovels. These are, in general, tenanted by two families in each, and truly it is a marvel and a mystery how human beings can, in such a position, escape disease in its most aggravated and pestilential forms. I know not whether it would service any valuable purpose to reveal the names of the proprietors of such horrid homesteads. But surely, they must be comparatively ignorant of the sanitary condition of the tenements from which their agents extract their weekly rents. That property has its duties as well as its rights, is a sentiment not less applicable on a small scale than upon one of the wildest dimensions; but the principle seems to be lost sight of in such squalid rotten nooks as the one now described.[132]

And as in the country, the loss of a breadwinner could spell disaster for the urban poor as Reverend O'Hanlon observed: 'In M'Tier's court we found fever doing its work; the husband of a poor woman had just gone to the hospital, leaving her, meanwhile, to starve or beg, or what seems to such persons, for some reason or other, the worse of all expedients, to knock on the poorhouse gate.' He contrasted the city dweller with poverty in the countryside. Walking through Samuel Street in Belfast, the Rev. O'Hanlon declared, 'Here, as I beheld the dense population, and felt the atmosphere, like a leaden weight, and looked at wan mothers, and sickly, emaciated children all around, it occurred to me to ask if these poor creatures ever breathe God's pure air, or look at nature, out amid fields, and trees, and hedgerows?'[133]

The fact that towns in Ireland were unhealthy places to live was confirmed by eminent Dublin surgeon Edward Dillon Mapother in his *The Unhealthiness of Irish Towns* (1866). The report focused on the poor sanitary conditions that caused sewage to infect water supplies. At Kells he was not surprised by the high epidemic rate:

> The sewers are too large, made of rubble masonry, flagged on the bottom, and are very imperfect, most of them having gratings which emit the effluvia of the decomposing sewage, and the stench-traps which had been laid were, at the time of my visit, out of order. The lanes and the yards behind the houses were covered with the most noxious kind of filth, for there was no accommodation for most of the houses.

He was alarmed by the state of the town's water supply. 'The water supply is by pumps, sunk, I was told, very superficially, two of them being in most dangerous proximity to the crowded church yard, one within ten, and the other within fifty yards of graves. Other pumps were in corners, which were also used as the filth depots of the town. The water was very hard in taste, and much complained of.'

Mapother was appalled by the contamination of the water supply in Sligo. He found the river polluted by the nearby churchyard:

> the impurities from the churchyard, which is but a few feet distant, percolate into it. It is disgraceful that some steps

are not taken to close this graveyard, as well as those of very many other Irish towns. That of Sligo is in the very midst of the town; its earth is dark, fetid, and overcharged with human remains, so that it cannot forward the decomposition of the bodies. So numerous have been the interments, that the surface of the ground outside has been raised three or four feet above the level of the floor, obscuring the Abbey walls, which are so interesting to the archaeologist.

Overcrowded graveyards were a feature of many Irish towns and cities. The graveyard of St Fin St Barre's Cathedral, Cork, had to be closed because 'whenever an interment was made several other bodies had to be displaced, some even in half a decomposed state, and that coffins had to be placed very near the surface. Bad smells pervade the grounds, and were complained of by the neighbouring inhabitants and those who attend the service of the Church. Very many cases of fever had been admitted into hospi[tal] from the neighbourhood.'134 The prohibitive cost of burials was a factor, as noted by the Chairman of North Union Guardians in February 1878. Dr R. Davys stated, 'that the poor people, to avoid expense of burial, leave the bodies of their dead infants in the vicinity of the graveyard in order that after their discovery they may meet with proper interment.'135

Chapter 6

Working Life

W orking life for many in Victorian Ireland was hard and grim. Although the standard working week was sixty hours, many worked much longer for low wages. Working conditions were often harsh and dangerous, particularly for women and children. Workers tended to live close to their place of employment until the expansion of railways and the tram networks. As the century progressed, the government, under sustained attack from social and religious reformers, legislated for better working conditions, fewer hours and to end the exploitation of children, often against the determined resistance of employers and political opponents.

Belfast, during the Victorian era, came to resemble the dark Dickensian world that was familiar to readers of *Hard Times* and *David Copperfield*. Already the cotton industry in the north was being eclipsed by the newly mechanised linen mills. Belfast stood at the heart of the linen industry. John Barrow, who visited the town in the mid-1830s, was struck by the pastoral aspect of the industry at the time:

> verdant fields, intersected by bleaching-grounds covered with linen as white as snow, which afforded a cheerful and lively prospect, more particularly to a stranger not accustomed in his own country to look upon the latter object. The linen is laid out in long strips, the width of the web, and, with the blades of grass standing up between them, has the effect, from a little distance, which is produced just when the snow is in the act of dissolving with the warmth of the sun.

By 1850, a third of the flax spinning mills, producing over half of the linen output for all of Ireland, were located in the Belfast area. William Makepeace Thackeray wrote in 1840, 'A fine night-exhibition in the town is that of the huge spinning-mills which surround it, and of which the thousand windows are lighted up at nightfall, and may be seen from almost all quarters of the city.' Thackeray visited Mulholland's factory in York Street. Originally a cotton factory, it had burned down in 1828 and was replaced by a five-storey factory with three steam engines driving some 8,000 flax spinning spindles. Thackeray was impressed by the scale of the operations:

> There are nearly five hundred girls employed in it. They work in huge long chambers, lighted by numbers of windows, hot with steam, buzzing and humming with hundreds of thousands of whirling wheels, that all take their motion from a steam-engine which lives apart in a hot cast-iron temple of its own, from which it communicates with the innumerable machines that the five hundred girls preside over ... They work for twelve hours daily, in rooms of which the heat is intolerable to a stranger; but in spite of it they looked gay, stout, and healthy; nor were their forms much concealed by the very simple clothes they wear while in the mill.

James Johnson, in his *A Tour of Ireland* (1844) reflected, 'On a first glance at an establishment of this kind, and at 500 young women busy at work, and earning good wages, one would be inclined to exclaim, what a blessing have steam and machinery conferred on Old England!' However, on reflection he conceded 'these five hundred girls produce, by aid of the engine, as much work as five thousand could do without it: – this throwing, as it were, four thousand people out of employment!'[136]

The spinning mills were built in green field sites along the lower Falls and Shankill roads and formed the nucleus of west Belfast.

The mill owners built row upon row of terraced houses for their rapidly expanding workforce. In these houses close-knit communities developed, with each generation following its predecessor into the spinning mills and factories. These areas soon developed along sectarian lines as Catholic workers settled in the Falls Road area while Protestants gravitated towards the Shankill, Ballymacarrett and Ballynafeigh region.

Newspapers championed local investment. The arrival of a new blacking and match factory in Belfast was welcomed by the *Belfast Morning News* of 30 August 1869, because 'it manifestly requires a broader variety of occupations than have yet been provided for its working classes, so that the inevitable vicissitudes of a particular trade may not disastrously affect an entire community, and that when one set of "hands" have to remain in comparative idleness, other employers of a different description will be actively engaged.' The new factory was erected in McAuley Street by R & D Anderson, already established in Upper Church Lane. 'The buildings, which are alike spacious and substantial, stand upon an ample plot of ground at the rear of the street. They comprise a series of workshops, not only thoroughly ventilated, but admirable adapted in every other respect of the various purposes for which they were designed, and altogether form the framework, as it were, of a model establishment.'

The new factories may have been spacious and substantial, but they were often dangerous places to work. Linen workers ran the risk of being maimed or killed by exposed machinery. Injury and death were endemic and frequent accounts of accidents appear in local newspapers. The *Belfast News-Letter* of 1 May 1854 reported that an employee of Messrs Rowan of York Street had suffered terrible injuries and was not expected to recover, 'She was engaged at the carding part of the machinery and her hair by some means got entangled in the machinery in which the greater part of the scalp was removed from the head.' The *Belfast News-Letter* of 24 May 1880 recounts the death that took place in the early hours of the previous Saturday morning at the extensive establishment of Combe, Barbour and Combe, Falls Foundry, 'A man named John Keown, residing in Woodburn Street, while engaged at a steam crane in the moulding shop … was caught in the crane, and received such injuries as to cause almost instantaneous death.'

Some employers could be more enlightened in their dealings with employees, although, in one case at least, this ended in tragedy:

DREADFUL ACCIDENT.

Some time ago a labouring man in the employment of the Messrs. Allen, millers, of Shannon Vale, about two miles from the town of Clonakilty, died, leaving a wife and family to deplore his loss. With a feeling of humanity which does them credit, the proprietors allowed his poor widow three shillings a week for her support, and she, to prove her gratitude for such extreme liberality, went to the mill every day, for the purpose of mending empty bags and keeping the place clean. One morning, about a week ago, as she was preparing for her accustomed labour, having gone too near the machinery, her clothes were caught by the clogs of one of the wheels, and before the slightest assistance could be given, she was crushed to death; – her two legs being completely severed from the body, which was otherwise shockingly disfigured. The mill was stopped as soon as possible, and the unfortunate woman conveyed to her own house, where an inquest was held, and a verdict of accidental death returned. What adds to this melancholy affair is the fact that the deceased was far advanced in a state of pregnancy.[137]

Few jobs were more dangerous than working in a match factory. In December 1882, a fire broke out at the Lucifer match factory of Samuel Osborne in Millfield Place and destroyed the entire building and contents. The *Belfast News-Letter* for 16 December 1882 acknowledged 'the great risk which workers' were expected to run. 'Small fires in a match factory are of almost daily occurrence. The most skilful worker often accidentally ignites a handful of matches, and as quickly extinguishes the flame. Spontaneous combustion sometimes takes place where excessive heat is applied, but prompt action nearly always arrests contagion.' In defence of the employers the paper declared, 'the greatest precaution is always taken to prevent the possibility of a fire, though it may be that, as in many equally dangerous trades, the workers are inclined to ignore the chances of danger, and to behave in certain circumstances as others less acquainted with the manufacture would fear to do'.

According to the 1871 census, domestic service accounted for almost 15 per cent of the female workforce. Servant life was not an easy one. Staff could be dismissed for unsatisfactory service. Mr and Mrs Hall condemned the treatment of Irish servants, 'They are insufficiently remunerated; little care is bestowed upon their wants; they are seldom properly fed and lodged ...' An 'odious and evil custom' they took objection to was the mode of paying servants what was called 'breakfast money', which was a small allowance allotted to them by their employers for food and the other necessities of life. 'The almost inevitable consequence is that of the weekly allowance they contrive to save a considerable portion, or nearly the whole, usually with a view to devoting the quarter's wages untouched to the necessities of their more miserable families "at home"... thus they are subjected to severe privations in the midst of plenty, if they scrupulously abstain from taking that which, by this rule, is not to belong to them.'[138]

Servants employed in inns and hotels unashamedly pressed guests for money, complained one Canadian visitor, 'In many places servants pay for their places for their chances of begging from passengers, instead of being paid, as they should be, by their masters. The system is demoralising.' He continued:

It is painful to see healthy, intelligent looking human beings stretch out their hands to you begging for money, which you don't owe them, and which you are not entitled to give. If you give liberally, you are rewarded with such acknowledgments as 'May the Lord's blessin' light on yer honor every day ye rise, and send ye safe to yer journey's end, and afterwards receive yer sowl to glory.' If you don't give as much as is expected, it is received with silence and a sullen countenance, and if you give nothing, they dare not curse you before your face lest the master's interest should suffer, and they should be dismissed, but won't you catch it among fellow servants when you are gone. Before leaving a hotel, you are accosted thus: – 'I'm the housekeeper, sir.' 'I'm the chambermaid, sir.' 'Remember boots, yer honor.' 'I carried your trunk, sir.' 'I'm the waiter, yer honor,' &c., &c., &c.[139]

Servants who were efficient and hard-working could be in great demand. The Society for the Encouragement and Reward of Good Conduct in Female Servants, established in Belfast in 1836, attempted to encourage servants to remain in their places of employment. According to the original prospectus of the society:

The periodical changes of servants which take place in this town, are universally acknowledged to be a great evil seriously to operate against the interest and comfort of families, and to have a most injurious effect upon the conduct of servants themselves.

By wandering continually from place to placc, young women encounter temptations of every description; and many a promising character has thus been ruined, and ultimately sunk to the lowest state of degradation, who might, in her station, have become a valuable member of society, if she had, in the first instance, retained a respectable situation.

The society guaranteed a servant who completed a fixed number of years, either four or seven years of uninterrupted service in one household, a sum of money to the amount of 4 to 10 guineas. Mr and Mrs Hall welcomed this initiative:

> The honest, faithful, long-serving attendant should be liberally rewarded as she should have (as in Belfast) her card of merit, (to her as precious as the Waterloo medal we see so frequently glittering on the breasts of our brave veterans) so that she might leave it as a legacy on her death-bed to some dear relative or friend; there should be a positive certainty that none would be rewarded who did not, in every sense of the word, deserve it; the knowledge of this would stimulate to good conduct.[140]

Servants who lost their positions could quickly fall upon hard times. A glance at the weekly return of admissions at the St Joseph's Night Refuge for the homeless poor, Cork Street, Dublin, for the week ending 13 July 1871 shows that servants made up the largest number of inhabitants, with 150 seeking shelter and food.[141] Homes for aged servants were also established and it was thought that if they were aware that they would be taken care of in old age it would be an incentive to them to behave well while employed. An advertisement in the *Dublin Daily Press* of 29 December 1888, offered 'Comfortable Lodgings for respectable Women Servants, temporarily out of place, in Protestant Servants' Home, 21 York Street'.

Nineteenth-century Belfast offered more opportunities for women's work than many British cities, especially from the mid-century with the rapid expansion of the linen industry. As a result, there were substantially more women in Belfast than men. In 1841 there were 38,000 females and 32,000 males; in 1901 the ratio was 188,000 to 162,000. Women worked in the linen industry, which in 1901 employed 24,000 females but only 7,000 males. Women were also found in large numbers in the clothing trades (11,000 compared with 4,000 males) and in domestic service, which employed almost 8,000 women and girls and provided 13 per cent of all female employment.

There were few areas of employment that middle-class women could enter. Teaching and governessing were two of the mainstays for those forced to support themselves. Shop work was also considered respectable work for young women. Shop assistants worked long hours, six days a week. Wages were not much better than that of factory workers, though shop assistants had to maintain a higher standard in appearance and dress. Office work also began to open up for women at the turn of the century. Women within offices had lower status than men and also became associated with the less well-paid areas of typing and bookkeeping. The expanding public sector also opened up clerical opportunities for women. The Post Office was regarded as the pioneer of women's employment, offering positions as telegraph operators or counter hands to intelligent, educated working-class girls. The country's female service typist took up her post in the Department of Agriculture and Technical Instruction in 1901.

Both boys and girls went out to work because of the overwhelming necessity to get every penny into the household. Children had, of course, worked since time immemorial, but the new mechanised age created working and living conditions that were shocking. Factories, now steam powered and no longer dependent upon a steady water supply, moved into the towns and cities where there was a plentiful supply of child labour. Many factories were operated by apprentice pauper children from the nearby workhouses. They were housed in barrack-like 'prentice houses so that they could not escape the confines of the factory for long. Only marginally better off were the so-called 'free' children who still lived at home in the surrounding slums. These juveniles or 'half-timers' attended school either in the mornings or afternoons, or on alternate days. But the law was largely ignored due to the absence of any means of enforcement. The minimum age for starting at the spinning mill or weaving factory was eight years until 1874, when it was raised to ten, eleven in 1891 and twelve in 1901. However, these laws were openly flouted as only four inspectors were appointed to monitor this legislation.

In 1863 the publication of *The Water-Babies*, a novel by Charles Kingsley, did much to raise public awareness about the gross mistreatment of children in this kind of employment through its central character, Tom, a child chimney sweep. But it was not until the 1870s that legislation required sweeps to be licensed and made it the duty of the police to enforce all previous legislation. It came too late to save one boy who died under horrible circumstances in Cork County Gaol in 1863. According to the *Cork Examiner* for 2 November of that year:

A boy lower case named Patrick Tansion [Tonson], about 14 years of age, was smothered in one of the chimneys of the County Gaol yesterday. He was apprentice of a sweep named Andrew M'Mahon, who has the contract of sweeping the chimneys of the gaol, and was on yesterday morning sent up one of the chimneys in the tower for the purpose of cleaning it. The chimney was rather narrow and when within some distance of the top the boy became jammed in it so he could neither go up nor down. In this position he was smothered, by the soot falling around him, before those beneath were aware of his danger. After he had been a short time in the chimney, his master became alarmed at his not returning, and called out to him. He received no answer, and on getting up found the unfortunate boy dead. The body was at once got down, and the police at the Victoria station were informed of the unhappy occurrence. Constable Real immediately proceeded to the gaol where he found M'Mahon, the deceased's employer. He asked who had sent the boy into the chimney, and on M'Mahon saying that he had done so, the constable took him into custody. M'Mahon was then carried before Mr. Leahy, J.P., and was committed to gaol until an inquest on the body of the boy should be held.

If the poor and destitute were vulnerable to a wide range of illness and disease, those in occupations were susceptible to a wide range of infirmities brought about by their trade. Many suffered because of the constrained position under which they worked. In 1867 Dr John Moore, writing on the influence of flax-spinning on the health of mill workers, was concerned about the spinning rooms where 'little girls are engaged, and here it is that the tender form of childhood is often in danger of being taxed beyond that it is able to bear'. 'The truth is,' noted the *Belfast Telegraph* in October 1877, 'that little seems to be known of the real struggles and physical dangers of factory existence, and that when people are in the habit taking pride over manufacturing progress, there is exceedingly small conception entertained of the trials which the factory worker is compelled to undergo.'

The death rate from phthisis was alarming. It was caused by the effects of dust constantly floating in the workrooms. The *Telegraph* continued:

> The class known as 'preparers' would appear to be the chief sufferers, but carders, hacklers, machine-boys, and spinners are also seriously afflicted, although the latter class not to the same extent the others. With regard to the spinners we are told that good deal of disease is generated by their garments being wetted by spray from the spindles, which so saturates them that in going out into the cold air in the evening their wet clothes gives them bronchitis almost immediately. The same results are entailed upon the doffers, among whom there is a still greater amount of mortality. Indeed, there does not seem to a department of the occupation that is not attended by fatal disease and the only surprise is that the deathrate is not far in excess of that given in the present elaborate returns.[142]

Workers also suffered from exhaustion. According to Dr Moore:

> Those who have been long in the atmosphere of the spinning-room generally become pale and anaemic, and consequently pre-disposed to those ailments which spring from such a state

of constitution. Children placed there early and compelled to keep upon their feet the entire day, as the nature of their employment obliges them to do often, suffer from the young and tender bones, which form the arch of the foot, being crushed and flattened.

It was not until 1874 that hours were successfully cut down to ten every weekday and six on Saturdays, and even then, employers added an extra duty of cleaning machines after hours. Until 1874 the usual working day began at 5 a.m. and ended at 7 or 8 p.m. Thereafter, until the beginning of the twentieth century, the working day began at 6.30 a.m. and finished at 6 p.m., with two three-quarter-hour breaks.[143]

At the British Association for the Advancement of Science, in September 1855, Dr Malcolm of Belfast, read a paper titled 'On the Influence of Factory Life on the Health of the Workpeople'. He directed attention to the influence of flax and tow dust, which materially injured the organs of respiration. 'The minute particles of this dust consisted of pointed angular fibres, armed, as seen through the microscope, with minute particles of silica, which, as was well known, was the chief ingredient of glass, and must, sooner or later, by inhalation, produce organic disease.'

This was not the only problem. 'The position of those workers, who were confined to a stooping posture, was, of course, unfavourable, and so was the high temperature. In the spinning room, the air was not only warm, but charged with vapor, so that the workers were constantly perspiring, and the skin, of course, exited to undue activity.'

In addition to this, there was the sudden transition from a warm and moist atmosphere to a cold and dry atmosphere, when the workers left the mill. Not everyone in the audience was convinced. A Mr Billing declared that 'much of the disease which exited among the factory workers was owing to the use of malt liquors, and the inordinate quantities of bad tea and coffee taken by the female workers especially'.[144]

A new source of employment for both skilled artisans and white collar workers was provided by railway companies. Over 30,000 men were engaged in railway building during the peak construction years of 1847 and 1848. This number would subsequently hover between 10,000 and 15,000 by 1860. Unskilled workers were recruited locally, but generally did not move on with the railway line: the navvies resented the intrusion of outsiders whether local or from further afield. English workers were assaulted on the Drogheda and on the Great Southern railways, and labourers on the Cork & Bandon refused to work not only with Englishmen but with Wexford men. The Midland and the South Eastern warned their contractors to employ local labour, although this was partially to placate local landowners who were faced with mass unemployment and a rise in the poor rate. It meant changing part of the workforce as the line progressed, while retaining experienced men for more skilled work such as cuttings, embankments and viaducts. For a time workers enjoyed unaccustomed luxuries of meat, bread and cheese, but returned to destitution when the line moved on. The Great Southern labourers at Knockardagannon in Offaly in 1847 reacted to their discharge by killing their ganger with a pickaxe when he protested that he had nothing to pay them with.

Recruitment of staff to work the railways faced difficulties only when recruiting for the managerial grades or more specialised skilled workers like engine drivers, who, before 1850, were mainly recruited from England. The younger sons of the professional classes filled the clerical posts while the better-educated element from the lower orders might aspire to the supervisory posts. The directors of the various railway companies regarded the appointment of even lowly staff as a privilege of their position. The posts were greatly sought after with good wages and fringe benefits. Departmental heads and station masters generally enjoyed free housing or paid only nominal rents and were supplied with free coal, while all companies supplied uniforms to their staff. Widows were granted lump sums ranging from £3 to £10, and sometimes funeral expenses, for the loss of their husbands through accident or injury, and some railway boards employed eligible orphans. The higher ranks also enjoyed sick pay and as early as 1835 the management of the Kingstown established a medical service for its workers and families that included the provision of hospital beds and medical attention in their homes. Later railway companies such as the Great Southern established contributory benefit societies to which it contributed £50 a year as well as fines.

There was also the possibility of promotion and a change of role: porters could become railway policemen or progress to guards, switchmen, ticket collectors, brakemen and occasionally station masters. Lower-class station masters in smaller stations were often promoted to higher classes on the opening of new sections of the line.[145] The workforce was overwhelmingly male, as the reaction to the appointment of a female station master by the West and South Clare Railway in 1898 in the Leinster Reporter shows:

> In this age of surprises the fair sex are taking their share; but so far as we know they have not hitherto stepped into the railway station except as passengers. Miss Lizzie Divine however has given a new lead to ladies who do not care to eat the bread of idleness. Her father, the later station master of Craggaknock, died some time back; and feeling like the military recruit 'free, able and willing,' she sent an application to the directors of the West and South Clare Railway to appoint her, and with a gallantry befitting Irishmen's character, these gentlemen responded to a man, not a single or married member being averse to a female station master.[146]

Chapter 7

Policing and Crime

Ireland was perceived in the popular English press as a lawless country rife with agrarian crime and assassination. Frequent periods of agrarian unrest, the murders of prominent landlords and their agents, and the Young Ireland and Fenian risings gave credence to this perception. On the other hand, as many visitors to the island were keen to point out, the inhabitants were a peaceable lot, time after time they recorded the small kindnesses they had enjoyed. Novelist Anthony Trollope, who spent several years in Ireland working for the Post Office, recalled in his autobiography:

> It was altogether a very jolly life that I led in Ireland. I was always moving about, and soon found myself to be in pecuniary circumstances which were opulent in comparison with those of my past life. The Irish people did not murder me, nor did they even break my head. I soon found them to be good-humoured, clever – the working classes very much more intelligent than those of England – economical, and hospitable.[147]

This certainly appears to be backed up by the judicial statistics from the later nineteenth century, which show a decline in crime and the numbers in prisons. This may have been in part due to the part played by increased policing and partially by the major devastation caused by the Great Famine and the palliative effects of mass emigration.

A strong army presence was a feature of nineteenth-century Ireland. Ostensibly it protected Ireland from foreign invasion; in fact it also assisted county authorities against internal discontent. For most of the Victorian period, around 25,000 troops were stationed across the country. On a visit to Limerick, which boasted four barracks, William Stevens Balch found the conditions in the barracks bordering on the sumptuous:

> We visited this morning, one of the barracks, occupying a large fort on the high ground in the eastern part of the city. We bolted in unasked, and looked at the comfortable quarters of the soldiers. English statesmen are wise in one thing, keeping strong the right arm of their power. The soldiers are well fed, and well paid, and have an easy time of it. None of the common people fare half so well. They are a sort of indigent nobility, furnished with red coats, glazed caps, and good rations at the public charge, and required to exercise barely enough to digest their food.

Balch found the citizens of Limerick in a state of agitation after prominent Young Ireland members William Smith O'Brien and John Mitchel had used strongly seditious language in the city a few evenings before. Stevens talked with a junior officer and quizzed him about his loyalty should he be called on to suppress rebellious activity:

> I found him loyal, in every particular, though he admitted the wrongs of government, and the miseries of his countrymen. I asked him if the government was willing to trust him to fight his own friends in case of an outbreak. He said he was not amongst his friends; he came from the north, and should certainly obey orders. He further told me that companies from the west and south had been generally sent out of the country, to England, Canada, or other places, while their places had been filled from England, Scotland, and the north. He did not think there would be any serious outbreak, but the

soldiers were fully prepared to quell any rebellion that might be undertaken.[148]

Most of the soldiers' time was spent in the daily round of drills, parades, fatigues and marches. Their chief responsibility was to assist the civil power in preserving the public peace. This involved supplying detachments to escort prisoners, to protect sub-sheriffs executing judgments against defaulting tenants and tithe payers, to guard wrecks, to keep the peace at fairs and race meetings and at elections, and to search the country for arms. As a result regiments were frequently split up into numerous small detachments, scattered at different posts, there being at one time more than 400 military stations in Ireland. The army could also be a source of friction with the local population:

AFFRAY BETWEEN MILITARY AND CIVILIANS. CORK, SUNDAY. – A serious affray occurred here to-night. A bad feeling appears to have arisen between the soldiers of this garrison and the people, owing to the recent homicide of a private of the 1st Dragoons. About eight o'clock a body of soldiers, comprising men of 1st Dragoons, and 72nd and 22nd Regiments, marched down to the city, with belts in their hands. They entered a public-house, and being told there was not room, they commenced to clear the place. This done, they proceeded to another public-house, and assaulted the proprietor. Before entering the taproom the civilians put up barricades, and a fierce struggle commenced. Those in the taproom assailed the military with pints and bottles and every available missile, while the soldiers used their belts. The persons who had been previously assaulted joined in the affray, and eventually the military were beaten back.

The fight was renewed in the street, where stones and red-hot pokers were used against the soldiers. Order was eventually restored by the police, who succeeded in separating the combatants. Several wounds were inflicted on both sides, and some Highlanders' bonnets were borne away in triumph by the crowd.[149]

As the nineteenth century progressed law and order became more and more a policing matter. Despite a series of acts of parliament passed during the eighteenth century, the Irish police force at the time of the Act of Union of 1800 was still composed only of small groups of sub-constables. These part-time policemen, appointed by the grand juries, were few in number and poorly paid out of the county funds. In 1814 Sir Robert Peel, then Chief Secretary in Ireland, created the Peace Preservation Force, popularly known as 'Peelers', which could be called upon by the Lord Lieutenant for use in a district that had been 'proclaimed' as a disturbed area. This force proved inadequate and in 1822 the County Constabulary were established to maintain law and order throughout the rest of the country, while the Peace Preservation Force worked in proclaimed districts.

Under the reforming Irish Executive of the Under Secretary Thomas Drummond in the late 1830s, the system was remodelled again. He absorbed all the existing police forces into a new body called the Irish Constabulary under an Inspector-General in Dublin. Power to appoint and discharge members of the force, to make rules and to fix salaries was vested in the Lord Lieutenant of Ireland. The Irish Constabulary was responsible for the preservation of law and order throughout the country except for Dublin and Belfast, which retained their own police force. By 1836 the Irish Constabulary had grown to around 5,000 men and by 1841 this had risen to over 8,000. Charlotte Elizabeth, in her *Letters from Ireland* (1837), found the new force very different to the one she was used to in London:

In occasionally naming the police, I must guard you against the mistake of identifying them with those peaceable-looking gentry, who, with blue coats well buttoned up, and respectable round hats, perambulate the streets of London, apparently not only inoffensive but defenceless too; and whose chief business, as a casual observer would surmise, is to answer the frequent queries of bewildered pedestrians, at a loss whether the right turning or the left will sooner bring them to their destination. The police force of Ireland present a far different aspect: their uniform is dark green, altogether of military fashion, with regimental cap, broad black belt, short musket, cartouche-box, and bayonet. The officers, or chief and deputy chief constables as they are called, wear swords. This is one of the saddening characteristics of poor Ireland.

The police force was a very visible presence in even the most remote parts of the country. Members of the force, who were mainly Catholic, were recruited from among the tenant farmer class and were removed to distant stations. The force was unpopular in many areas because it was used to assist at evictions and because it supplied Dublin Castle with most of its intelligence information. The duties of the constabulary were gradually extended from peacekeeping to include the collection of agricultural statistics, enforcement of fishery laws, census enumerators and a variety of duties under the laws relating to food and drugs, weights and measures, explosives and petroleum. For this work they were poorly paid, there were no recognised off-duty periods or annual leave and a constable was confined to barracks at night. He could only marry after seven years' service, and then his proposed bride had to meet with the approval of the authorities. A constable could not vote in elections and it was forbidden for policemen and their wives to sell produce, take lodgers or engage in certain forms of trade.

By the end of the nineteenth century there were a total of around 1,600 barracks dotted around the Irish countryside with four or five policemen living in each barrack the norm. The sergeant had to ensure that the barracks was clean: the walls were regularly freshly whitewashed; the constables' bedsteads and blankets were neatly rolled up; the floors of the barracks were spotlessly clean. The local barracks was a popular source of information for many well-intentioned visitors to Ireland during the period. Mr and Mrs Hall visited the police station near Dunmanway, Co. Cork, in the 1840s.

> It contained five men, strong and active fellows; the rooms were all whitewashed, the little garden was well-cultivated and free from weeds. The men slept on iron bedsteads, and the palliasses, blankets, pillows, etc., were neatly rolled up and placed at the head of each. The firearms and bayonets, each as polished as a mirror, were hung up over each bed and the floors were as clean 'as a new pin'. Each man had his small box at his bed foot. All was in as perfect order as if all had been prepared in this little out-of-the-way place for the accustomed call of the inspector ... In this barrack the men were all bachelors; but it is usual to assign one married man with his wife to each barrack – the wife, of course, arranging the rooms, and providing the meals of the men who always mess together.

Visitors were impressed by the calibre of men recruited. In 1852 Sir John Forbes commented, 'They are, I believe, the picked men of Ireland; and being so, I verily believe it scarcely an exaggeration to say that they are also the picked men of mankind. They are not merely all tall, well-grown, and muscular, but they are almost all ... well-knit, of fine carriage, and of handsome countenances.' S. Reynolds Hole, Dean of Rochester, who visited Ireland in the early 1890s agreed, 'There is no exaggeration in stating, that if a regiment could be formed from the Irish constables, it would be the finest regiment in arms. See them wherever you may, they are, almost without exception, handsome, heroic.'

The constabulary were a very visible presence at court sessions in any small Irish town. Twice a year the common law judges went on circuit to try major civil and criminal cases including murder, infanticide, rape, robbery, burglary and arson at the assizes in county towns. The selection of cases to go before them was the responsibility of the county grand jury, which for much of its history consisted of twenty-three landowners chosen by the county sheriff. The judge was received with great pomp and treated to lavish hospitality, which was always an event in any town. The novelist William Makepeace Thackeray left an account of the assize at Waterford in his *Irish Sketchbook*:

> The witness is here placed on a table instead of a witness-box; nor was there much farther peculiarity to remark, except in the dirt of the court, the absence of the barristerial wig and gown, and the great coolness with which a fellow who seemed a sort of clerk, usher, and Irish interpreter to the court, recommended a prisoner, who was making rather a long defence, to be quiet. I asked him why the man might not have his say. 'Sure,' says he, 'he's said all he has to say, and there's no use in anymore.' But there was no use in attempting to convince Mr. Usher that the prisoner was best judge on this point: in fact the poor devil shut his mouth at the admonition, and was found guilty with perfect justice.

Being a member of the jury could be an onerous and thankless task. Sir Charles Cameron, in his *Reminiscences*, recalled the murder trial at Maryborough Queen's County, in August 1873 of James Moore:

> The jury in this case were kept forty-six days virtually in confinement. They were allowed a jaunt into the country under police escort, but practically they had no exercise. They were placed upon a good diet, allowed a liberal supply of whiskey, and provided with packs of playing cards. It was noticed that under these conditions some of the jurors increased in weight. On their enlargement one of them found

a very youthful addition to his family, another juror lost one of his. Several became bankrupt, due, they alleged, to their prolonged absence from business.

Murder cases were followed with great enthusiasm in the papers, the more sensational the better. Although they attracted great public attention, murder in nineteenth century was a relatively rare event. Executions were public events and were reported in considerable detail in the local press, as is shown by that of Francis Berry in front of Armagh jail in August 1852. He had been convicted at the Armagh Assizes for conspiracy to murder Meredyth Chambre:

Execution at Armagh

It is stated that he slept tranquilly for a few hours, but awoke about five, and at half-past eight was visited again by the Rev. Mr. Galloghy, who celebrated mass in the apartment, and continued with him for an hour. At half-past ten, he was removed to a room in the vicinity of the drop, and was engaged in religious exercises up to the period appointed for the execution, in company with the Rev. Mr. Rogers and the Rev. Mr. Crinian, Roman Catholic clergymen of the city. Shortly before twelve o'clock, the hour appointed for the execution, a detachment of the 46th regiment, at present occupying the barracks, consisting of two officers, Lieutenants Shervington and Chambers, two sergeants, one drummer, and 50 rank and file, under the command of Lieut. Shervington, and 50 of the constabulary, under the command of Sub-Inspector Kelly, were drawn up in front of the prison. The number of spectators was not large, consisting principally of the very lowest of the town population, and embracing a considerable number of females. There were not more than a dozen of the respectable inhabitants within the railings ...

At noon the door leading to the drop opened, and the convict, dressed in his shroud, stepped out and advanced to the drop which was hung round with black crape. In a short speech he urged his friends to 'attend to the advice of your clergy, which, if you do, you will not bring yourselves to the unhappy end which I have done. If I had taken my clergy's advice, I would not have been here this day ... I have been a great sinner, and I hope you will pray to God and the blessed Virgin Mary for me.' Having concluded his short address, the executioner pulled the cap over the culprit's face and shortly afterwards he was launched into eternity. The body was allowed to hang for forty minutes, when it was lowered down, placed in a coffin that was in readiness, and put on a hearse, which proceeded immediately along the Newry Road, in the direction of Forkhill, where Berry had formerly resided. The corpse was accompanied by a considerable number of persons, all of the peasant class, and it was expected would be met by great numbers on the way.[150]

The last public hanging in Ireland was in 1868, with executions thereafter confined behind prison walls. The details of the execution continued to be reported in gruesome detail in the newspapers. On Saturday, 30 July 1870 the *Cork Constitution* provided a comprehensive account of the execution of Andrew Carr, who had been convicted of the murder of Margaret Murphy six weeks earlier. The execution took place within the walls of Richmond Bridewell, by an executioner who was 'secured from one of the low haunts the city' and despite tests being carried out the previous night, the event turned into a bloodbath:

The rope having been adjusted, and a white cap having been pulled over the head and face the convict, the chaplain who stood by him to the last, bid him an affectionate farewell and, as the noisy bell of the prison was ringing, the bolt was drawn by the executioner, and the drop fell. Down came the wretched man, and when the rope stretched with a kind of burring sound, the headless body of him who but few seconds before was full of vigorous life rolled over in the bloody shingle with which the yard was covered, and soon after the head encased in the gore-saturated cap which covered it fell from the noose beside the lifeless corpse, from the neck of which protruded the lacerated muscle and bleeding vessels which had been wrenched asunder in the terrible fall. Unspeakable horror was depicted in every face, and quick and appalling was the fearful circumstance that for a considerable time no person moved from the place where they had been standing, and the empty noose of the rope swung to and fro in the morning breeze.

The Quarter Sessions in each county were made up of two or more justices of the peace. The sessions took place in the weeks around the dates of Epiphany (6 January), Easter (moveable), Midsummer (24 June) and Michaelmas (29 September) and took their name. They dealt with less serious crimes such as bigamy, assault, concealment of birth, bribery, criminal damage, prostitution, theft and vagrancy. Nineteenth-century justice was often arbitrary in nature, as can been seen in the following extract from the *Belfast News-Letter*:

BELFAST QUARTER SESSIONS
Tuesday, 9 July 1839

Charles Magennis, for stealing a coat, at Belfast, on 12 June, the property of Francis McIlwaine. Pleaded guilty; four months' imprisonment.

Thomas Hunter, for stealing a piece of bacon, on 12th June, the property of John Finlay. Guilty; seven years' transportation.

John McBride, for having in his possession a grate, on the 4th June last; same stolen from J. Hunter. Pleaded guilty; six weeks' imprisonment.

Margaret McKeown, for stealing a cap and cloak, at Belfast, on 13th June last, from Matilda Patterson. – Pleaded guilty; two months' imprisonment.

Michael Dyer, for having in his possession a piece of baize, at Belfast, on 29th May, the property of Isabella Toole; same having been stolen. Seven years' transportation.

Sarah Green, for stealing two half-crown pieces and a sovereign from Hiram Griffith, on the 24th June last. – Three months' imprisonment.

The Petty Sessions Court was presided over by two or more unpaid justices of the peace, or by a single paid (stipendiary) magistrate without the need for a jury. Each court met daily, weekly or monthly, depending on the volume of cases to be heard, and dealt with less serious cases. William Makepeace Thackeray visited Roundstone Petty Sessions in 1842:

> the Sessions-room at Roundstone, is an apartment of some twelve feet square, with a deal table and a couple of chairs for the accommodation of the magistrates, and a testament with a paper cross pasted on it to be kissed by the witnesses and complainants who frequent the court. The law-papers, warrants, &c., are kept on the Sessions-clerk's bed in an adjoining apartment, which commands a fine view of the courtyard, where there is a stack of turf, a pig, and a shed beneath which the magistrate's horses were sheltered during the sitting. The Sessions-clerk is a gentlemen 'having', as the phrase is here, both the English and Irish languages, and interpreting for the benefit of the worshipful bench.[151]

At Parsonstown Petty Sessions, a young lad named Kennedy, who was under ten years of age, was charged with hiding in a sugar hogshead of Martin Kennedy's shop with the aim, the policemen who charged him believed, of 'opening the shop to others during the night'. His mother, who brought a statement of character from Mr Hammersly, a local magistrate, did not help her son's cause when she told the magistrates that the previous week 'she sent the prisoner with his father's dinner to where he was at work, and also gave him two pence to purchase eggs with which he absconded'. Their worships ordered him to whipped and then discharged.[152]

Magistrates tended to take a strong line against gambling in the streets. In June 1882 three small boys named George Hamill, William M'Loughlin, and Francis Bradley were charged with 'having played pitch and toss in the public thoroughfare yesterday'. According to the local newspaper, 'The prisoners, who were under eleven years of age, said that they were sorry for what they did, and would not again be guilty of the offence.' The magistrate Mr Johnston fined them 5s each and costs.[153] At Cork Police Court before magistrate Felix Mullan:

Five newsboys were brought up for playing pitch and toss. Three of the youths were remanded since yesterday, and two more were charged with the same offence; having been arrested by Constable Kilfedder while in the act. Mr Mullan observed that they were beginning to infest the city; their mania (or playing pitch and toss) was so great with them that they gambled every farthing they earned, and then slept in the door ways, or under any other shelter they could procure at night, being afraid to go home. The lads in reply to the Bench said that they were never in jail before. The gamblers were discharged with a caution.[154]

Playing marbles was enough to land children in Belfast in trouble. At Belfast Police Court before resident magistrate J.C. O'Donnell, John Donnelly was summoned for having obstructed the thoroughfare in Little George's Street, playing marbles, on the 27th of the previous month. The policeman said that on Sunday morning last he saw a number of boys playing marbles on the footpath and ordered them away. They then commenced to 'boo' him. There were seven or eight boys there at the time. Mr. O'Donnell said the boys should have been at their place of worship instead of playing marbles. The defendant was fined with costs.[155]

In an attempt to find an alternative to jail for young offenders, the English model of Industrial Schools was introduced to Ireland in 1869. This enabled magistrates to send children under the age of twelve found begging, or else needing care and protection, to Industrial Schools to learn a trade. Industrial Schools were similar to National Schools except that offenders were required to spend only two hours a day on literary work and the rest on industrial training. Offenders between the ages of twelve and sixteen were dispatched to reformatories. John Fagan, the inspector of reformatories and industrial schools, reported in 1867 that of 1,410 children admitted to the schools that year, 904 had been classified as children found begging in public. The inspector claimed that in a large number of cases this situation had been deliberately contrived by destitute parents in order to qualify their children for admission.

Children were sent to the appropriate reformatory schools as dedicated by their religious background. As with the workhouses, disputes frequently arose when children were sent to the reformatory of a different religion. In a letter to the *Irish Times*, dated 29 December 1860, the writer complained that fourteen-year-old James Tyrrell, a Protestant, had been sent to a Catholic reformatory. Under the emotive heading 'New Mode of Kidnapping – Reformatory Schools' the writer complained that no one had enquired of the delinquent's mother as to his religious background.

Before the 1880s, the Irish prison system was an amalgam of state-run convict prisons, which became increasingly important with the gradual abolition of transportation. Men, women and children were transported, sometimes for the most trivial offences. A Co. Antrim man, William McKeown, received a seven-year sentence for stealing

A Funeral in Connemara Illustrated London News. 21 May 1870

A soccer match at the Admiralty Recreation Ground, Castletown, National Archives of Ireland

All Hallow Eve Kilkenny, Illustrated London News 6 November 1858

An Irish Peasant Family is visited by the Fairy Doctor London Illustrated News

Argideen Vale Lawn Tennis and Croquet Club, 1890s c.Argideen Vale Lawn Tennis and Croquet club

FARMING UNDER DIFFICULTIES IN COUNTY MAYO.

Armed Constables in co Mayo *The Graphic* 1880

Connaught Cabin, Richard Lovett, *Ireland Illustrated with pen & pencil* c1891

Consulting the priest: A Sketch at Claremorris, County Mayo Illustrated London News
26 November 1881

Customs House, Dublin, Leitch Ritchie *Ireland Picturesque and Romantic* (1837)

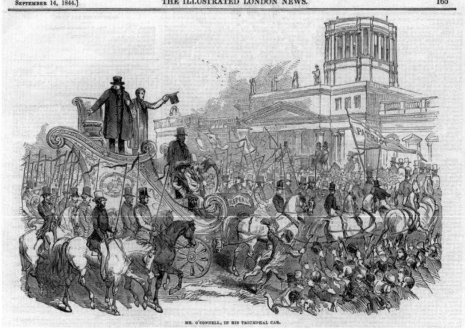

MR. O'CONNELL, IN HIS TRIUMPHAL CAR.

Daniel O'Connell, standing on his triumphal Chariot celebrates his release from prion
Illustrated London News 6 September 1844

Dublin Castle c1900, The National Archives of Ireland

Dublin Slums, Library of the Royal Society of Antiquities of Ireland

THE EJECTMENT.

Ejectments, Illustrated London News 16 December 1848

Sackville Street, Dublin, Portfolio of Famous Scenes, Cities and Paintings by John L Stoddard, (1899)

19th century photograph of Trinity College Dublin c 1890s unknown source

Lord Spencer Lord Lieutenant of Ireland from
Charles O'Mahony The Viceroys of Ireland (1912)

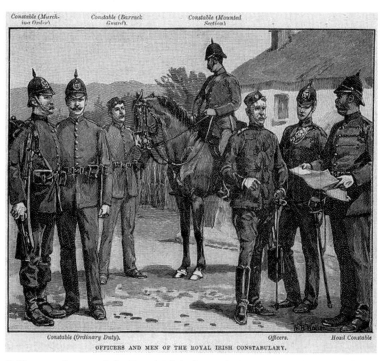

OFFICERS AND MEN OF THE ROYAL IRISH CONSTABULARY.

Officers and men of the Royal Irish Constabulary Illustration by William
Barnes Wollen from Cassell's Century Edition History of England (1901)

Mienies Illustrated London News 20 February 1847

THE VILLAGE OF MIENIES.

News Years Night in an old Irish Cottage, Illustrated London News 30 December 1848

Paul Cullen Archbishop of Dublin, by unknown 19th century photographer

PEASANT GIRLS.

Peasant Girls, Illustrated London News 7 October 1843

Queen Victoria bidding adieu to the Lord Lieutenant of Ireland from Queen Victoria, her grand life and glorious reign, John Coulter ed (1901)

Queen's visit to Dublin Ireland, Robert L'Estrange, 1900

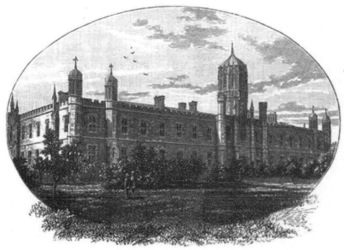

Queens College Galway,
Richard Lovett, *Ireland
Illustrated with pen &
pencil* c1891

Saturday Night in
Dublin, Madame
de Bovet, *Three
Month's Tour in
Ireland*, 1891

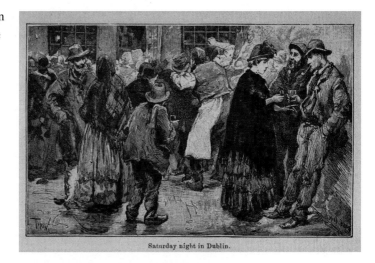

Saturday night in Dublin.

Top Row—Pidgeon, Penston, Doherty, Ronan (Treas.), Abbey, Kelly, Monks (Trainer), Cunningham (Secty.)
Lawless.   Second Row—Wimble, Jack Owens, Heslin, James Owens, Ledwidge.
Cleary.
SHELBOURNE F.C.   Webster's Series, Grosvenor Road, Belfast.

Shelbourne FC
National Archives
Ireland

Soup depot Cork,
Illustrated London
News 13 March 1847

Terminus of the
Midland and Great
Western Railway
Handbook to
Galway, Connemara
and the Irish
Highlands, (1854)

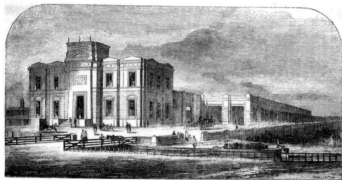

A car to Killarney,
William Makepeace
Thackeray, *The Irish
Sketch Book* (1843)

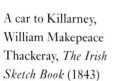

The Irish Jig, Leitch Ritchie *Ireland Picturesque and Romantic* (1837)

The Music Hall, Dublin Illustrated London News 1844

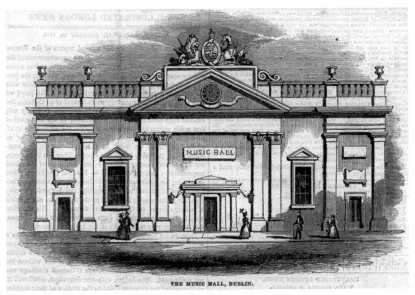

Trinity College Dublin, Illustrated London News 1851

Trinity College Dublin, Illustrated London News 1851

Waterford Courthouse,
William Makepeace Thackeray,
The Irish Sketch Book (1843)

The Pig fair, Meath, William Makepeace Thackeray, *The Irish Sketch Book* (1843)

Women at field work Roscommon, Illustrated London News 7 May 1870

Youghal Church, Leitch Ritchie *Ireland Picturesque and Romantic* (1837)

two and a half yards of cloth. Boys of twelve and under were sent to the penal colonies for pilfering, and women, often with infants or small children, for 'being vagabonds'.

Australia was the chief destination until 1853. New South Wales was removed from the system in 1840, and this was followed by Tasmania in 1852 and Western Australia in 1867. The main reason for this was that the Australian colonists came to regard the convict system as a stigma on those who had chosen to emigrate, as well as criticism in both Britain and Australia of the brutality of certain aspects of the convict system. During the first half of the nineteenth century transportation had proved a cheaper alternative to imprison. Local prisons were run under the authority of county grand juries and funded on the rates, as were bridewells for short-term detention of minor offenders. The author of the *Bible in Ireland* visited the jail in Tullamore in the mid-1840s, which contained a number of persons engaged in various activities:

> In the afternoon I visited the jail, which contained eighty-one prisoners; seventeen had been that morning sent to Dublin for transportation. They were all at work; some cracking stones, some making shoes, and others tailoring or weaving. Their food is one pound of stirabout, and milk in the morning, and four pounds of potatoes for dinner. There are two hospitals, one for males and the other for females. The drop where criminals are executed is in front. Four had suffered upon it within the last two years.

Mr and Mrs Hall found the jails of Cork, city and country, 'models of management, cleanliness and order'. However, they were critical of Irish jails for their 'want of classification' so that 'atrocious criminals and petty offenders are mixed together in a manner sadly prejudicial'. They found this particularly true of Clonmel jail, where 'the prisoners were placed before us in files; among them we saw an elderly and respectable-looking man striving to hide his face with his hat and stepping back to elude observation. We found that he had been confined for drunkenness, but that the person next to whom he stood was about to be tried for sheep stealing, and had previously been in custody on suspicion of murder.'[156] Kohl observed in the mid-1840s, after a visit to the same county gaol, that for many prison offered a more luxurious life than they could hope for at home:

> The entire prison is built of iron and stone; and as Paddy's dwelling is usually constructed of earth or mud, it may be said, without exaggeration, that for the commission of a wicked crime an Irishman is removed from a hole to a palace. His diet is also, in general, very much improved, for while he remained at home, with unimpeached honour, he had only watery potatoes; but as an offender in prison, he receives daily two pounds of bread and an allowance of milk along with it. It would, indeed, be difficult to make Paddy more uncomfortable in gaol than he is at home.

In his opinion such a system produced 'a peculiar and numerous class of offenders, who have entirely lost their love of freedom, and who because they live as well or better in gaol, do not scruple, after being set free, to offend again, and again to be imprisoned'.[157]

In 1878 the establishment of the General Prison Board brought prison administration under government control. This coincided with poor harvests and agrarian unrest, and a series of high-profile prisoners including Charles Stewart Parnell, John Dillon, and William O'Brien. The incarceration of such men and women turned the attention of many to the prison system. Tim Harrington, who spent two months in Mullingar Gaol in 1883, later testified before the Royal Commission that he had refused to participate in the twice-daily dumping of the prisoners' chamber pots outside the prison walls into the nearby river by means of a line up of the convicts.[158]

Transportation of women ended in 1853 and this increased the female prison population. They entered a system where there was no segregation of the sexes and where the harshness of the regime reflected its male intake. From 1878 all males serving sentences of twelve months or more, and females sentenced to over six months, were removed from most local prisons to convict prisons in Dublin, Cork and Limerick. The town gaols of Cork and Limerick became exclusively female prisons, as did Dublin Grangegorman and Belfast. For female prisoners there was little educational provision and work programmes if they existed were confined to cleaning, cooking and laundry duties. In Galway Gaol, according to the *thirty-eighth report of the Inspectors-General of Prisons in Ireland* (1860), female prisoners were granted one luxury over their male counterparts, 'There are baths in which all the females are washed on admission, throughout the year, and the males in the summer ...'[159]

The most common offences committed by women were linked to prostitution including soliciting, drunkenness, being drunk and disorderly and vagrancy. Prostitution was common in Irish towns and cities, especially where military garrisons were located. Many women were forced into prostitution through losing their employment or desertion by a spouse or breadwinner. Police were slow to take action in case it drove these women into new areas. Those areas that gained the reputation as the haunts of prostitutes pressed Dublin Corporation to rename their streets. In 1885 Lower Temple Street became Hill Street to placate local residents who 'had suffered serious deterioration in the value of [their] property'.[160]

Other offences associated with women were the desertion of infants, 'withholding sustenance from infants and concealing births'. More shocking was infanticide, which is a regular feature of Victorian newspapers. These young women had given birth to illegitimate babies, making them outcasts in their own communities. There was often a degree of sympathy among magistrates and neighbours for these unfortunate girls. The *Dublin Evening Mail* of 1 November

1864 recounted the story of a servant girl named Elizabeth Park, who confessed to leaving the body of her newly born infant in the manure pit at the rear of a house in Coleraine Co., Londonderry. The case caused a great deal of resentment locally when rumours spread that 'the poor unfortunate creature, having been taken in the act by which she sought to hide the miserable story of her shame and crime, was not permitted to put on one article of dress save what she wore at the time, but was marched barefooted, first to the police barrack, and hence, nearly half a mile, to the union workhouse'.

Domestic violence rarely came before the courts because it continued to have a degree of tolerance and was seen by many as bringing a family's name into disrepute. According to the *Kilkenny Journal* for 23 October 1872, at the City Petty Sessions:

> A man named Wall, from King Street, was brought upon remand from the county for beating his wife in a most brutal manner. Mrs. Wall, a respectable-looking woman, came forward, but declined to press the charge, at the same time interceding for the delinquent, and begging their worships to let him go. The bench, in accordance with the woman's application, let him off – at the same time giving him severe caution, and making him aware that had his wife pressed the charge against him be would imprisoned for six months.[161]

Domestic violence was not an exclusively Irish vice according to the *Dublin Weekly News*, which reported a case of wife beating in Norwich. The newspaper noted that the magistrate had expressed the hope that parliament would pass a law to enable courts to use the cat as a corrective in cases of gross violence against women. The newspaper smugly agreed that, 'The women of England are surely in need of all the protection laws can give them against their husbands.'[162]

Life for female prisoners differed little from that of their male counterparts. According to an account of female convict life in Mountjoy Prison, published in 1882, 'They are here from fifteen years old to sixty, and even more; innocent-looking girls who seem as if their consciences were not all seared, and who will probably yet become useful and respectable members of society; and withered, hardened specimens of humanity, who look as if they were at war with all the world, and never had such a thing as a conscience at all.' An initial probationary period of nine months was spent in their cells, apart from an hour's recreation and an hour in school. As probationers they learned to keep their cells clean, including the folding of their bedclothes in military fashion. These women were employed knitting or sewing in their cells. The daily routine did not vary:

> They rise all over the establishment at 6.30 a.m. this winter season, when they are allowed fifteen minutes to dress and clean their cells. The doors are unlocked at 6.45, and the convicts conducted to their respective places of worship for prayers, the others performing that morning duty where they slept. Prayers continue twenty minutes. The convicts are re-conducted to their cells, where they occupy their time in reading until 7.45, when breakfast is served. Dinner follows at 12.45, and supper at 5.15. Gas is furnished in each cell, and the inmates read the religious book, provided for them until a quarter to eight o'clock, when the bell rings for bed, and eight o'clock sharp the lights are turned out, and inmates tucked up for the night.[163]

Much of the violence and crime in Ireland was blamed on alcohol, which came under sustained attack from religious quarters during the nineteenth century. By the Victorian period, whiskey had replaced ale and cider as the most common alcoholic drink for most of the population, and for the poorer classes it was safer to drink than the water. On his visit to the old part of Limerick, William Stevens Balch commented:

> All along the street, centre and sides, were grouped masses of human beings, of both sexes and all ages, who exhibited

the lowest depths of poverty, intemperance and vice. The gin, beer, junk, and slopshops were in character with all the rest, in the style of Orange-street, though on a much larger scale. Smutty childhood, wrinkled age, hobbling decrepitude, gaunt distress, bloated drunkenness, shameless vice, barefaced crime – all the odiousness of ignorance, depravity and famine were mingled in a confused mass, the most loathsome and forbidding.[164]

The more sympathetic Sir Charles Cameron could not deny that there was a great deal of intemperance among the working dosses, and, as the Victorian period progressed noted that women, 'who formerly were rarely seen intoxicated, are now frequently to be observed in that state'.[165]

Bishop James Dole of Kildare and Leighlin believed that the main problems of alcohol consumption was to be found in the towns, where most of the licensed premises were to be found. But the rural population who visited the towns during fairs, markets and race meetings, were not dependent on licenced premises for their supply of drink, as Charlotte Elizabeth found out in her visit to the Mandeville Estate in Tandragee, Co. Armagh, where the agent was taking action against Shebeen houses: 'The Shebeen houses, as they are called, are to be found in every neighbourhood; and though no outward sign denotes the business carried on within, everybody knows that the occupier 'keeps a bottle'. She asked the land agent:

'Does not a great deal of the mischief perpetrated in Ireland, originate in meetings at these Shebeen houses?' 'Nearly all of it,' my friend replied. 'Many a respectable female dates her ruin and disgrace from them; and here political offences are plotted and ripened for execution. The profit netted by the owners of such unlicensed places is very great; I have known frequent instances, especially in Meath, and on the borders of Cavan, where a man having made his corn into whiskey, appoints a night, and issues regular cards of invitation, to this effect – 'A ball will take place at Pat Lavery's on Sunday evening, the – day of –'. This is a signal for a gathering of all ages; lads, lasses, and old folks who came to get a sup of the 'drink'. The lads treat the maidens, nothing being provided by the person giving the ball but music and lights; and liquor is paid for; the night is spent in carousing and all manner of revelry; and next morning, Pat Lavery has realized a sum to pay his rent, satisfy his priest, and do many other things beside.[166]

One Co. Kerry land agent, Samuel Hussey, a bitter opponent of the Land League, blamed drink for much of the agrarian crime in Ireland, 'There never was an outrage committed without an empty whisky bottle being found close to the scene of the murder.' 'Did you never hear the parish priest's sermon?', he declared. 'It's whisky makes you bate your wives; it's whisky makes your homes desolate; it's whisky makes you shoot your landlords. And – with emphasis, as he thumped the pulpit – 'it's whisky makes you miss them.'[167]

The first important temperance societies were established in Ireland in 1829, mainly inspired by the success of the anti-spirits movements in the United States. However, temperance did not become a major popular movement in Ireland until total abstinence was introduced from England in 1835 and the coming of Father Theobald Mathew, a Capuchin from Cork who took up the teetotal cause early in 1838. His crusade was a phenomenal success, particularly among rural Catholics. In the years before the Famine alcohol consumption decreased dramatically in Ireland: Temperance Reports record a few cases where publicans and brewers were forced to change their line of work. In Gort, for example, 'four public houses have been closed down ... and reopened as bakeries'. Although the figures are unreliable, there was a substantial reduction in crimes, especially those relating to intoxication. Kohl was convinced that the temperance movement had reduced 'riots and outbreaks arising from party hatred' even in counties as disaffected as Tipperary.

Kohl witnessed Fr. Mathew's reception at Kilrush in the 1840s and was impressed by the influence he had on his followers, 'Almost every Irishman wears the temperance medal, and no less than five million (this number I have from his own mouth) are said to have taken the pledge from Father Mathew'. Kohl's guide told him, 'When Father Mathew has once laid his hands on a man's head, and blessed him, and hung the medal around his neck, he is dedicated to temperance for his entire life: from that moment he hates all intoxicating liquors, and can no longer endure those who are given to drinking. So great is the effect of the blessing of our Apostle of Temperance.'[168]

Although many police inspectors welcomed the decline in drunkenness, by the early 1840s they were expressing concerns that the temperance movement might be subsumed by religious or political groups for their own purposes. O'Connell had taken the pledge in 1840 and his movement made use of temperance bands and reading rooms. Although Father Mathew made efforts to avoid this, more than half the county police inspectors and magistrates, asked if there was a connection between O'Connell's Repeal Association and the temperance societies, believed there was a connection between the two movements.[169]

Teetotalism suffered a rapid decline after the Great Famine and the death of Father Mathew in 1856. In Ulster, Presbyterians, Methodists and other dissenters were strong advocates of total abstinence and campaigned for anti-drink legislation for much of the second half of the century. A high point for temperance was the achievement of Sunday closing, which was introduced to Ireland in 1878. Significantly it excluded the five largest cities in the country (Dublin, Belfast, Cork, Waterford and Limerick). Also the fact that 'bona fide travellers', those who had travelled a distance of more than 3 miles, could be served ensured the laws were widely flouted outside the cities.

The link between crime and drink remained a popular cause of debate for the remainder of the century and was reported with great solemnity in the newspapers, combining as it did two of their readers' favourite subjects: crime and religion. Occasionally these columns were enlivened by a story that offered the newspapers the opportunity to poke fun at their betters: on the morning of Wednesday, 29 April 1840, the court correspondents were treated to the sight of a number of red-faced aristocrats and gentry who had been arrested while attending a grand fancy ball given in an unlicensed house by a woman named Booth in Little Grafton Street Dublin, according to a gleeful account that appeared in the *Freeman's Journal* on 1 May:

On Wednesday Morning the board-room of this office presented an unusually busy appearance, no less than 94 prisoners being brought up to have their cases decided by the bench, and the great majority of them consisted of fashionably dressed gentlemen on town [sic], military officers, and ladies of a questionable character. It appeared from the proceedings, that on the previous evening the police had been well acquainted with the fact of a grand fancy ball being about to be given in an unlicensed house kept by a woman named Booth, residing in Little Grafton-street, and they made arrangements to capture the whole of the delinquents ... When Mr. Tudor, the presiding magistrate, took his seat on the bench, he seemed to be much surprised at the figures presented by the prisoners. Were it not for the tell tale daylight, a person might have supposed he was in a ballroom. Most of the males were in full dress, and the women shone in all the colours of the rainbow; pearls were twined in the hair of those who had convenient ringlets, others wore guilt Malibrans, and white and red roses were in sufficient abundance to stock the shop of any dealer in artificial flowers.

It was curious to note the various demeanour of the accused, as they were brought up in several batches, and exposed to the gaze of the casual spectators present. Some tried to laugh off the affair, but their merriment was forced; and the majority of the women had their shawls pinned over their heads, and with averted eyes handed the amount of the fine imposed on them to the magistrates' clerk, and made their exit with great precipitation.

Chapter 8

Religion and Superstition

'In this unhappy country,' wrote James Johnson in *A Tour in Ireland* (1844), 'RELIGION, instead of cementing Christians together in one common faith and friendship, appears to be a corrosive agent that dissolves all cementing ties, and repulses man from man.' Even those, like William Le Fanu who considered the nineteenth century as one of unimpeded progress, conceded, 'Since my early days I have seen a vast improvement in everything but intolerance in religion; that, I grieve to say is as strong as ever.' These religious divisions had deep roots and were dictated not only by class but by ancestry, as Kohl found on his tour of Ireland in the 1840s, 'The three religions of Ireland, the Presbyterian, the Episcopalian, and the Roman Catholic, correspond with the three races which inhabit it – with the descendants of the original Irish, and of the earliest English colonists, who are all Catholics; with those of the later English immigrants, who are Protestants; and with the Scottish, who profess Presbyterianism.'[170]

Queen Victoria was unusually broad-minded, for her time, 'Sincerely Protestant as I have always been I cannot bear the abuse of the Catholic religion.' Her Irish subjects were not always so magnanimous. Religion was a badge of difference rather than a unifying factor in Ireland throughout the nineteenth century, as James Johnson complained: 'The Jew and Mahamodan do not more cordially despise and detest each other's creeds, than do the Protestant and Catholic sections of the same religion! This sectarian bigotry (for it does not deserve the name of religion) insinuates itself into and mingles with all the transactions of private life. It is carried even to exclusive dealing.

The tea of a Protestant grocer would stick in the gorge of a Catholic consumer, and *vice versa*.'

Schools, hospitals, and other charitable institutions, orphan societies, voluntary organisations, even sporting clubs, tended to organised along denominational lines. Kohl noticed:

> in Cork I lodged at an hotel, the landlord of which was a Protestant and a Tory, and received Protestants only as his guests. Another hotel in the city was, in like manner, exclusively frequented by Whigs and Catholics. In many other towns of Ireland these exclusively Protestant or Catholic hotels are to be found; and I have been told that there are even public conveyances in which Protestants chiefly travel, and others regularly preferred by the Catholics.

The evangelical Charlotte Elizabeth, who had toured the Manchester estates in Tandragee with land agent Henry John Porter, found that in Portadown she quickly forfeited her hard-earned Protestant reputation in the eyes of the locals simply by taking the wrong coach:

> Two coaches pass from Armagh to Belfast, nearly at the same time; Mr Porter had advised me to take advantage of the first, if possible, lest there might be no vacancies in the other. We learned from our little driver, that one of these was a Protestant coach, and the other a Roman one; and it was evident which way his predilection lay, by his frequent assurance that there was every prospect of the Protestant coach coming up first.

This was not the case, and when Elizabeth secured passage on the first coach that drew up, one of the locals shouted, 'That is the Popish coach; you won't get into Belfast in any time. The Protestant coach is just coming up. Sure you won't go in that!' and finding me resolved, he at last exclaimed, 'Mr. Porter would not go in that coach for ten pounds.'

Marie Anne de Bovet found similar conditions prevailing in Limerick:

> Here, as elsewhere in Ireland, they are very devout, and it
> is only by keeping apart from each other that the different
> religions can get on peaceably together. The double poison
> of political hatred and religious dislike ruins all sociability
> – in a country where the people are the most amiable of any
> in the world. Needless to add, neither social nor business
> relations are easy here: it is necessary to maintain an attitude
> of strict reserve, and avoid giving offence, while still holding
> your own opinions. Strangers benefit by it; nothing can equal
> the kindness and cordiality of Irish hospitality.[171]

One thing the churches broadly agreed on and that was the roles of
men and women. The Rev. John Gregg, a Church of Ireland cleric,
presented a series of lectures and sermons in Trinity Church in 1856
including one directed at women in which he asserted that the different
roles of men and women were preordained, 'The larger portion of the
labours of life – of public life – fall almost exclusively to the lot of men;
but a most important portion of the duties of life, especially of private
life, falls to the share of women … [God] has adapted your sex to the
peculiar duties to which you are called.' His sermons were advertised
for sale in The *Catholic Layman* at 2d each. The *Irish Homestead*
agreed that, 'neatness, order, and thrift are religious duties with the
women to whom the domestic care of a family is entrusted'.[172]

From 1537 until 1870 and disestablishment, the Church of
Ireland was the state church in Ireland. In order to preserve the
English interest in Ireland, nearly all the higher posts in the Irish
Church were filled with Englishmen, often persons who had missed
promotions in England. The lower ranks were largely recruited
from the ranks of the smaller Irish gentry. Co. Kerry land agent
S.M. Hussey commented that while they were 'perhaps, richer in
proportion than many of the curates and incumbents in England,

there are no "fat" livings'. He calculated that, 'The average in Kerry, and over most of the south of Ireland, is a stipend of two hundred pounds a year, which involves reading services in two churches each Sunday, and therefore puts the clergyman to the expense of keeping a horse and trap.'[173]As members of the established church they were expected to maintain a certain standing in the local community. John Fitzgibbon commented in 1868:

> The Protestant rector of a parish must support the rank of a gentleman. That he shall have a family is not only allowed, but expected; and that he shall maintain them with decency in his proper rank is imperative upon him. The curates also must keep their place as gentlemen upon stipends which seldom exceed the wages now paid to carpenters and bricklayers, and other skilled labourers, in Dublin, and other cities in Ireland.

The vast majority of landowners were Anglican, and, outside Ulster, its membership consisted mostly of the professional classes. Fifty per cent or more of all barristers, solicitors, civil engineers, medical men, architects and bankers are listed in the 1861 census as members of the Church of Ireland. Unlike the Church of England, which claimed to represent the majority of Englishmen, the Church of Ireland embraced only a minority of the population – no more than 12 per cent according to the census returns of 1861. Marcus Beresford, Archbishop of Armagh and Primate of Ireland, declared when its critics dismissed it as a minority church that, 'A Church that embraces so large a proportion of the educated classes, which numbers among its members the inheritors of the great historic names of the Country, a majority of the learned professions, and the mercantile classes, and which has implanted the principles of industry, order and loyalty for which the protestant population is so remarkable, cannot be said to have failed in its mission.'

Those with social ambitions were attracted to the church of the establishment. Mr and Mrs Hall found that:

> At one time many of the principal families in Ulster, particularly in Antrim and Down, were Presbyterians; but their descendants with very few exceptions, conformed to the Established Church; and their example is pretty generally followed by such of the mercantile and manufacturing classes as have attained to that wealth and standing which enable them to associate with the higher ranks.

Membership of the Anglican church had a certain prestige: the Church of Ireland was tasked with civil administration, being responsible for the upkeep of parish schools and roads; for the burial of the destitute; the welfare of foundling or deserted children; and for looking after the poor. This gave the Anglican clergy considerable authority in their parish, and this was reinforced by their close relationship with the local gentry, a fact that contributed to their unpopularity among Catholics and dissenters.

The concept of an Established Church meant that every person in the parish was considered to be a parishioner regardless of denomination, even though he or she did not worship at the local parish church. The vestry meeting was therefore a meeting of all the inhabitants of the parish. However, religious antagonisms often emerged. At a meeting of St Mary Shandon vestry, the unlikely named Mr H. Bible moved that Catholics should be excluded as it was an exclusively Protestant vestry. According to the *Cork Examiner*:

> Mr O'Flyn protested against such a shameful and exclusive proposition. It was true that Catholics could not vote at this vestry election of Church Wardens ... but the law authorised every parishioner, no matter what creed or sect, to be present

at every public Vestry. He was determined to insist upon that right, which he came there to try, no matter what resolution a few common exclusionists may come to (cheers). Messrs. Shepherd and Dowman moved, as an amendment, that Catholics may attend, which on being put from the Chair was carried by an overwhelming majority. The doors, which were previously closed, were now thrown open, and a numerous body of the parishioners entered.[174]

At St Mark's Parish this was disputed. Mr W. McGuinness, a Roman Catholic, was proposed for the office of churchwarden, but this was objected to by Dr Ringland, who claimed that none but Protestants could vote at the first vestry. The churchman acknowledged that 'the law is strange enough on this point, for although it allows a Catholic to fill the office of churchwarden, yet it prevents a Catholic from voting at the election for that office.'[175]

The vestry was also obliged to manage the tithe system, which nominally earmarked one tenth of the produce of the land for the maintenance of the established clergy and was payable in kind such as the tenth cow or sheep. The tithe was paid half-yearly in November and May but in many parts of Ireland payment was made in cash. The tithe was generally collected by a tithe proctor rather than by the incumbent clergyman. The clergyman received a fixed sum and the excess was retained by the proctor, who had therefore strong motivation to exact every last penny for himself. Agrarian secret societies sprang up in the 1830s to oppose its collection, which led to widespread intimidation and violence on both sides. Spasmodic violence broke out in various parts of Ireland, particularly in counties Kilkenny, Tipperary and Wexford, and reached its climax at the beginning of Victoria's reign. In 1839 parliament introduced the Tithe Commutation Act, which reduced the amount payable directly by about a quarter and made the remainder payable in rent to landlords. They in turn were to pass payment to the authorities, which meant that tithes were effectively added to a tenant's rent payment.

The Tithe Composition Act was to mark the beginning of a series of legislative changes that the Church of Ireland was subjected to during the nineteenth century. Opposition to the church was increasingly fervent from the 1850s, partly because the Roman Catholic bishops were increasingly alarmed at the missionary activity of some established clergy, which, especially in Connaught, had considerable, if temporary, success. But the real turning point was the census of 1861, which provided for the first time, reliable figures of denominational distributions. Out of a population of 4½ million, the members of the established church were under 700,000, of whom well over half were concentrated in the province of Ulster. It provided ammunition for those who opposed its privileged position.

Prime Minister William Gladstone's Irish Church Act of 1869 dissolved the union between the churches of England and Ireland and ended the Church of Ireland's position as the established church. 'So long as that Establishment lives,' Gladstone had warned, 'painful and bitter memories of Ascendancy can never be effaced.' The legislation was carried through its various stages in the face of a united and powerful opposition. William Lee, Archdeacon of Dublin, referred scornfully to those politicians who would 'deal with the worship of God as with a question of free trade'. Undeterred, Gladstone successfully guided the legislation through against considerable opposition in both the Lords and Commons in less than five months, which was described by the *Annual Register*, 1869, as 'the most remarkable legislative achievement of modern times'.

From 1 January 1871 the property of the church, which consisted almost entirely of lands, buildings and tithe, was, apart from churches and churchyards, confiscated and vested in a body of commissioners for Irish church temporalities. The commissioners were to provide for the life interests of clergy, schoolmasters and other ecclesiastical officials of the disestablished church, to make similar provision for Presbyterian ministers in receipt of regium donum and to pay a lump sum to Maynooth in lieu of the annual grant. Tenants on church lands were given the option of buying their holdings, or leaving three quarters of the purchase money on mortgage at 4 per cent. By 1880 over 6,000 tenants, out of some 8,400, had taken advantage of this opportunity.

The Roman Catholic Church remained the overwhelmingly predominate creed in Ireland. In 1861 Catholics were a substantial majority of the population, making up 86 per cent in Leinster, and more than 90 per cent in both Munster and Connacht. They were a minority only in four Ulster counties (Antrim, Armagh, Down and Londonderry) as well as in the towns of Belfast and Carrickfergus. In two other Ulster counties, Fermanagh and Tyrone, they accounted for not much more than half the population. John Forbes, who toured Ireland in the middle of the nineteenth century, commented, 'My experience in Ireland, hitherto, had certainly been almost entirely that of a man travelling in a Catholic country; so small a portion of the whole field of observation did the Protestant element seem to occupy: and … this decided Catholic character assumes even a still more striking aspect when presented in its Sunday dress.'[176]

The nineteenth century was a period of progress and reform for the Catholic Church following the removal of almost all of the legal obstacles imposed on it in the previous century. Significant building work was carried out throughout the century and a new generation of reforming bishops brought their influence to bear on the lower clergy through regular conferences, retreats and visitations. Under Archbishop Cullen, who became Ireland's first cardinal in 1866, the church was brought back into full discipline with Rome. Symbolically Roman dress became the fashion among the priesthood during the Cullen era.

Strong efforts were also made to regulate the behaviour of the wider Catholic community, particularly in regard to the rituals of faith. The restrictions of the previous century had led to a wide variation in religious practice and the merging of popular folk customs with Christian events. Spring wells were one such phenomenon that came in for clerical opposition. The *Ordnance Survey Memoirs* for the parish of Down, written in 1836, noted that local people were in the habit of coming at certain times of the year to Struell Wells and carrying off portions of the earth and stones as preventatives of disease. It is perhaps not surprising that such a gathering provoked a hostile response from the church for it was custom for penitents to bath in the wells at two specially constructed bathhouses. 'Even within the last 5 or 6 years the practice existed to an extent that appears extraordinary,' declares the *Memoirs* 'and the bathing house ... was seen filled by from 30 to 40 people of both sexes in a state of perfect nudity. During the time that these ceremonies were going on, the ground in the neighbourhood used to be covered with tents for the sale of whiskey, and the Sunday after St John's Eve was devoted to all kinds of mirth and festival.'

An astonishing number of parish churches were built during the Victorian era, reflecting a new self-confidence. The second half of the nineteenth century also saw the effective return of the religious orders to Ireland. Some, such as the Jesuits, the Franciscans and Dominicans, had a long history in Ireland. Archbishop Cullen was supportive of the newer orders such as the Vincentians and Redemptionists, with their Roman devotions and nationwide parish missions. The *Cork Examiner* welcomed the presence of these missions to counteract the activities of evangelical groups in the south and west. The newspaper was convinced that a mission led by the order of St Vincent from Castleknock to Castletown, Berehaven, to preach to locals in the Irish language would help support the activities of the local priest in resisting attempts by Protestant missionaries to encroach on his parish:

> Our readers are no doubt aware that this remote and ill-conditioned district has long since attracted the particular attention of the enemies of Catholicity, where it was once

hoped a flourishing and devoted colony might be permanently established. For the last six years neither effort nor expense was spared to ensure such a result, though we are glad to say nothing in accordance with the extravagant expectations entertained has been realised. The Priests led on by the Vicar of the District, the Very Rev. Michael Enright, P.P., whose exertions in encountering and defeating the foe's morality and religion are entitled to the highest praise, have manfully struggled against fearful odds, and in the worst of times in defence of their persecuted Religion, and if a few had fallen it is consoling to know that the good cause is safe and likely to receive additional security from the presence of the good Fathers of St. Vincent, &c.[177]

Such missions were also a calming influence during times of political and agrarian unrest. The *Carlow Post* welcomed the Vincentian Fathers in the town, which had been seriously disturbed during the Fenian uprising. It was aware that, 'efforts have been made by infatuated, misguided, and, in too many instances, unscrupulous persons, to implicate the people in general in hopeless and desperate rebellion, which had been undermined by the presence of missionaries in the district.' In its opinion:

The visit of these holy and indefatigable guides, directors and admonishers, so uniformly attended with beneficial results during the Holy Season of Lent, has been even far more conductive to good than usual on the present occasion, not only in our town but in its vicinity, at the distance of many miles in every direction. The confessionals have been continuously thronged from early hour every day till late at night, and the stirring instructions, eloquent discourses and exhortations delivered during the mission have been attended by thousands and listened to with depth of attention and intensity of interest that are already bearing and showing their good fruits.[178]

The dedication of Irish Catholics to the church was remarked upon by numerous travellers. In 1887, Paschal Grousset, noted that the Catholics he met were, 'Catholics not so only in name. The greater number follow the services of the Church, observe all the rites, maintain a direct and constant intercourse with priests. The sincerity of their faith is particularly striking, and is not to be found in the same degree even in Italy or in Spain.'[179] This devotion became more marked as the century progressed as many sought refuge in the church from the immense cultural, social and economic changes that were taking place around them. This devotion sometimes manifested itself in the sort of phenomenon that took place at the village of Knock, Co. Mayo, on the evening of 21 August 1879 when a group of men, women, teenagers and children witnessed an apparition of the Virgin Mary, Joseph and Saint John the Evangelist at the south gable end of the local small parish church. The site quickly became a place of pilgrimage. On her travels in Ireland, Margaret Dixon McDougall visited Knock and noted:

> As I stood looking, the car man came in after tying his horse, and knelt down on the damp earth before the Virgin's shrine and repeated a prayer. He was not ashamed to practice what he believed before the world and in the sight of the sun. When his prayer was over he joined me, and drew my attention to the number of crutches and sticks left behind by those who were benefited. I pointed out to him a very handsome blackthorn stick among the votive offerings, and asked him would it be a sin to steal it, as black-thorns were in demand over the water. He told me if I did that whatever disease was laid down there by the owner of the stick would cleave to me.

Religious life in towns, villages and rural areas, was centred on the chapel. Individuals and families depended on the Church for the celebration of the rites of passage – baptism, marriage and death. Until 1870 mixed marriages performed by Roman Catholic priests was illegal but marriages between Catholics had always been regarded as valid. The Catholic clergies relied on the contributions of their parishioners for their subsistence. This helped create a close bond between them and their flock, as Alexis de Tocqueville noted in 1835:

> There is an unbelievable unity between the Irish clergy and the Catholic population. The reason for that is not only that the clergy are paid by the people, but also because all the upper classes are Protestants and enemies. The clergy, rebuffed by high society, has turned all its attention to the lower classes; it has the same instincts, the same interests and the same passions as the people; state of affairs altogether peculiar to Ireland, a point which one should keep well in mind in speaking of the advantages of voluntary remuneration.

Presbyterian ministers enjoyed a similar place in the affections of the congregation in the north-east of Ireland. The Presbyterian population was heavily concentrated in Ulster, where 96 per cent of its members lived. In the counties of Antrim and Down, and in Belfast and Carrickfergus, Presbyterians were the largest single religious group and it had a strong presence in Co. Donegal. Congregations of Presbyterian settlers were also established during the Cromwellian period at Athlone, Clonmel, Dublin, Limerick and Mullingar. Margaret Dixon McDougall, who toured Ireland in the late nineteenth, visited Duncairn Presbyterian church and was struck by a singular fact:

> Found myself half an hour too early, so watched the congregation assemble. The Scottish face everywhere, an utter absence of anything like even a modified copy of a

Milesian face. Presbyterianism in Ulster must have kept itself severely aloof from the natives; there could have been no proselytizing or there would have been a mixture of faces typical of the absorption of one creed in another.[180]

The Presbyterians had long been an object of suspicion with the authorities. For much of the eighteenth century their freedom of action was severely curtailed by the penal laws so that it was technically illegal for Presbyterian ministers to perform marriages of members of their congregation until 1782. It was not until 1845 that they could legally marry a Presbyterian and a member of the Church of Ireland. In 1840, the Armagh Consistorial Court declared a marriage between a Presbyterian and an Episcopalian celebrated by a Presbyterian minister illegal. The following year, a man convicted of bigamy carried the matter to a higher court, on the grounds that his first marriage had been between a Presbyterian and Episcopalian performed by a Presbyterian minister and so was illegal. The Queen's Bench found in his favour. So great was the subsequent controversy that the government passed an Act in 1844 declaring valid not only future mixed marriages performed by Presbyterian ministers, but any past marriages.

By the middle of the nineteenth century the dominant figure in Ulster Presbyterianism, cleric Dr Henry Cooke, played a major role in guiding the Presbyterians of Ulster away from their old alliance with the Liberals and Catholics against the Anglican Establishment, and substituting a new alliance with the Unionist Episcopalians against the Catholics, which became increasingly marked after Gladstone's conversion to Irish home rule. Presbyterianism also became increasingly evangelical in tone during the Victorian period, emphasising faith, the literal truth of the Bible and personal conversion.

Among the larger religious denominations in Ireland differences became more marked as the century progressed, particularly in the north-east of the country and especially in Belfast. Religious rivalries were also a constant problem in many parts of rural Ulster throughout the nineteenth century. It was in the tiny farms of these areas where the linen industry flourished that increasing competition for land once thought uneconomic resulted in faction fighting at local fairs and markets. This culminated in the battle of the Diamond in September 1796, which led to the formation of the Orange Order. Despite early government attempts to suppress the organisation, it remained the largest Protestant organisation in Ireland with its annual Twelfth of July demonstrations. By the 1870s more than five thousand lodges met across the British Empire. At the Triennial Council of Orangeism held in Londonderry in July 1876, an address was issued to the Orange Brotherhood to set out its cherished principles:

> To you who know them there is no need to reiterate the reasons which render such brotherhood necessary. An ever restless and potent influence, working from the Vatican, seeks to bring under the Papal sway the minds of all men. Against this influence it is requisite that all who love truth and freedom should ceaselessly contend, and, that this may be done effectually, to unite and organize in such a brotherhood as ours is the duty of all true Protestants. The services rendered to the empire by the Orange Order have been many and great. At home and in the colonies it has ever presented an obstacle in the way of those who desired to bring about the disintegration of the empire, and statesmen would do well to recognise the spirit and the principles which, notwithstanding passive dislike and active hostility, in quarters that least ought to have shown such, have not caused to swerve from their loyalty a vast and increasing body of men, who are animated by attachment to Bible truth and to the British Constitution.[181]

By the 1880s the Orange Order had become increasingly vocal in its opposition to the Land League and Home Rule for Ireland.

The symbols of Orangeism were very visible during the month of July, as Margaret Dixon McDougall noted on her visit to Clones:

> I was quartered in the most loyal corner of all the loyal places in Clones. Every wall on which my eyes rested proclaimed that fact. Here was framed all the mysterious symbols of Orangeism, which are very like the mysterious symbols of masonry to ignorant eyes. There was King William in scarlet, holding out his arm to someone in crimson, who informed the world that 'a bullet from the Irish came that grazed King William's arm'.

One of the most remarkable events of the nineteenth century was the 1859 revival, which swept through most of the towns and villages in Ulster and in due course brought 100,000 converts into the churches. One of the most interesting aspects of this phenomenon was the almost electric speed with which it spread among female workers in several mills simultaneously.

At one linen mill it was reported in the *Banner of Ulster* of 9 June 1859 that on Tuesday, 7 June in one of the departments of a local spinning mill a number of female staff were suddenly affected:

> Within two or three hours on the morning mentioned, nearly twenty of these girls were struck down – each in an instant – at their work; several becoming apparently insensible at once, and others uttering agonising cries for mercy. The scene produced the greatest excitement throughout the entire works, and not a little alarm. The persons prostrated were, however, promptly attended to by the humane manager and by their companions. Cars were provided for those who could not otherwise be removed to their homes, and the rest were assisted out of the premises, and taken to their respective places of abode. Orders were given that the workrooms

should be closed for the day; but some additional cases of visitation occurred even as the young women were leaving the place and passing down the stairs. Some of those attacked have not yet been able to return to work.

Many local mill and factory owners were less than happy about this sort of disruption to their businesses. Measures were taken to stop such manifestations, with workers being warned that if they dared to attend any revival meetings or were to fall down at their work they would immediately be discharged. According to the *Banner of Ulster* 'One little boy ... was seen pointing out a passage of Scripture to two female workers, when the manager took the Bible from him, locked it up, and in the evening discharged all three.'

For many, particularly among middle-class Protestants and Catholics, Sunday was a gloomy day. Almost all activities were forbidden, and only improving reading matter was allowed. Charles Russell later Baron Russell of Killowen, recalled in his memories:

No cooking that might be done on Saturday was allowed. After dinner each of us had to read a chapter of the Bible aloud, while mamma and dada listened respectfully. The piano was never heard, except to accompany a hymn; no game of cards was allowed; but all sorts of childish games, such as riddles, conundrums, stories etc. made our evenings cheerful.[182]

A rigid observation of Sunday was a feature of the north of Ireland that was remarked on by many visitors. In 1891, Marie Anne de Bovet wrote:

Sunday is no joke in Belfast. As the hotels generally have a public bar, the door is locked during the hours of Divine service, and travellers are obliged to have it opened for each entry. Needless to say that every kind of spirituous liquor is freely supplied in the dining-room, or that drunkenness goes on at a great rate in the suburbs all Sunday evening. But the moral discipline of this very religious town forbids all entry into public-houses during service; I say entry, because those who are in can remain behind drawn blinds all the time of mass or sermon. This exterior rigidity of Sunday manners hardly exists to-day save under Protestant auspices.[183]

In the cities, religion did not feature strongly in the lives of many people. According to the Rev. W.M. O'Hanlon, Congregationalist minister for the church in Upper Donegall Street, there were parts of Belfast where few Protestant or Roman Catholic clergy braved the streets unless sent for on special occasions. On one walk through the town he calculated '307 families who are connected with no denomination of Christians, and never enjoy the ministrations of the Sabbath or the Sanctuary'. At Beatty's Entry and Hamill's Court, in the Millfield area, O'Hanlon recalled:

We found the moral and religious condition of the people here quite in keeping, as it generally is everywhere, with their external circumstances. We were given to understand that the face of a Christian instructor is never seen there, nor could we find that the people attend any place of worship on the day of rest. We inquired of a woman, who professes to be a Presbyterian, how long it was since she had been at her meeting house or Church, and she replied, it was twelve months. Her pleas was the common one – the want of suitable clothes to appear in among respectable people; and I suppose her case might be regarded as a fair sample of the ordinary state of things, in this respect, among all parties in this and similar districts.

This was, he pointed out, 'by no means the worst quarter of the town'.[184]

Outside the towns, tourists and folklorists alike were intrigued by the superstitions and customs of the Irish peasantry. Many observed that marriage was highly valued. In the 1840s Mr and Mrs Hall noted on a visit to Kerry that, 'second marriages are very rare amongst the peasantry, and comparatively so among the higher classes. This affords strong proof of the depth of their attachment, and they do not hold it to be strictly right for either men or women to marry again'. Some of the customs surrounding marriage surprised English visitors. Mr and Mrs Hall were amazed by a local custom for choosing a bride:

> A few days before our arrival, an occurrence took place which we understand is by no means uncommon – a race for a wife. A young man, a carpenter, named Linchigan, applied to the father of a girl named Corrigan, for his daughter in marriage. A rival, called Lavelle, asked for her also, on the plea that as he was richer, he wouldn't ask so much with her. Whereupon, the factions 'of the swains' were about to join issue and fight; when a peacemaker suggested that 'the boys should run for her'. The race was run accordingly, a distance of some miles up and down a mountain; Linchigan won and wedded the maiden.

The usual age for the marriage of women seems to have been between fifteen and twenty, and a young man would marry from the age of twenty upwards. Early marriage was blamed by contemporary writers for the poverty of the cottier and labouring classes in Ireland. Lieutenant J. Greatorex, in his memoir for Aghalurcher in Co. Fermanagh, published in the 1830s, declared, 'It is customary as soon as the children of a family grow up for them to marry, usually at an early age, and begin the work on their own account, building mud huts wherever a few acres of land are to be obtained, and struggling through life in poverty and wretchedness, but apparently contented and cheerful'. According to the *First Report from His Majesty's Commissioners for Inquiring into the Conditions of the Poorer Classes in Ireland*, 1835, early marriage was a strategy for survival among the poor. One witness told the inquiry, 'I think early marriages are most useful here a man looks forward to being supported in age by his family ... if a man marry at the age of 35, he will be broken down and unable to work before his children can be grown enough to support him ... but when a man marries young, his children will be able to support him before he is beyond his labour.'

This was confirmed by Charlotte Elizabeth, in her *Letters from Ireland*, published in 1837:

> You must imagine, first, a state of society where the individual past work has no public asylum, no gratuitous provision of any sort whatever in store: the only prospect is that of having children grown up, who, through the powerful influence of natural feelings, cherished as most sacred among these people, will be constrained to shelter and sustain an infirm parent. Go where you will among the Irish poor, you may hear this motive expressly assigned for the very early marriages that they contract. If they deferred the engagement until they might have realized some little matter to begin the world with, their children would not be sufficiently grown to take charge of them, on the approach of the premature old age induced by their severe privations and over-work.[185]

It is hardly surprising, given the fight for survival many in Ireland faced throughout their lives, that any travel writers during the Victorian period commented that the Irish placed great emphasis on the manner of their send-off. Mr and Mrs Hall noted:

> The most anxious thoughts of the Irish peasant all through his life are concerned with his death, and he will endure the extreme of poverty in order that he may scrape together the means of obtaining a 'fine wake' and a 'decent funeral'. He will, indeed, hoard for this purpose, although he will

economise for no other, and it is by no means rare to find among a family clothed with rags and living in entire wretchedness, a few untouched garments laid aside for the day of burial. Only a month ago we gave a poor woman, an inmate of our parish workhouse, a few shillings. On asking her soon afterwards what she had done with the money, she said she had purchased a fine calico under-garment to be kept for her shroud so that she might be buried decently.

Leitch Ritchie, in his book *Ireland Picturesque and Romantic* (1837), left a vivid account of a wake:

On the death of a person, the nearest neighbours cease working till the body is interred. Within the house where the deceased is, the dishes, and all other kitchen utensils, are removed from the shelves or dressers; looking-glasses covered or taken down; clocks are stopped, and their dial-plates covered. Except in cases deemed very infectious, the corpse is always kept one night, and sometimes two. This sitting with the corpse is called the wake, from Like-wake (Scottish), the meeting of the friends before the funeral. These meetings are generally conducted with great decorum; portions of the Scriptures are read, and frequently a prayer is pronounced, and a psalm given out, fitting for the solemn occasion. Pipes and tobacco are always laid out on a table, and spirits and other refreshments are distributed during the night. If a dog or cat passes over the dead body, it is immediately killed, as it is believed that the first person it would pass over afterwards would take the falling sickness. A plate with salt is frequently set on the breast of the corpse, which is said to keep the same from swelling. Salt was originally used in this way as an emblem of the immortal spirit.[186]

Mr and Mrs Hall were struck by the role of women during the event, 'The women of the household range themselves at either side, and the keen (caoine) at once commences. They rise with one accord and, moving their bodies with a slow motion to and fro, their arms apart, they continue to keep up a heart-rending cry.' During pauses of the women's wailing, the men, seated in groups by the fire, or in the corners of the room, are indulging in jokes, stories and bantering with each other – the subject of their conversation 'prices and politics, priests and parsons'. Margaret Dixon McDougall found it:

> a most unearthly sound, sweet like singing, sad like crying, rising up among the ruined towers, and clinging ivy and floating up heavenwards. I believe the stories of banshees must have arisen from the sound of the caoine. These mourning women were very skilful, I was told, and were relations of the dead whom they mourned, and whose good qualities mingled with their love and grief rose in wailing cry and floated weirdly over the ruins and up to the clouds.

Such was the fame of the Irish wake that it was greatly sought after by tourists. According to Marie Anne de Bovet in the 1890s:

> A driver, hearing two Englishmen speak of their desire to witness one of these strange ceremonies, told them that unfortunately his cousin had just died, and if their honours would gratify the family with their presence, the preparations for the evening could be hurried on. In order not to be outdone in politeness the tourists naturally offered to pay for the whisky, and in the evening the whole village was getting drunk at the deceased man's house at their expense. But at the height of the revel, one of the tourists thought he saw the corpse move slightly, and became suspicious. He therefore

approached the corpse in a careless manner, and quickly applied a burning cigar to its nose. In a moment the corpse had thrown off its shroud, and was off as hard as it could go, pursued by the angry Englishman: had not the dead man been a better runner than the living, the comedy would probably have ended in a real wake.[187]

For a people who set such store in burial customs, the abandonment of these during the dreadful mortality of the Great Famine was all the more traumatic. Asenath Nicholson observed the following scene during the height of the pestilence:

The chapel bell tolled one morning early, when a respectable young woman was brought into the yard for interment. No bells tolled for the starving, they must have the 'burial of an ass,' or none at all. A young lad improved this opportunity while the gate was open, and carried in a large sack on his back, which contained two brothers, one seventeen, the other a little boy, who had died by starvation. In one corner he dug, with his own emaciated feeble hands, a grave, and put them in, uncoffined, and covered them, while the clods were falling upon the coffin of the respectable young woman. I never witnessed a more stirring striking contrast between civilized and savage life – Christianity and heathenism – wealth and poverty, than in this instance; it said so much for the mockery of death, with all its trappings and ceremonies – the mockery of pompous funerals, and their black retinue. This poor boy unheeded had stayed in the dark cabin with those dead brothers, not even getting admittance into the gate, till some respectable one should want a burial; then he might follow this procession at a suitable distance, with two dead brothers upon his back, and put them in with his own hands, with none to compassionate him!

The Irish peasantry was both celebrated and condemned for their belief in superstition. According to *Ireland Picturesque and Romantic* (1838):

> A belief still prevails of the existence of fairies; and their non-appearance at present is alleged to arise from the general circulation of the Scriptures. Fairies are described as little spirits, who were always clad in green, and inhabited the green mounts called forths. Numerous stories are told of their being seen at those places, 'dancing on the circling wind' to the music of the common bagpipe.

The *Wicklow People* in the 1890s noted that, 'The educated classes thought the beliefs of the Irish peasantry delightfully romantic. Deprive them of their fairies and their superstitions, and they are mere ordinary mortals: with these adjuncts, they are [the] most primitive and interesting people to be found on the civilised globe.'[188] Surgeon Sir William Wilde, father of Oscar, was concerned that the devastation of the countryside caused by the Great Famine and the changes brought about by the railways would undermine traditional beliefs and customs, 'In the state of things, with depopulation the most terrific which any country ever experienced, on the one hand, and the spread of education, and the introduction of railroads, colleges, industrial and other educational schools, on the other – together with the rapid decay of our Irish vernacular, in which most of our legends, romantic tales, ballads, and bardic annals, the vestiges of Pagan rites, and the relics of fairy charms were preserved – can superstition, or if superstitious belief, can superstitious practices continue to exist? 'His wife, Lady Jane Wilde, wrote in her preface to her *Ancient Legends*:

> The superstition ... of the Irish peasant is the instinctive belief in the existence of certain unseen agencies that influence all human life; and with the highly sensitive organization of their race, it is not wonderful that the people live habitually under

the shadow and dread of invisible powers which, whether working for good or evil, are awful and mysterious to the uncultured mind that sees only the strange results produced by certain forces, but knows nothing of approximate causes.

Poet W.B. Yeats was equally passionate about the folktales and superstitions of the Irish peasantry. He was consoled by the fact that Ireland had not been transformed by the industrial revolution as Britain had been over the course of the nineteenth century. Yeats liked to challenge the ideas of utilitarian thinkers like Jeremy Bentham, who regarded the rise of the newspapers and the spread of industrialisation as a victory of reason and progress over the forces of myth, superstition and folk beliefs. From Yeats's perspective, however, such modernising forces were to blame for emptying the world of mystery and imagination. His essay, published in the London magazine *The Leisure Hour* in October 1890, was an attempt to offer a positive reappraisal of the Irish folk imagination at a time when secular and rationalist thinking was in the ascendant:

When I tell people that the Irish peasantry still believe in fairies, I am often doubted. They think that I am merely trying to weave a forlorn piece of gilt thread into the dull grey worsted of this century. They do not imagine it possible that our highly thought of philosophies so soon grow silent outside the walls of the lecture room, or that any kind of ghost or goblin can live within the range of our daily papers. If the papers and the lectures have not done it, they think, surely at any rate the steam-whistle has scared the whole tribe out of the world. They are quite wrong. The ghosts and goblins do still live and rule in the imaginations of the innumerable Irish men and women, and not merely in remote places, but close even to big cities.

Chapter 9

A National Education

Ireland witnessed a remarkable growth in education during the Victorian era. The national system of primary education established in 1831 preceded the establishment of a similar system in England by almost four decades. National schoolhouses sprang up rapidly across the country: the 4,500 schools established by 1848 had roughly doubled at the end of the century. Mr and Mrs Hall, who remembered the old schoolhouses as 'for the most part, wretched hovels, in which the boys and girls mixed indiscriminately', were impressed by the transformation brought about by the Board of Education. 'The schoolhouses instead of being dark, close, dirty and unwholesome, are neat and commodious buildings, well-ventilated and in all respects healthful.'[189]

Before the 1830s there were numerous schools, hedge schools and pay schools in Ireland, most of which catered for either Catholic or Protestant children; the general standard was low and many were badly conducted. Those, like the Charter Schools and the Kildare Place Society, which received public support, encountered a great deal of Catholic opposition because of their overtly Protestant outlook. The *Second Report of the Commissioners of Irish Education Enquiry*, published in 1826, found that the majority of Catholic children received their education in hedge schools. These varied in nature with comments like 'held in a barn', 'wretched mud cabin, thatched' and 'an upper room in a wretched house'. German traveller Johann Kohl visited one of the last of the old hedge schools during his stay in Ireland in the 1840s:

The schoolhouse was a mud hovel, covered with green sods, without windows or any other comforts. The little pupils, wrapped up as well as their rags would cover them, sat beside the low open door, towards which they were all holding their books in order to obtain a portion of the scanty light it admitted ... The school-house stood close by the roadside, but many of the children resided several miles off, and even the schoolmaster did not live near it. At a certain hour they all met here; and when the day's task is over the boys put their primers in their pockets and scamper off home; whilst the schoolmaster fastens the door as well as he can, puts his turf fees into his bag, takes his stick and trudges off to his remote cottage across the bog.

After the repeal of the Penal Laws at the end of the eighteenth century many schools were set up, especially in the towns, by religious orders such as the Presentation Congregation, and the Sisters of Mercy. Edmund Ignatius Rice established the first Irish Christian Brothers school in Carrick-on-Suir in 1816, and by 1867 there were fifty-five Christian Brothers schools across Ireland.

Many children of all denominations depended upon the generosity of the local landlord for their education. Mr and Mrs Hall commented in the 1840s:

The principal proprietor of Tandragee is Lord Manderville, who, with his neighbours, Lords Farnham and Roden, Colonel Blacker and the Marquess of Downshire, have contributed largely to the present cheering condition of the county of Armagh. Lord Manderville has established no fewer than sixteen district schools on his estate in this neighbourhood, for the support of which he devotes £1000 per annum, out of an income which is by no means large.

It was against this background of haphazard education that the Irish system of National Education was founded in 1831 under the direction of the Chief Secretary, E.G. Stanley. A superintending board was established that would exercise control over schools. The commissioners would be responsible for the funds voted by parliament and over the textbooks used in the school. The curriculum was to be secular in content, though provision was made for separate religious instruction at special stated times. All teaching and printed material was in English; it was not until 1878 that Irish was recognised as an additional subject that would be taught outside school hours for a fee.

As well as receiving an education, girls were taught needlework and the National Education Board encouraged the teaching of agriculture and gardening for boys and girls. The priorities of the Commissioners of National Education are indicated in a set of instructions given to inspectors in 1836: 'He [the inspector] will ascertain the advancement of education among the children, noting the proportion of children who can read fluently; what progress they have made in writing and arithmetic; whether any be taught geography, grammar, book-keeping and mensuration; whether girls be taught sewing or knitting.'

The school building costs required a one-third contribution from local trustees and local managers, who had the right to appoint and dismiss teachers. In practice this gave them considerable control over the religious outlook of the school. Practical considerations did come into play when local managers advertised for teachers. Major S.W. Blackhall, MP, stipulated that a male and female teacher were wanted for Lysnyan National School in Co. Longford immediately: 'The Schoolhouses and School Furniture are of the first character. The Teachers' Houses are most comfortable, and in the best condition. An agricultural Farm will be attached to the Male School, and under the direction of the Board.' The only qualifications specifically requested were agricultural, 'As the Male Teacher will have the Produce of the Agricultural Farm, with other advantages, none need apply but those who are capable of giving improved Agricultural Instruction, and to be, at least, one of the Second Class Teachers of the Board.' In practical terms Major Blackhall wanted a married couple: 'The situation would be most comfortable for a Husband and Wife to be the Teachers of the Schools – therefore such would be preferred.'[190]

More commonly the appointment of teachers reflected the sensitivities of the predominant religious denomination in the area. This reflected the fact that the main criticism of the new system had come from the churches. The Established Church was suspicious of these attempts to remove its influence over the education system. In 1839 the Church Education Society was established. Its declared object was to maintain an independent system of schools conducted under the auspices of the Established Church. By 1850 it had 1,800 schools affiliated to it but by the 1870s the expense of maintaining the society drove it into the state system. For a short time in the 1830s the Presbyterian Synod of Ulster also refused to have anything to do with the Education Board, reflecting its concern at the restrictions placed on the use of the Bible. The Roman Catholic clergy remained suspicious of what they continued to see as a proselytising organisation. The system at first enjoyed the support of the majority of bishops but opposition soon emerged among a minority, most prominent of whom was Dr McHale, bishop of Tuam from 1836. He believed that the scheme was anti-Catholic and anti-national, and argued that education for Irish Catholics should be characteristically Irish and exclusively Catholic. A papal decision in 1841 allowed each bishop to decide whether the schools in his diocese might participate in the national school system.

The influence of the churches eventually led, in practice, to segregated schools under the control of clerical managers from the different religious bodies. In Catholic schools the manager was almost always the parish priest, and in Protestant schools the rector, minister, or landlord. They were charged with the daily oversight of the school and had the right to appoint and dismiss teachers, who were to be hired from model or training schools established by the board. The manager also chose which of the several approved sets of textbooks the school would use, and, within broad limits, arranged the school's timetable.

The need to ensure a steady supply of suitably qualified teachers was an early problem. At a meeting of the teachers of Ulster in Banbridge in July 1840 one of the speakers, Mr Geoghegan of Newry, looked upon it with regret, that, 'while the Apothecary, the Surgeon, or a member of the Clerical profession, could only be admitted to the exercise of his important duties on possessing indispensable qualifications, every one who thought fit to call himself by the name was thought fit to be a teacher'.[191] As part of the new national school system a teacher training school was established at Marlborough Street and a college for women was opened in 1844. By the end of the century seven teacher training colleges existed including St Patrick's, Drumcondra or De La Selle for Catholic men and Our Lady of Mercy College, Baggot Street, for Catholic women.

From 1845 promising pupils at the age of eighteen could become monitors working in the schools and taking extra lessons, so that at the end of three years they could sit the King's or Queen's scholarship examination. If they were successful, they could attend a training college, although this was not compulsory. Model schools were set up gradually throughout the county specifically to train monitors. The Irish Education Commissioners underlined the importance of the influence teachers could have of inducing competent persons to become candidates for 'teacherships' 'through a fair prospect of remuneration and advancement ... whose conduct and influence must be highly beneficial in promoting morality, harmony and good order, in the country parts of Ireland'. Their influence would ensure an element of social control. 'Living in friendly habits with the people, not greatly elevated above them, but so provided for as to be able to maintain a respectable station; trained to good habits; identified in interest with the State, and therefore anxious to promote a spirit of obedience to lawful authority ...'[192]

Although by the end of the nineteenth century free elementary schooling was provided for all children, the numbers attending schools in many areas was sparse. Dr John Forbes found that attendance at school varied from place to place. At Kenmare, although there were fifty-four boys on the books, only twenty-seven were present on the day he paid his visit. He was told that numbers had dropped because of recent emigration and due to the demands of the present harvest season. According to evidence given to the Powis Commission of 1868–70, only 33.5 per cent of pupils made an annual attendance of 100 days, and from 50 per cent to 65 per cent in some counties were found unable to read or write. Although Acts of 1876 and 1880 prohibited the employment of children under ten years old and children up to thirteen were required to attend school, the Reports of the Commission for Education make it clear that many children made only infrequent attendance.

Though there was some regional variation, overall levels of illiteracy fell rapidly, from 53 per cent in 1841 to 18 per cent in 1891. Nationalist politician and journalist A.M. Sullivan noted the quiet revolution brought about by the national schools:

> The average standard of proficiency attained, especially in rural districts, is even still very low, owing to the short and broken periods for which children are allowed to attend school rather than help to earn for home by work in the fields. But, slight as the actual achievement may be in a strictly educational point of view, socially and politically considered, nothing short of a revolution has been affected. There is now scarcely a farmhouse or working-man's home in all the land in which the boy or girl of fifteen, or the young man or woman of twenty-five, cannot read the newspaper for 'the old people,' and transact their correspondence. Our amusing friend the parish letter-writer has almost disappeared. His occupation is gone.[193]

There remained an underclass, however, who never saw the inside of a national school. Vagrant children remained a feature of city life in nineteenth-century Ireland. According to the *Report of the*

Inter-Departmental Committee of the Employment of Children During School Age, published in 1902, there were in Dublin 433 boys under sixteen selling chiefly newspapers, and 144 girls selling newspapers, fruit or fish, while in Belfast 1,240 boys and 45 girls were truant. Ragged schools aimed to tackle this problem. They were non-residential, providing a meal and a few hours' education each day for vagrant children. In 1853 there were nine ragged schools in Dublin attended by about 700 children, of whom about two thirds 'were probably thieves', according to evidence given to a parliamentary committee. In 1856 the ragged schools were condemned as centres of proselytism by Catholic Archbishop Cullen. Marie Anne de Bovet, who visited the Ragged School in Coombe Street Dublin opened by the evangelical Irish Church Missions, deplored the attempts to proselytise:

> It does not really make much difference whether the ragged urchins, who are educated at the Coombe Street school, go to mass or to church, but it does matter a good deal that children, who might receive a good education, are allowed to play in the gutter because their parents refuse to have them taught to deny their national faith.[194]

The nineteenth century saw a dramatic improvement in educational opportunities for girls. Free primary education enabled parents to send daughters to school at no cost and their numbers gradually overtook that of boys, particularly in rural districts and urban areas of low female employment. This also improved employment opportunities for girls, so that by 1900 over half of all national teachers were women. Prior to the introduction of compulsory education in 1892, girls' attendance was highest in areas with low female employment, and lowest in the northeast, where the mill and the factory beckoned, and there was much home-based garment and textile work. The improvement in female education also opened up a wider range of employment opportunities for women in office work, the expanding public sector and in nursing.

For much of the nineteenth century there was no state system of secondary education and what was available was provided by a small number of voluntary schools. When the national system of education was introduced in 1831 many schools that had provided intermediate education ceased to do so because the new Board of Education would only support primary education. In 1837 the Wyse Committee recommended the provision of a centrally funded non-denominational system of intermediate education but until the passage of the 1878 Intermediate Education Act, second-level education was available predominately in the Protestant diocesan, royal and Erasmus Smith Schools. By the 1860s a number of fee-paying schools were established in Dublin and Belfast to cater for girls entering higher-level education. These colleges trained girls in the classics and mathematics, and their existence ultimately led to girls being admitted on equal terms with boys to the intermediate school-leaving examination when it was established in 1878.

By the mid-1860s a number of Catholic grammar and diocesan schools were established: the *Catholic Directory*, published in 1865, listed sixty intermediate schools, which did not include the fifty-five Christian Brothers' Schools that were by then in existence and in the higher classes of which there were some intermediate studies. These schools were to the Catholic middle class what, for example, the Belfast Academical Institution (opened in 1814) was to the Presbyterian middle class or a public school like St Columba's was to the Church of Ireland middle class.

The Intermediate Education Act (1878) funded secondary education on a payment-by-results basis. To avoid criticism that it was bolstering denominational education, the government proposed to indirectly aid schools by conducting annual examinations, rewarding successful candidates with scholarships and certificates and by paying results-based fees to school managers. It marked a great advance in the provision of education generally, and particularly for girls. Students could sit any number of subjects, but they had to include two of the following: Latin, Greek, English, mathematics and modern languages. The marks allocated to subjects varied. Latin, Greek, English and mathematics were worth 1,200 marks; German and French 700, Celtic (i.e. Irish) 600. Valuable exhibitions (i.e. scholarships) were awarded on a candidate's aggregate marks. Girls' schools competed on an equal basis, and the curriculum in girls' schools changed dramatically as a result. Examinations were held at three levels; junior, middle and senior (and at preparatory level from 1890). Between 1881 and 1911 the number of intermediate schools rose only slightly from 488 to 489 but the number of pupils doubled from 20,000 to 40,000, figures that represented but a tiny fraction of the school-age population.[195]

University education remained a controversial subject for much of the Victorian period. For centuries university education was limited to Trinity College, Dublin. Founded in 1592, Trinity College was the centre of the Protestant Ascendancy, where graduates were required to subscribe to the Oath of Supremacy and Roman Catholics were unable to take degrees until after 1793. Despite the abolition of the penal laws, as long as Episcopalian Protestants had the exclusive control of Trinity neither Catholics nor Protestant Dissenters felt they were receiving equality of treatment in matters of higher education. It was not until 1873 that all religious tests were abolished but Trinity remained a bastion of the Protestant ascendancy, as noted by Marie Anne de Bovet in the 1890s. She found that Catholics and Dissenters, 'are very low in profiting by this liberal measure if we can believe the last list of undergraduates, which has 771 members of the Episcopalian Church (which are improperly call Anglicans), 80 Presbyterians, 64 Protestants of different sects, and only 81 Roman Catholics'.

Trinity College in mid-century had a total of 1,500 students, making Dublin the second-largest University City in the British Isles, after London. Behind its high iron railings the Victorian university had become something of a self-contained community, out of sympathy with the increasingly nationalist city and focused on an expanding British empire for opportunities for its graduates. The students would on occasion emerge from the college to attack political and religious antagonists. According to the *Dublin Daily Nation*, tensions created by nationalist opposition to the Boer War resulted in clashes between students and a hostile crowd:

> Last night the Dublin public were again treated by the students of Trinity College to one of those scandalous scenes which characterised their conduct in the city yesterday. About 11 o'clock a large crowd of the College gentlemen left the Gaiety Theatre where a performance under the auspices of the University Dramatic Club had taken place. Entering South King street they started cheering for Chamberlain and shouting down with the Boers, Rule Britannia, and God Save the Queen, of course, formed part of the programme which they went through. Before leaving the thoroughfare they were unfortunate to meet a small hostile crowd. A free fight at once ensued, with the result that the students were badly treated, and some of them beat a hasty retreat. During the progress the encounter sticks were freely used on the heads of the collegians, who in turn, wielded their canes. The police arrived on the scene and put an end to the fight. No arrests were made. Sometime afterwards about 20 students were treated in Mercer's Hospital for cut heads, while one young fellow was suffering from a broken shoulder. None of them were detained patients. There were no other disturbances during the night.[196]

In 1845 Prime Minister Robert Peel introduced a bill into parliament proposing the establishment of the Queen's Colleges in Belfast, Cork and Galway, which were to be strictly non-denominational. Peel believed that the development of a well-educated middle class would be the best counter to the political influence of the clergy. The seeming success of 'mixed education' under the National Board misled him into supposing that the same principle would be readily acceptable at university level; the Queen's Colleges were established as secular institutions, though arrangements were made by which the various denominations could provide for the pastoral care and religious instruction of their own students. The college fees were low, and the provision of scholarships generous, so that university education was made more widely and generally accessible in Ireland than it was in contemporary England. Sir Robert Peel declared in 1845:

> In founding these Colleges we shall promote social concord between the youth of different religious persuasions, who, hitherto too much estranged by religious differences, will acquire new methods of creating and interchanging mutual esteem. I sincerely believe that, as well as receiving temporal advantages, so far from preventing any advantages with respect to Christianity, the more successfully will you labour to make men good Christians the more they are imbued with that great principle of our faith – a principle which, I grieve to say, many individuals are too apt to forget – the principle, I mean, of reciprocal charity.[197]

Presbyterians, after initial reservations, made the most of the opportunity provided by the establishment of the Queen's College in Belfast. But the colleges were opposed by Daniel O'Connell and many Catholic bishops led by Archbishop MacHale of Tuam, who warned Peel that 'nothing but separate grants for separate education will ever give satisfaction to the Catholics of Ireland'. Under MacHale's influence the bishops insisted that Roman Catholic students could not attend lectures in history, logic, metaphysics, moral philosophy, geology, or anatomy 'without exposing their faith and morals to imminent danger', unless those subjects were taught by Roman Catholic professors. Despite opposition from many Catholic bishops, the colleges were opened in 1848. Papal rescripts condemned the colleges and this contributed to the relative lack of success of the colleges in Cork and Galway with the number of Roman Catholic students attending the colleges remaining comparatively small.

Archbishop Cullen had long harboured an ambition to establish a Catholic university, which was founded in 1854 with controversial English theologian John Henry Newman installed as rector in 1854. Without a government charter its degrees were without legal recognition, and without state endowment it faced financial difficulties. In the first twenty-five years of its existence from 1854 to 1870 (after which the Catholic University became University College Dublin, administered by the Jesuits) the average yearly intake of students was about twenty-five. The Medical School, which opened in Cecilia Street in 1855, was the Catholic University's great success story. Its examinations were recognised by the Royal College of Surgeons in Ireland and links with the Mater and St Vincent's hospitals ensured the career prospects of its students.

Women's right to a university education made rather slower progress. As the nineteenth century progressed middle-class women were demanding greater educational opportunities that would enable them to engage in more suitable employment. A leading campaigner for women's educational rights, Isabella Tod, summed up the prevailing attitude amongst many middle-class families to their daughters in her pamphlet *On the Education of Girls of the Middle-Classes*, published in 1874. In it she declared middle-class parents, looked forward to 'all their daughters marrying, to all these marriages being satisfactory, and to the husbands being always able and willing to take the active management of everything; neither death, illness, nor untoward circumstances occurring to throw the wives on their own resources...they cling to it and will not prepare their girls for anything else.' The Royal University of Ireland Act (1879) finally allowed females to take university degrees on the same basis as males. Catholic girls' schools were slower than Protestant girls' school in doing so but, despite the opposition of senior Catholic leaders, the more progressive religious orders gradually began to enter their female students for the university examinations.

The improvements in education produced a better-educated population keen on reading, especially newspapers. Marie Anne de Bovet noted in 1891, 'The cheap Victorian printing press which could turn out pamphlets and tracts fed the appetites of the growing reading public. Millions of new readers had been created by rises in the standard of living throughout society, by more leisure time, and by the Education Acts which made elementary education free and compulsory.' Rapid advances in printing techniques made possible for the first time publishing for a mass market. Newspapers and literature of all kinds was a great deal more widely available to Victorians than it had ever been before. The reading public had now access to 'cheap editions', 'pocket editions', 'abridged editions' and 'collected editions' of the classics and lowbrow fiction that included sensational literature by Irish writers such as Sheridan Le Fanu and Bram Stoker.

The early years of the century had witnessed a spread of libraries including subscription libraries, Mechanics' Institute libraries and public libraries. This trend increased during the Victorian period as labourers and artisans now had access to cheap subscription libraries requiring the payment of an initial fee and then a subscription of a penny a week or so that offered newspapers, novels and textbooks. There were also reading rooms set up by the temperance movement as an alternative to public houses. The *Northern Constitution*, 21 October 1882, proudly declared, 'The working men and inhabitants generally of the town of Bushmills are fortunate in having a capital institution of this kind lately opened in their midst. In the very heart of the town the eye catches sight of a neatly painted exterior with the title "Reading Room" printed on the signboard.' Inside the reporter was impressed by the facilities:

> Two large reading tables occupy the centre of the room, and on them we notices the following papers, &c, lying for the use of the members: The Illustrated London News, Graphic, Punch, Belfast News-Letter, Northern Whig, Boy's Own Paper,

> Temperance Journal, Carpenter and Builder, British Workman,
> Cottager and Artisan ... Passing from this larger room through
> a curtained doorway we entered another apartment which is to
> be devoted to such games as draughts &c.

Finally there was a smoking room, which the reporter examined with
particular interest.

Increased literacy had a profound impact on the spread of news
within a district, as noted by Irish politician A.M. Sullivan:

> For public news the peasant no longer relies on the Sunday
> gossip after mass. For political views he is no longer absolutely
> dependent on the advice and guidance of Father Tom. He
> may never find counsellor more devoted and faithful; the
> political course he may now follow may be more rash or more
> profitable, more wise or more wrong; but for good or ill it
> will be his own. He will still, indeed, trust largely to those
> whom he judges worthy of his confidence, and largely follow
> their lead; but not in the same way as of yore.[198]

This new literary was English in character and until the end of the
nineteenth century, rural Ireland was the custodian of the Irish
language. The National Education Board made no provision for
teaching in Irish until 1879, when it was introduced as an optional
extra subject outside school hours.[199] Irish was not taught in national
schools during school hours until 1900.[200] According to the opinion
of Commissioners of National Education, expressed in a formal reply
to the Chief Secretary in 1884, 'the anxiety of the promoters of the
National System was to encourage the cultivation of the English
language and to make English the language of the schools. No
question appears to have been mooted by any of those concerned in
the foundation of the National System, or even by its hostile critics, as
to the engrafting of instruction in the Irish language upon the English

programme of the schools.' By the end of the nineteenth century this would change dramatically.

Sir Patrick Keenan, a former teacher, and by 1854 head inspector of national schools, was a keen proponent of the Irish language. He published reports during the 1850s in which he urged the view that those Irish-speaking children in Donegal, in whom he was interested, should be taught English through the medium of the Irish language. However, he acknowledged the resistance of many of the parents who favoured English. In his report for 1856, he noted the strong passion for education among the population.

> This passion may be traced to one predominant desire – the desire to speak English. They see, whenever a stranger visits their islands, that prosperity has its peculiar tongue as well as its fine coat; they see that whilst the traffickers who occasionally approach them to deal in fish, or in kelp, or in food, display the yellow gold, they count it out in English; and if they ever cross over to the mainland for the 'law', as they call any legal process, they see that the solemn words of judgment have to come second hand to them through the offices of an interpreter. Again, English is spoken by the landlord, by the stray official who visits them, by the sailors of the ships that lie occasionally in their roadsteads, and by the school-master himself; and whilst they may love the cadences, and mellowness, and homeliness the language which their fathers gave them, they yet see that obscurity and poverty distinguish their lot from the English-speaking people; and, accordingly, no matter what the sacrifice to their feelings, they long for the acquisition of the 'new tongue', with all its prizes and social privileges.[201]

The heavy mortality rate among rural peasantry in the west of the country during the Great Famine decimated the number of Irish speakers. Meanwhile, the national school system, the expanding rail network, the influence of newspapers and books, and emigration all led to the expansion of the English language.[202] The Irish language became equated with poverty, while English was the language of trade, business and commerce and offered the prosect of advancement. According to the *Royal Commission of Inquiry into Primary Education – Ireland* (1890), 'the parents have never manifested any disposition that their children should cultivate the Irish ... They have energetically demonstrated an anxiety that their children should know English'. This attitude met with the tacit acceptance and approval of the Catholic Church, parents, and political leaders.

Attempts to revive the Irish language were taken forward by organisations such as the Society for the Preservation of the Irish Language (1876), the Gaelic Athletic Association (1884) and the Gaelic League (1893). In 1892, Douglas Hyde, the driving force behind the League, gave a lecture to the National Literary School entitled 'The Necessity for De-Anglicising Ireland'. He urged his fellow Irishmen to turn away from English books and periodicals, which he described as 'garbage'. 'It has always been very curious to me,' he declared, 'how Irish sentiment sticks in this halfway house – how it continues to imitate them; how it continues to clamour for recognition as a distinct nationality, and at the same time throws away with both hands what would make it so.'

The study of Irish should not to be confined inside the walls of the schools or university, as the *Evening Herald* pointed out in July 1896, 'Now that the holiday season is upon us a good deal of useful work in the cause can be done, not alone by Irish speakers, but also by learners and others interested in the matter who intend to spend few weeks in the country.' It condemned those who promoted the pernicious doctrine that Irish was a vulgar language. Instead 'an acquaintance with Irish should be the proudest boast of any man or woman born within the four seas of Erin. Speakers of Irish are expected to use it as their conversational medium on every available occasion, and those able to read and write it should lose no opportunity in taking down some of the numberless poems and proverbs still extant in the country.'[203]

The movement was remarkably successful. 'Evidence is daily accumulating to prove that the movement for the revival of the Irish Language has taken a firm hold,' declared the *Drogheda Independent* proudly, 'and that the prospects of Irish being once more the language of Ireland is brighter than ever before.'[204] In its account of the Feis at Macroom in April 1899 the *Cork Daily Herald* welcomed the rapid advancement of the Irish language in the district in recent years:

> A typically cheering and reassuring thought suggested by the number of the young children who participated in the competitions. In all cases their mastery of the language was almost perfect, and the thorough appreciation of the ideas conveyed by the words was palpable from the manner in which they were uttered. This is all the more a matter for congratulation when the fact is taken into account that scarcely one of these children understood a word of the language a few years ago, and the majority of them, more particularly girls, commenced its study during the year.[205]

The founding of the Gaelic League helped retrieve the language from antiquarian studies to a vehicle for shaping a reawakened national identity in the later nineteenth century.[206]

However, in a letter to the *Derry Journal*, J.J. Doyle condemned the marketing of Irishness for purely marketing purposes. He lamented the decay of the smaller market towns and local industries, and complained, 'Our country is yearly becoming more and more a tourist resort. See the miserable specimens of Irish art (bless the mark) we have to sell the visitors in the way of bog oak or Irish marble ornaments. They are a disgrace, and most of them are doubles made out of Ireland.'[207]

Chapter 10

Disease and Intervention

F ear of illness and disease were an everyday feature of Victorian life. Death rates were high, and all classes were vulnerable to outbreaks of whooping cough, cholera, typhus, influenza, smallpox, measles and many other illnesses. There were few doctors and treatment for a wide variety of ailments and conditions was often primitive and available almost exclusively for those who could pay for it. However, by the middle of the nineteenth century the workhouses had taken disabled vagrants off the streets, and the government was tackling disease and disability with an ambitious programme of legislation that transformed public health. The *Dublin Medical Press* welcomed these developments in characteristically forthright language, 'Although our streets are now free from the offensive and dangerous practice of the exposure of frightful cases of disease, yet living memory can recall the time when the senses were wont to be disgusted by the sight of cripples and other loathsome objects, who were carried to a frequented thoroughfare and there exposed to excite the compassion of passers-by.'[208]

There were all sorts of contributory factors to the prevalence of disease in the Victorian period. These included poor housing, contaminated water, inadequate sanitation and poor diet. Fear of the spread of infectious diseases among the poor prompted the government to play a major role in the establishment of hospitals in Ireland from the late eighteenth century onwards. Before that, voluntary hospitals developed in the cities on a denominational basis. As time went on many of these voluntary hospitals were given state aid so that no fewer than seven hospitals in Dublin were receiving annual grants, despite many efforts at Westminster to stop the payments upon the ground that no other hospitals in the entire British Empire were state supported. The country districts had access to county infirmaries and fever hospitals, and the benevolence of their local landlords.

Lying-in hospitals were found in many towns financed by local subscription with the aim of providing medical aid and attendance for women during the later stages of pregnancy. A woman's marital status was not considered relevant for admission because it was generally accepted that unmarried women claimed to have husbands. Those who were admitted to Coombe Lying-in hospital were required to do needlework and help in the care of other patients. They were forbidden to smoke, spit on the walls or floor, be insolent, swear or use insolent language, unnecessarily soil the bedclothes, or play at any game.[209] However, for a great many women, particularly in rural areas, the only assistance was the local midwife or the help of an experienced neighbour.

With the introduction of the Poor Law in 1838, Ireland acquired a new type of medical practitioner, the Poor Law medical officer, and a new location for hospital services, the workhouse, although the patient had to qualify as a pauper to access this. Initially a relatively minor part of the Poor Law system, medical provision became an increasingly important element of its administration. In 1847, as part of the expansion of the Poor Law system in response to the Great Famine, boards of guardians were empowered to establish separate hospitals 'for the reception and treatment of "poor persons" affected by dangerous contagious disease'. As a result, many of the fever hospitals that had been set up by grand juries under previous legislation closed.

The expansion of Poor Law medical services continued in the decades after the Great Famine. In 1851 the haphazard dispensary provision financed by private subscription was reorganised and reconstituted as part of the Poor Law system. Ireland was divided into 723 dispensary districts with 776 dedicated dispensary doctors and ten midwives. The dispensary service was a major step forward because it provided outdoor relief for the sick poor at dispensaries and at their homes. Another advance took place in 1862 when workhouse hospitals were opened to the non-destitute poor, some of whom would be asked to pay for at least part of the cost of their maintenance and treatment in hospital.

The medical dispensary system, local infirmaries and workhouses provided considerable employment to the growing number of Irish doctors. This group became the local family doctor. Their medical education was likely to include medical and surgical training as well as a qualification in midwifery. When and where possible they had private practices, seeking out a more affluent clientele. The *Irish Medical Directory* of 1852 lists medical practitioners, and members of scientific associations and societies, in Ireland in the mid-nineteenth century. Included in each entry is a notation of where the doctor or pharmacist received their training, previous places of employment and a list of their notable publications. Some doctors made startling claims for their work. Leslie Hamilton is described as having cured cancer, although there are no further details about what the cure entailed.

Having originated as a largely Protestant profession, medicine had become one of the few careers open to Catholics in the eighteenth century. Throughout the Victorian period, Catholic doctors medical training had a distinct denominational character. The impetus behind the establishment in the nineteenth century of Catholic voluntary hospitals such as St Vincent's in Dublin (1834), the Mercy in Cork (1857) and the Mater Infirmorum in Belfast (1883) was in part to provide training institutions for Catholic doctors. By 1883 there were nineteen medical schools and training hospitals in Ireland, all with a particular denominational character. While this did nothing to break down sectarian divisions, it may have helped to make the Irish medical profession more open in other respects.

Doctors were overwhelmingly male throughout the Victorian period. Irish medical women pioneers tried to change the situation but found themselves frustrated by the negative attitudes of many professional men. In 1885 the Royal College of Surgeons in Ireland agreed to extend its educational facilities to women and to recognise the examination results from the London School of Medicine for Women, earning it the distinction of being the first college in Great Britain and Ireland that allowed women to take its examination. In 1886 the Royal College and the chief Irish training body, the Institute of Medicine, agreed to a conjoint degree that made it obligatory for all candidates to pass medicine, surgery and midwifery before admission to the General Medical Council register, and by that date there were already fifty women registered.

As in Britain, the introduction of trained nurses to voluntary hospitals in Ireland was the result of pressure from within the medical profession for competent nurses and this was supported by social campaigners, who saw nursing reform as a way of improving public health. Inspired by the activities of national heroine Florence Nightingale, the status of nursing as a professional was greatly enhanced. In Ireland, however, nursing was closely associated with the various religious orders. By the 1890s, in response to official pressure through the Dublin Hospital Commission, which had reported in 1887, nurse training schemes had been established at all the major voluntary hospitals in Dublin of both denominations. Probationary nurses paid fees and nurse training became an important source of funding for voluntary hospitals.

A major shift took place in the provision of care for the mentally ill and destitute in Ireland during the nineteenth century. The minimal provision for the destitute mentally ill, which generally involved incarceration in workhouses or prisons, gave way to a system of large district asylums dotted around the country, mostly filled to capacity, and some twenty private asylums registered in 1893, located chiefly in Dublin and its surrounding towns. The District Lunatic Asylum on the Falls Road, Belfast, raised money by the novel method of holding its annual festival inside the walls of the asylum. According to the correspondent from the *Belfast News-Letter*:

Many, who have not experienced the pleasure which we felt on the occasion, would be likely to suppose that no sight could be sadder than the display of so vast a wreck of human capacity – such an aggregate of shattered intellects; but such were not the sensations we experienced. We perceived nothing but smiling content, and a kind of infantile happiness and innocence around us; and we retired, after witnessing the strange scene, convinced that madness, in its gentler moods at least, and under humane and enlightened treatment, is not the worst calamity, in a physical sense, which may fall upon the children of men.[210]

Not all regimes were so enlightened and, as a sensational case in Queenstown showed, failure to keep up with payments could lead to very public embarrassment. A young man named Twomey, whose family owned a victuallers business in the town, had, after seven years in a private asylum run by Dr Bull at the cost of £50 annually, been transferred to the District Lunatic Asylum, where his family contributed £17 a year for his upkeep. The stipend was to be paid quarterly and when a payment was missed the young man was returned to his family:

The family of the young man are most respectable, and the idea that they would be distrusted for a few pounds never crossed the minds of any of them. But on Tuesday, a quarter to two o'clock the afternoon, what was their horror to see the poor lunatic, in a straight waistcoat, brought into them between two keepers. In that condition he had been brought at mid-day through the streets of Cork, then paraded through Queenstown, and marched into Mr. Twomey's shop, the customers in which at once fled in terror, as the lunatic was a powerful young man, and it was known had been so violent that during the whole time he was in the asylum he had never been allowed to quit his cell. It is easy to imagine with what consternation such an event was regarded by the mother of the lunatic, a woman nearly sixty years old. Mr. Twomey was compelled at once to proceed to Cork and get a magistrate's order to have his lunatic brother taken to Dr. Bulls asylum, where he now is.'[211]

There was a number of institutes for the treatment of the 'deaf, dumb and blind'. The Richmond National Institution for the Industrious Blind, in Sackville Street, provided instruction to forty male inmates in weaving, basket-making, netting, various kinds of handicraft, and a sale room for the disposal of the manufactured articles. The Asylum for the Deaf and Dumb at Claremont, near Glasnevin, provided for more than 100 inmates:

who are wholly maintained, clothed, and instructed; the boys, after school hours, are occupied in gardening, farming, and other mechanical works; and the girls in needlework, housewifery, laundry work, and in the management of the dairy; a printing-press has been purchased for the instruction of some of the boys in that business, and for the printing of lessons adapted to the use of the pupils. The building contained separate schoolrooms for male and female pupils and was wholly supported by subscription and private benefactions.[212]

Despite the elaborate system of medical provision developed in Ireland during the Victorian period, disease was an everyday feature of existence. Many diseases were seasonal, with the spring and winter months particularly bad. The records of the Cork fever hospital in the early 1840s showed that the greatest number of patients was received in April and May, and in November and December. Johann Kohl explained:

The former are the months in which the distress of the poor in Ireland is at its greatest height; and the latter months are

those in which the greatest quantity of rain falls, it is also
remarked that in years of extreme wetness or scarcity the
typhus fever is most prevalent. The increased humidity of
a year works not only directly on the constitution, but also
increases disease indirectly, by preventing the preparation and
drying of the turf, and increasing the price of this necessary
article so much that it is unattainable by the poor. How often
does it happen, in Ireland, that they are compelled to break
up and burn their tables, bedsteads, and other furniture, to
procure a little warmth![213]

Typhus, also known as typhus fever, is a group of infectious diseases
that was particularly acute during cold, wet weather and scarcity. The
common symptoms include fever, headache, and a rash, and it was
transmitted by body lice that lived in the clothing of the poor.[214] The
appalling conditions endured by the urban poor were particularly
conducive to typhus, with little or no access to washing facilities and
people forced to huddle together in winter for warmth. A major epidemic
occurred in Ireland during the Great Irish Famine between 1846 and
1849. The epidemic spread to England, where it was dubbed the 'Irish
fever' and was noted for its virulence. The patterns of the disease varied
according to class. Among the poor the disease spread throughout the
entire household, while in better-class families the disease was confined
to the fever victim and the rest of the household remained untouched.
The virulent nature of typhus generated great fear among the population
and prompted many to conceal the existence of typhus in the family.
Tradespeople and shopkeepers tried to keep secret the visits of physicians
and the removal of those affected to hospital, while hotels and various
forms of public transport were avoided by nervous customers.

Cholera was also greatly feared: a water-borne disease endemic,
it is characterised by diarrhoea and vomiting. Cholera was usually
contracted by drinking contaminated water or by eating contaminated
food, two ever-present dangers for the poor, but is not otherwise

transmissible by contact. It struck Britain and Ireland in 1831–32, 1848–49, 1853–54 and 1866. In Belfast during the winter of 1847–48, more than 2,500 died during the cholera epidemic. Lack of knowledge about the causes of the disease added to its horror. The contagiousness of the disease excited great debate as noted by the *Clare Journal and Ennis Advertiser*, 16 April 1849:

> Contagiousness of Cholera – if experience is the best test of the truth of any doctrine, there are now a sufficient number of facts on record to prove the errors of the non-contagionists in reference to cholera. A few days since two gentlemen arrived at a friend's house in Ballinderry, having been driven thence from Hillsborough. Some hours after they found the man who had drove the car very ill, and a medical gentleman pronounced the disease cholera. The poor fellow got rapidly worse, and was removed to a cottier house in the vicinity, where all efforts to save his life proved ineffectual, and he died in a few hours. In a short time afterwards the tenant of that house caught the distemper, and died, and a child of his also took ill, with the same fatal result. Previous to that time cholera had never been known in Ballinderry, and there is not the slightest doubt the car-driver, coming from Hillsborough, where the disease existed, brought the infection to the house of the poor man, in whose bed he died, and a child of his also took ill, with the same fatal result.

The newspaper called on the Central Board of Health, 'with its host of theoretical philosophers', to 'throw some light on these strange facts, which go far to set at defiance all their recent assertions on the non-infectious nature of cholera. We might furnish twenty additional instances of a similar nature from the Dublin and other papers.'

The Central Board, established in 1820, co-ordinated reports from localities and the distribution of information about preventive measures. Gradually it established local boards and appointed health officers.[215] The Central Board had already concluded that, although hospitals had been established to deal with epidemic fever, cholera, because it was not contagious, was better dealt with at home. It set out the details in the local press:

> The Commissioners of Health are anxious to impress upon all persons the important difference that exists between cholera and fever, with respect to the mode of propagation of the epidemic diseases. Fever, it is well known, is highly contagious, or easily propagated from one individual to another, while all experience shows that cholera is rarely, if ever, contagious; consequently, the separation of the sick from the healthy – a measure so essential in checking the spread of fever – is not required in cholera; and the friends and relatives of persons attacked with cholera may be under no apprehension of catching the disease, and need not be deterred from affording to the sick, in their own dwellings, every needful assistance and attention.[216]

According to the Report of the Commissioners of Health for Ireland on the epidemics of 1846–50, the total number of cases for the whole country was 45,698, with deaths numbering 19,325. Although cities like Dublin and Belfast suffered badly, cholera spread to larger institutions like prisons, workhouses and schools in smaller towns. In the small county town of Gort, 403 died and in Ballinasloe 756 deaths were reported. These figures may only represent part of the picture because rural workhouses were still crowded with refugees from the famine.

Scarlatina was another scourge. The signs and symptoms included a sore throat, fever, headaches, swollen lymph nodes, and a characteristic rash. Long-term complications as a result of scarlet fever included kidney disease, rheumatic heart disease, and arthritis. Outbreaks were reported regularly in local newspapers, particularly during April to June. The *Dublin Evening Mail*, 3 June 1861, announced:

> We regret to learn that, in Belfast and its neighbourhood, scarlatina, of a more than usually virulent type, is at present extensively prevalent. It is not confined to infancy or childhood, many persons well advanced in youth and some adults having been attacked. Instances have very recently occurred in which the disease has terminated fatally in two, and even three, cases in the same family, in rapid succession. Some of these have taken place in localities, in the environs of the town, remarkable for salubrity of situation. Other maladies of a similar character, as measles, smallpox, &c., are not more common than is ordinarily the case at this season.

In 1854 the Towns Improvement Act allowed the smaller towns to set up a local authority to deal with public health issues. These bodies were allowed to enforce cleanliness, not only in the streets, but in backyards and premises, to disinfect dwellings in time of contagious disease at the expense of the owners or occupiers, to regulate slaughter houses, and cleanse and construct sewers and arrange for a water supply.[217] Under the Sanitary Act, 1866, action could be taken against those who wilfully engaged in activities that could lead to the spread of dangerous or contagious disease. Anyone suffering from an infectious disease was forbidden to enter any public conveyance without notifying the owner or driver of his or her condition. Any owner or driver who did not immediately disinfect his conveyance, or any person, who, without previously disinfecting, gave, lent or sold any bedding, clothes, rags, or other things that had been exposed to infection from such disorders was liable to prosecution. Likewise, action could be taken against any person who let any house or room in which any person suffering from a dangerous contagious disorder had been, without having disinfected it to the satisfaction of a medical practitioner, who supplied a certificate as proof.

The *Irish Times* of 16 January 1888 reported that:

> At the Police Court to-day, a poor man named Patrick Noonan was charged by the Corporation with a breach of the Public Health Act by 'waking' his child who died of measles, thus endangering the spread of disease. Dr Donovan, Corporation medical officer, expressed his opinion that the recent spread of measles was owing to such conduct as the defendant was charged with. All the persons who attended the wake (about 20 in number) were liable to spread the disease, and might communicate the disease to two or three hundred persons. From the evidence it appeared that Noonan was drunk on the night of the wake, and that since another of his children had been attacked by the disease. Mr Gardiner, RM said he hoped it would go to the public that persons were liable to a fine of £5 for holding wakes on persons dying of infectious diseases. A fine of 40s was imposed on Noonan, but on his promising to go to the workhouse the fine was remitted.[218]

Throughout the nineteenth century there were recurrent epidemics of smallpox that caused suffering, disfigurement and death, despite the fact that vaccination was freely available. John Milner Barry introduced vaccination into Ireland in 1800, but it was not until the second half of the nineteenth century that the Boards of Guardians in Ireland were empowered to carry out vaccinations under the compulsory Vaccination (Ireland) Acts, 1863 and 1879. Nevertheless, implementation remained patchy, as the number of court cases that appear in local papers continued to demonstrate well beyond the end of the nineteenth century. It proved impossible to enforce compulsory vaccination against smallpox because of the absence of reliable information about births and deaths. The authorities took action against parents who refused to have their children vaccinated without a valid certificate of exemption. Thomas Strain, of Meadowbank Street, was summoned at the instance of the Belfast Board of Guardians for failing to have his child vaccinated. According to The *Belfast Telegraph*, 12 August 1881, 'The evidence showed that the defendant had been fined on a former occasion when brought before the Court on a similar charge. He now stated that he objected to vaccination, and would persist in disobeying the law in that respect. A fine of 10s and costs was imposed.'

Rumours of smallpox could be enough to affect businesses in the city. On 4 November 1894, the *Freemans Journal* published letters from several large drapery establishments in Dublin denying the presence of the disease at their establishments. However, the newspaper warned:

> At all events, the truth of the matter is sufficiently serious. It is beyond question that smallpox has got a hold in the city, and apparently, though it is said to be most prevalent on the south side, it is not confined to any quarter. Thirty-nine cases were admitted to hospital during last week, an increase of nine on the admissions of the previous week, and 22 over the number for the week ended the 27th ultimo. The deaths from smallpox during last week were four – two women, a girl aged nine, and a man aged 34 years, who had not been vaccinated. On Saturday last 81 Smallpox patients remained under treatment in the hospitals. The outbreak, though it is, as will be seen from these figures, pretty widespread, does not seem to be of a virulent type.

Tuberculosis was a silent killer in Ireland and frequently disguised as bronchitis on medical certificates by those who thought the term more gentile. The spread of the disease was not fully understood until Koch's discovery in 1882 of the bacillus that caused the disease. However, the symptoms were clear enough: fatigue, weight loss, night sweats, the production of sputum, haemorrhaging and above all the characteristic cough. Tuberculosis eventually led to the destruction of the lungs. The census of 1841 calculated that, in the proceeding ten years, 135,590 people had died from consumption, compared with only 23,518 from fever. By the 1880s and 1890s tuberculosis had reached epidemic proportions. The *Ballymena Observer* of 23 August 1889 warned that 'the germs are coughed by sufferers, and become lodged in carpets, clothing, hand kerchiefs, etc. They may be even converted dust and float about the atmosphere, still retaining their noxious properties. This has been proved over and over again by experiment.'

It was only in the 1890s that tuberculosis became a major concern of public health officials. Two great public campaigns were launched in Ireland with the objective of educating the public about the disease. The main aim was to alert the public to its contagious nature and for that reason they recommended better ventilation and more frequent sweeping of public buildings. They discouraged any form of oral contact between people, including the sharing of eating and drinking vessels and the practice of kissing the Bible before giving evidence in court, and they advocated restrictions upon spitting in public places.

With such much disease about, middle- and upper-class Victorians anxious to avoid the cost of a private doctor frequently turned for guidance to printed medical guides. Victorians were quick to consult a wide range of household guides including *Mrs Beeton's Book of Household Management* (1861), *Mrs Humphrey's Manners for Women* (1897) and *Buchan's Domestic Medicine* (1848). Many sought relief from the medicines advertised in the local newspapers that claimed to have miraculous powers. Holloway's Pills is perhaps the most famous of these confections. Its ingredients, which were a long-held secret, included ginger, cardamom, saffron, cinnamon, rhubarb root and 'confection of roses'. It was brilliantly marketed by its creator Thomas Holloway, who adjusted his newspaper advertisements to different localities. Holloway claimed that his pills cured almost all ailments, including rheumatism, aches and pains, disorders of the chest and throat, and sores and ulcers. Readers of the *Enniskillen Chronicle and Erne Packet*, 3 January 1850, were informed:

A respectable female in the neighbourhood of Loughgall was attacked with typhus fever, and lay for five days without having tasted any description of food. She was given over by the surgeon, and preparations were made for her demise. Mr Benjamin Mackie, the Quaker ... heard of the circumstances, and knowing the immense benefit that he himself had derived from Holloway's Pills, recommended an immediate trial, and eight were given to her, and the same number was continued night and morning for three days, and in a very short time she was completely cured.

The number of medicines and drugs such as arsenic kept in the average household led to frequent accidental poisoning cases. The *Anglo-Celt* of 17 June 1852, reported one such grisly case in Co. Monaghan:

Eight unfortunate persons, the family of a peasant named GIBNEY, living near Virginia, narrowly escaped death on Sunday last, from partaking of a large quantity of arsenic accidentally administered to them in place of soda, on some vegetables. One child, who was providentially absent at the time of the meal, was the only person left to procure assistance for her suffering relatives, whom the acute pains of the poison had rendered utterly incapable of any exertion. This creature was obliged to travel a distance of four miles to the residence of the nearest medical gentleman, who on learning the afflicting circumstances, hurried to the relief of the suffers. The scene which presented itself on his arrival cannot be readily imagined. Clustered together in a wretched hovel were these eight beings, father, mother, and children, each suffering intense torture, and deprived of anyone who might afford them the smallest consolation, or relief. Truly, the severity of such an accident cannot be more aggravated than when it is accompanied by a total want of the comforts, and even necessaries of life.

Arsenic was also found in the green dye used in wallpaper and paints. A letter to the *Irish Times* in June 1859 warned of 'the dangers arising from green paper hanging'. The writer had examined the wallpapers and carpet dust of a sick gentlemen, at the request of a physician. 'In each of the papers I found a great quantity of arsenic, and even the dust contained a very large proportion of that fearful poison.'[219]

Laudanum was available over the counter. Many of the opium-based preparations were marketed as 'women's friends'; these were widely prescribed by doctors for problems with menstruation and childbirth, and even for fashionable female maladies of the day such as 'the vapours', which included hysteria, depression and fainting fits. Children were also given opiates. To keep them quiet, children were often spoon-fed Godfrey's Cordial (also called Mother's Friend), consisting of opium, water and treacle and recommended for colic, hiccups and coughs. Overuse of this dangerous concoction is known to have resulted in the severe illness or death of many infants and children. Parents used it to sooth sick children, as the death of five-week-old William Shiels at his home in Malt Street, Belfast, demonstrates. The case was examined by the coroner and a jury in the recorder's court in the city:

Evidence was given that on Friday last the child took ill, and that its mother then administered laudanum in whiskey punch. The illness after this only became worse, and on Saturday morning at seven o'clock death ensured. Dr Caul, who was called in, but found the child dead, noted that death was due to Laudanum poisoning. He said he thought that greater restriction should be placed upon the sale of that drug, and in his opinion it should be placed in Schedule 1 of the Sale of Poison Act.[220]

The 1868 Pharmacy Act attempted to control the sale and supply of opium-based preparations by ensuring that they could only be sold by registered chemists.

For most of the nineteenth century, unqualified dentists were the last resort for those who needed a tooth extracted. It was not until the Dentists Act of 1878 that the title of 'dentist' and 'dental surgeon' was restricted to registered practitioners. Even so many patients died from botched treatment, infections and other complications, so it was hardly surprising that the dentist's chair was regarded with sheer terror. The *Belfast News-Letter* reported:

> A labourer on the Belfast and Co. Down Railway, a young man, named Denis Murray, having, for some time, been annoyed by toothache, on Tuesday last got a tooth extracted. An unusual loss of blood was, however, the immediate consequence; and the bleeding continued, notwithstanding surgical assistance was resorted to, till Thursday, when he died, apparently from exhaustion. He was a native of Downpatrick, where his mother, a widow, resides –unmarried, and was much respected, both by his fellow-labourers, and in the vicinity where he lodged (Lagan Street), for his quiet and inoffensive conduct.[221]

If you were lucky there might be a tot of whiskey to numb the pain but otherwise all that was offered was a prayer. Later gas became available, and this could prove a potent mix, as one patient found out in October 1851, as reported by the *Belfast News-Letter*.

> The Recorder, in dealing with appeals from decisions of the police magistrate, to-day disposed of a peculiar case. Mr Moran had a tooth extracted by a dentist in Camden

Street, who in order to perform the operation administered gas. After the tooth was out the patient took two small drinks, and while going home was arrested for being drunk. The police-sergeant who arrested Moran said he had no doubt he was drunk. When brought to the Police Station he produced a tooth, which he said he had just got extracted. The police magistrate had fined Moran for being drunk. Moran appealed to the Recorder in order to clear his name, claiming he had been to another dentist who failed to extract the tooth, and after the suffering he had undergone he had gone into the public house and had two half-glasses of whisky. The Recorder found in Moran's favour, declaring the arrest to be illegal because it had taken place while he had been inside the public house.[222]

Chapter 11

Transport and Communications

The advances in transport and travel during the Victorian era changed forever the landscape of Ireland, revolutionised the working practices of a large proportion of its people and altered the conception of time. It was an age of marvels, with the arrival of the steam engine, the invention of the bicycle, and the first appearance of the motorcar. 'We who have lived before railways were made belong to another world,' wrote William Makepeace Thackeray in the 1840s. 'It was only yesterday, but what a gulf between now and then! Then was the old world. Stagecoaches, more or less swift, riding-horses, pack-horses, highwaymen, knights in armour, Norman invaders, Roman legions, Druids, Ancient Britons painted blue, and so forth …We who lived before railways, and survive out of the ancient world are like Father Noah and his family out of the Ark.'[223]

Before the development of the railways, roads were the principal form of communication across the country. Novelist Anthony Trollope, then serving in the Post Office, walked a great many of these roads in order to establish a number of postal routes. The hungry labourer often walked great distances in search of work or charity, while farmers depended upon roads to get their produce to market. In the early years of the nineteenth century parliamentary grants were available to help road building and from 1831 the newly formed Board of Works, with its qualified engineers, took on responsibility for public works, including roads and bridges. The construction that followed brought considerable change to many regions of the country. When a new road had been built at Iveragh in Co. Kerry, for instance, 'the old inhabitants of the hill left their cabins and built new ones along the new road sides'.

Farmers welcomed them as they improved access to local towns, which benefited from the burgeoning markets. According to an 1838 report, 'even small portions of those roads were scarcely out of the engineers' hands before they were covered with the carts of the farmers, eager to take advantage of the improvement'.[224] The new road building was not always welcomed by locals because they also provided better access to the local military and police authorities. German journalist Johann Kohl noted when travelling from Killarney to Bantry in the 1840s, 'These roads are some of the benefits which Ireland reaps from the English. From these improved roads have arisen other improvements, which the Irish will probably hardly feel disposed to regard as such – namely, the new police stations, which are always erected upon them.'

William Makepeace Thackeray was appalled by many of the roads he encountered in various parts of Ireland. He commented:

> of all the roads over which human bones were ever jolted, the first part of this from Listowel to Tarbert deserves the palm. It shook us all into headaches; it shook some nails out of the side of a box I had; it shook all the cords loose in a twinkling, and sent the baggage bumping about the passengers' shoulders. The coachman at the call of another English bagman, who was a fellow-traveller, – the postillion at the call of the coachman, descended to re-cord the baggage.[225]

The stagecoaches that were such a feature of the Irish roads were largely the work of one man, Charles Bianconi, who was able to seize the opportunities provided by the new carriage tax (which led many people to sell their jaunting cars) and the ending of the Napoleonic wars (which made good horses available cheaply). He secured a major mail contract through personal contact with the postmaster-general, the Duke of Richmond, and expanded his services rapidly until they covered 3,800 miles and 120 centres by 1845. Bianconi's cars, 'Bians' as they were popularly called, had by the 1840s opened up Ireland to trade, with Bianconi boasting that 'the farmer who formerly drove and spent three days in making his market, can now do so in one for a few shillings; thereby saving two clear days and the expense of his horses'. He also claimed that in 1856 after the more remote parts of Ireland had been opened up by his cars, calico, which had previously cost 8d or 9d a yard, was sold for 3d and 4d.[226]

With admirable foresight he purchased shares in some of the railway companies and even after their arrival continued a brisk business offering connections to the railway stations.[227]Kohl did not have a very high opinion of his coaches, however:

> It is in vain that he seeks where to sit most comfortably on the coach. In the inside, which is as narrow as a herring-barrel, he thinks himself in danger of suffocation; and on the outside, where nothing but a single slight iron rail, four inches high, separates him from an abyss of fifteen feet, he grows dizzy. In fact, the seats, whether inside or out, of the English stage and mail-coaches, are the most uncomfortable to be found on earth; and it was at first very difficult for me to discover how those seats are consistent with the great love of comfort which characterizes the English nation ...[228]

The arrival of one of Bianconi's coaches caused a great deal of excitement in town and villages, as observed by Sir Francis Head when stopping at a post house close to the Galway–Mayo border:

> On arriving at the post-house I found playing very sweetly before it a piper, at whose feet, knitting socks, were sitting four women and three children, in old ragged red petticoats. I had never before heard the Irish bagpipe, which is played with bellows instead of by the breath, and I was particularly admiring its bass notes, when, all of a sudden, the women

and girls jumped up, and, casting my eyes down the road, I saw, rocking, and reeling, and rapidly approaching me, one of Bianconi's three-horsed cars, accompanied on each side by a swarm of girls from twelve to eighteen, all in red petticoats, and all with extended hands offering to passengers, whose knees they could touch, scarlet and white socks. As soon as the car reached the post-house, at which it was to change horses, the arms and stockings were, if possible, more earnestly extended than before.

In a few minutes the fresh horses were affixed, and the coach and passengers drove away at a brisk trot, followed by their young escort. As Sir Francis Head watched them disappear, a local constable told him that the young people had joined the coach 2 or 3 miles from the post house and would follow it now for about the same distance.[229] Those used to the bustling English railroads were greatly amused by the old world stagecoaches and stagecoach establishments to be found in Ireland. Kohl, on travelling through Co. Clare found:

At times we stopped at a mean inn to change horses. The walls were generally tapestried with proclamations offering rewards for the apprehension of criminals. Fifty pounds were promised for the apprehension of those who had murdered farmer so-and-so; thirty pounds for information that would lead to the conviction of those who had burned a mill, and ill-treated the inmates to such a degree, that two of them had since died; and many others of the same kind. I had not time to read all these placards, instructive as they were respecting the condition of the country ...[230]

The alternative to travel on public transport was the Irish jaunting car, which was a light two-wheeled carriage pulled by a single horse. It had the novel arrangement of either two or four seats in which passengers sat back-to-back. A French visitor in the late 1880s noted, 'Imagine a pleasure car where the seats, instead of being perpendicular to the shafts, are parallel with them, disposed back-to-back and perched on two very high wheels. You climb to your place under difficulties; then the driver seated sideways like you (unless the number of travellers obliges him to assume the rational position), lashes his horse, which plunges straightway into a mad career.'[231]

Bernard H. Becker, who toured Ireland in the winter of 1880–81, considered it:

> the most abominable of all civilised vehicles. Why the numskull who invented the crab-like machine turned it round sidewise is as absolutely inconceivable as that since dogcarts have been introduced into the West the car should survive. But it does survive to the discomfort and fatigue of everybody, and the especial disgust of the writer. This style of locomotion rather startles you at first, not only on account of its novelty, but also by reason of the indifferent equilibrium you are able to maintain. Jostled over the pavement, threatened every moment to see yourself projected into space, at a tangent, you involuntarily grasp the nickel handle which is there for that purpose, just as a tyro horseman instinctively clutches the mane of his steed. But one gets used in time to the Irish car, and even comes to like it.[232]

In the early Victorian era, before the arrival of the railways, those who wished to avoid Ireland's variable roads turned to its rivers as the only alternative. From the 1730s a series of canals were constructed in various parts of Ireland, and although they were never as commercially successful as their counterparts in the heavily industrialised north of England or Scotland, canal transport was much cheaper and much more reliable than road transport and could also carry heavier and bigger loads. Apart from freight, the canals also offered barge-like 'passage boat' and 'fly-boat' passenger services. The Grand and Royal Canals developed a flourishing passenger service, with canal boats making their way from Dublin to the Shannon at a leisurely pace. On the Grand Canal, hotels were built for passengers at Portobello (Dublin), Sallins, Robertstown, Tullamore and Shannon Harbour. The Royal Canal had four passenger boats in regular service taking passengers from Dublin to Mullingar, a distance of 53 miles, taking thirteen and a half hours. Because of the slowness of canal travel, each boat was equipped with facilities for serving meals on board. A German visitor in 1842 commented, 'As there are no railways in Ireland, with the exception of two miniature ones ... the canals which transverse the country are much used for travelling, and boats, generally full to overflowing, ply regularly from and to Dublin. The boats, like the trekschuiten in Holland, are drawn by horses that move along at a smart trot ...'[233]

Steamboat trips remained popular with tourists throughout the Victorian period. Paschal Grousset in the 1880s noted the popularity of the steamers with tourists, who were a mixed lot:

merchants bent on a pleasure trip; judges and barristers, having taken leave of briefs; professors enjoying their holidays, with wives, daughters, sons, goods, and chattels – all have the sun-burnt complexion and the satisfied look one brings back from the seaside. They have been staying on the beautiful shores of the Co. Clare, and are returning home with a provision of health for one year.

He noted the number of passengers in holy orders, 'Here the proportion is far greater than in the ancient coach; it is not one priest we have on board, but a dozen, all sleek, fat, and prosperous, dressed in good stout broadcloth, as smooth as their rubicund faces, and provided with gold chains resting on comfortable abdomens.'

In 1834 the 6-mile-long Dublin and Kingstown was the first railway to be opened in Ireland. The line's construction did much to open up the coastal area south of Dublin for residential development, although it was not always welcomed by the leisured classes. Mrs Frederick West, while enjoying the view from the sitting room of Rathbone's hotel in Kingstown, complained, 'The eternal racket of the Kingstown Railway, alone districted from the scene: those straight lines, and ugly monsters of machines, forms a hideous background to every landscape.'[234] Although the Dublin and Kingstown line was a success, investors were slow to put their money into railways because there was not the same need for cheap, efficient transport as in heavily industrialised England.

In the more industrialised north-east, manufacturers set up the Ulster Railway Company, which launched the second Irish line, between Belfast and Portadown, in 1842. The Dublin and Drogheda Railway built the line between Dublin and Drogheda and the Dublin and Belfast Junction Railway linked the Dublin and Drogheda and the Ulster Railway at Portadown in 1855, having overcome the major obstacle of the River Boyne. Opening up the interior in the north was more important to Ulster businessmen than establishing links with the south, however, and the result was to draw more and more of the province's commerce towards Belfast.[235] Armagh came online with the Ulster Railway in 1848 and a line from Derry opened up west Ulster. They encountered some opposition from the Sabbatarians, who objected to the running of trains on Sundays. One minister told his congregation that he 'would rather join a company for theft and murder than the Ulster Railway Company, since its business is sending souls to the devil at the rate of 6d a piece' and that 'every blast of the railway whistle was answered by a shout in Hell'.[236]

The railways also drew criticism from those trades and industries that saw their services decline locally, as noted by a speaker at a meeting of the trades of Dublin in January 1848 in the city's Royal Exchange.

Its secretary, Mr McCormick, told an audience of house carpenters, house painters, bricklayers and stucco plasterers that:

> if the times did not change a great number of artisans in the city of Dublin must go [to] the workhouse, and it therefore behoved the ratepayers to afford the tradesmen every facility in their power for obtaining employment. Most of the contractors for public works in this city, instead of employing the tradesmen of Dublin, were getting the work executed in different parts of the country, and then conveyed it here by railway.[237]

The railways had a major impact on Irish society and economy. Bridges, viaducts and tracks transformed the landscape. In towns and cities, properties had to be demolished to clear the way. The jury convened to consider compensation to property owners impacted by the works of the Dublin and Drogheda Railway were told that:

> The line of railway will run from the Custom House Dock-wall, near Commons Street, through Harte's Row, where all the houses will be taken down. It will then run through Halpin's Row, where twelve houses will be levelled; from thence to the low ground and pass through Seville Place and Aldborough Court where six houses will be levelled; and it will cross the canal below Newcomen Bridge, extending in a direct line, until it joins the embankment at the estuary across the sea at the Crescent of Clontarf.

The legal team representing the railway company declared that the claimant was offered a fair price 'which he could not make sale of for upwards of twenty years'. [238] Engineer William Le Fanu, brother of the novelist Sheridan, recalled the horrors of driving the railway lines across a country ravaged by famine:

As I, with my assistant engineer, was walking along the railway works which had just been commenced near Mallow, and which during the remainder of the famine gave much employment and relief, we passed near the old churchyard at Burnfort. Several dogs were fighting and howling there, my assistant ran down to see what they were about. He found them fighting over the bodies of some poor creatures who had died of famine, and had that morning been buried – if buried it can be called – without coffins, and so close to the surface, that they were barely covered with earth. We had coffins made for them, and had them buried at a proper depth.[239]

On another occasion he went in a half-way house for a few minutes, where 'a poor woman, barefooted and miserably clad, with three children, came in, so stricken with famine was she, that she could barely speak. I ordered coffee and bread for them. No sooner had she taken a little than she fainted'.

The railways provided work for an army of artisans and labourers:

The Dublin and Cashel Railway

There is at present upwards of 2000 men employed on the above railway between Sallins and Dublin, independently of carpenters and other mechanics; and we learn from a correspondent that the contractors have adopted every practical measure to secure comfort and accommodation for the workmen. Shops have sprung up like magic at different points, and no complaint is made of the manner in which they are conducted, as the contractors exhibit a laudable zeal to prevent fraud or extortion on the workmen.[240]

Gangs of navvies were recruited from the canal and railway construction industry in England and Scotland, many of them Irishmen who had learned their trade in the railway mania of the previous decade.

They were paid a piece work rate, which was essentially earning according to the amount of muck they could shift, the quantity being assessed by overseers who measured the loads in wheelbarrows. An experienced navvy could shift about 20 tons of clay in a twelve-hour day using a pick and shovel and could put away 2lb of beef per day washed down with a dozen quarts of beer. Little wonder that their life expectancy was short. A clergyman, the Rev. St George Sargent, recalled his time at the Mendacity Institute in Dublin, 'I think they are the most neglected and spiritually destitute people I ever met ... ignorant of Bible religion and gospel truth, infected with infidelity and very often with revolutionary principles.'[241]

The construction of the railways across Ireland opened up large tracts of countryside to visitors and locals alike for the first time. One visitor to the works at Dalkey and Bray Head welcomed the employment the railways gave to the unskilled labourer:

> It is a most cheering sight to behold the most inaccessible spots occupied by groups of labourers engaged in all the heavy operations of quarrying, levelling, etc. Several hundred pounds of gunpowder are daily expended in blasting, and as many as from fifty to one hundred explosions of blasts take place, from which the visitor need be under no apprehension, as the workmen's movements if followed will be a certain guide to avoid danger.[242]

Accidents were nevertheless frequent. One hundred and sixty-two deaths from falling embankments alone were recorded among railway builders between 1846 and 1857. According to Malahide Dispensary records, it treated 103 cases of injury in one month during the building of the Drogheda line.[243]

A visitor from Canada, when reflecting on the positive impact of the railways, took a fairly original viewpoint, being convinced that it had reduced the level of crime, 'by shutting up of those roadside public houses ... which were the indirect cause of half the crime of the country'.

> Some were obliged to stop there in returning from markets, others by fatigue or inclemency of the weather during their journey, and some resorted there from the pure love of liquor, but none with malice aforethought, to raise rows. However, the liquor invariably did its work; drunken brawls, assaults, robberies, and sometime murder ensured, and fearful have been the consequences . . . Should riots take place, or any serious disturbance be apprehended, large forces of troops in reply to a telegram can be conveyed in a few hours to the most distant parts of Ireland; and large parties who collect at given points for political demonstrations are conveyed with speed to their homes, by the railway, thereby avoiding a delay which would bring them in contact with opposite parties. In furthering the ends of justice, railroads effect a great saving to the country by expeditiously sending criminals to their destinations without exposure to rescue; by saving road making, in the reduction of the police force, &c.[244]

The *Dublin Penny Journal* had no doubts of the benefits the railways would bring to Ireland:

> It is hardly necessary to speak of the advantages to be derived from the execution of railroads, in the giving of employment to the poor peasantry; not merely their temporary labour, while the works are in progress, but also the constant service, which the preservation of the roads, and the increase of commerce and intercourse, will require. Facilities will be afforded for the reclaiming of waste lands, and the draining of bogs; and stimulus will be given to agriculture, to trade, and the arts,

by opening markets for the productions of the interior, and providing coal for manufacturing purposes. The swift and easy transport of troops, the rapid conveyance of the mails, the inducements to travellers and tourists to visit Ireland, are a very imperfect enumeration of the minor benefits, which will arise from the formation of roads for speedy and certain communication throughout the kingdom.[245]

Travellers and tourists had mixed reactions to the Irish railway system. W.H. Richardson and a group of friends toured the north of Ireland in August 1880 and commented, 'We always travelled second class in Ireland, which is about the same in point of comfort, as the second class on English railways, though the third class appears to be rather inferior. Travelling is very reasonable in Ireland if special tourist tickets are taken, and we never had experience of more courteous railway officials.'[246] However, Margaret Dixon McDougall, travelling in the 1880s, had a less pleasant experience:

Between Omagh and Strabane I took a third-class car. It was dirty, of course, horribly dirty, but, as Mrs. McClarty said, 'the dirt was well dried on,' and it was almost empty, so I entered. At a way station a great crowd, great compared to the size of the compartment, came surging in. Every man had a clay pipe, every man had a supply of the most villainous tobacco. I do not wonder the Government taxes such tobacco, that it has to be sold by license – some would not grieve if the duty were prohibitory. Soon matches were struck, a tiny flash and ammunition of reports like toy pistols – all matches here go off like that. Every man began to smoke for dear life, and smoked furiously with great smacks and puffs. And the floor! When the mud of many days that had hardened and dried there was moistened again by tobacco juice! Soon the compartment was filled with smoke, there was literally nothing else to breathe. The car began to heave about like a ship at sea. Fortunately we stopped at a station and some on board got out, so that there was an opportunity of getting close to the door and letting down the glass and a faint was prevented. It was not pleasant to sit there craning one's neck round to breathe at the window, for the seats ran lengthways of the carriage, and keeping all crushed up to keep out of the way of a cross fire of tobacco juice from the opposite benches. Made a vow there and then against third-class carriages.[247]

A branch of tourism that attracted local people to the seaside was sea bathing which was boosted by the railways. Small resorts were already growing along the coast to serve the towns or the prosperous agricultural hinterland. Blackrock, Co. Louth, according to *Lewis* in 1837, was 'much frequented, during the summer seasons, by the farmers of the inland counties, both for the purposes of bathing and drinking the sea-water'. Railway excursions encouraged numbers to increase rapidly according to Paschal Grousset who observed in the 1880s:

Portrush is a delicious sea-side place, at the mouth of Lough Foyle, on the most wonderful coast in Europe; it is seated on the edge of the Antrim table-land, which is of volcanic origin: probably a dependency of Scotland geologically, rather than belonging properly to Ireland, to which it came and welded itself, at some unknown epoch. The traveller has there the agreeable surprise of a delightful hotel – one should say a perfect one – a regular miracle of comfort; and the still greater surprise of seeing there the only electric railway actually working on this planet. That bijou-line is used to take the visitors to the wonder of Ireland, the Giant's Causeway ... As it rises higher the prospect gets wider and wider, and you get a view of the Scotch mountains only fifteen miles distant, while the most extraordinary basaltic formations are following one another under your eye along the coast.

The railways changed the Victorian concept of time. The journey between Belfast and Dublin in 1857 took five hours and twenty minutes, half the time it had taken the stagecoach. In a letter to the *Newry Telegraph*, dated 31 December 1849, 'Watchman' pointed out the impact of the steam age on time keeping. It was directed to Mr Blackham and Mr Cordner 'to whom we chiefly look for a note of time'. According to the letter writer:

> One of them winds and regulates our Church clocks, by which the hours for labour and attendance on Divine worship are fixed; the other manages the railway time, and also the clocks of at least two of the Banks; yet, strange to say, there is always from six to ten minutes difference. This might be, and really is, a matter of very serious moment, and should not be submitted to. I would, therefore, propose, that we should agree to keep the same time. The latter I would much prefer, and would suggest that they should be regulated by either Dublin or Belfast.

His suggestion was not acted upon for more than thirty years, which resulted in many missed trains. Problems with developing railway timetables was critical to the passing of the Time Act, 1880, establishing Dublin Mean Time across Ireland, which was about twenty-five minutes twenty-one seconds behind Greenwich Mean Time (GMT), that was defined by the same act to be the legal time for Great Britain. Previously, clocks in Cork were eleven minutes behind those of Dublin, while those in Belfast were one minute and nineteen seconds ahead.[248]

Another revolution went hand in hand with the spread of the railways across Ireland and this was the arrival of the electric telegraph, the lines for which were located initially beside the railway. The electric telegraph was invented in the 1830s and it allowed messages to be transmitted over great distances and at a faster speed than the posted mail. According to the *Athlone Sentinel* of 21 April 1852:

> the construction of the Electric Telegraph between Dublin and Galway, is fast progressing towards completion. A few days ago, some of the Directors of the Railway came down the line to inspect it. An experimental application of the wires was tried from this town to Dublin, and resulted most satisfactorily – a message being sent from here to Dublin, and an answer received, in the space of three minutes and a half!

Ireland was officially connected with Britain in 1852 when lines were laid on the seabed from Holyhead and they connected Dublin to the British telegraph network. The *Northern Standard* commented:

> The electric telegraph had already been completed from Dublin to Galway, and thus we possess an unbroken line of communication with the shores of the Atlantic, requiring but a few minutes to carry information back and forwards. It is impossible to overrate the importance of this event, in whatever point of view we may regard it. We hail it in fact, as one of those material agencies by which incalculable benefit may be conferred upon Ireland, and the interest of the two countries be indissolubly connected.[249]

In 1868 the government bought out the private companies and handed over control to the Post Office. Already the arrival of the railways had dramatically improved the mail service in Ireland and with services from British towns and cities the Post Office started to use special sorting carriages on trains.

In January 1878, Scottish-born scientist, inventor, engineer, and innovator Alexander Graham Bell demonstrated his new invention, the telephone, to Queen Victoria, Princess Beatrice and the Duke of Connaught at Osborne House on the Isle of Wight. After Bell had explained his new invention to the Queen, Her Majesty spoke to Sir Thomas and Lady Biddulph, who lived in Osborne Cottage situated within the grounds of the estate. Within two years the first telephone exchange in Ireland was opened on the top floor of Commercial Buildings in Dame Street Dublin. It had five subscribers initially but within a decade this had risen to 500. In 1884 a trunk line was constructed between Dublin and Belfast and by 1893 the National Telephone Company was providing a service in Cork, Limerick, Dundalk, Drogheda and Derry. The Post Office, anxious about the losses on its telegraph service, purchased the trunk lines in 1892 and by the end of the century Ireland was connected to Britain through a submarine cable between Newcastle, Co. Wicklow, and north Wales.

The first petrol car seen in Ireland was owned by a Dubliner, Dr John Colohan, who imported a Benz Velo in 1896. He was quickly followed by other prominent Dublin citizens such as H.M. Gillie, the editor of the *Freeman's Journal*, and Lord Iveagh. When the Royal Irish Automobile Club was founded in 1901, the majority of its members were titled landowners, military officers, or wealthy brewers and distillers. For those of more modest means the bicycle offered the possibility of independence. Ireland was at the forefront of the cycling craze that swept the western world in the late Victorian era. It was not merely that the Irish adopted the bicycle, they also contributed to its development. John Boyd Dunlop invented the pneumatic tyre in the 1880s after his son had complained of the pain caused by cycling on solid wheels over cobblestones. The tyre was an immediate success and Dunlop went into business with Harvey du Cros, a paper manufacturer of Huguenot origin, manufacturing the tyres at Stephen's Street in Dublin. All across the capital, the tyres were fitted on the growing number of bicycles seen along the city's streets.

However, the enthusiasm was far from universal. According to the *Cork Examiner* for 27 May 1881:

> CAUTION TO BICYCLISTS. – At the Police Office yesterday, Mr. W. Harrington referred to the practice of riding bicycles through the streets of the city. He saw a bicycle running through Prince's-street, one of the greatest thoroughfares and one of the most obstructed streets in the city of Cork. He did not know what the law was, or whether there was any law in reference to those machines having bells. If bicycles were to be allowed in the streets they ought not to be allowed to go through the narrow streets. He wished to bring it forward there to see if there were any redress for the danger that the public were exposed to by those machines.

Chapter 12

Sport and Leisure

D uring Queen Victoria's reign big changes took place in the way people spent their leisure time. More traditional blood sports like bear baiting and cockfighting were banned, while new sports like lawn tennis and croquet became popular among the middle classes. Older sports, such as rugby, football and cricket, were codified by agreed rules and increased in popularity through national competitions facilitated by the railways. Gaelic sports also enjoyed a revival and renewed a strong sense of county and national allegiance. Theatres, music halls, libraries, museums and art galleries were built in every major town and many minor ones while seaside towns were no longer the preserve of the rich, and places like Bray and Bangor developed as popular resorts for the working classes.

Originating in saloon bars within public houses during the 1830s, music hall entertainment became increasingly popular with audiences as the century progressed; so much so, that during the 1850s, some public houses were demolished and specialised music hall theatres developed in their place. These theatres were designed chiefly so people could eat, drink and smoke tobacco in the auditorium while the entertainment took place. These were rowdy events as acts were cheered or booed off and objects thrown at the stage. The audience joined in by singing along to favourite popular songs, or watched entertainments as diverse as acrobats, trapeze artists, 'operatic selections', 'black-face minstrels', or can-can dancers. According to the *Dublin Evening Telegraph* of 28 April 1894, 'among the many attractions of the "Araby" bazaar, will be the character impersonations by Mr Charles Gladwin of Mr. Albert Chevalier, whose coster songs will be reproduced, and of Mr. Eugene Stratton, 'the whistling coon,' whose plantation ditties will also be sung.'

Dublin was liberally supplied with music halls, of which Jude's in Grafton Street was the most characteristic, according to the *Dublin Evening Telegraph* of 26 December 1896, 'There are, no doubt, numerous citizens of Dublin who have enjoyed their chop or glass of punch – both reputed to have been of the best – accompanied with a "little harmony", and who have spiritedly beaten time to the chairman's mallet with the well battered spoons of the hostelry.'

A terrible accident occurred in March 1882 at the Star of Erin Musical Hall in Dame Street, Dublin. One of the items in the performance was the aerial flights of Artois, surnamed "The Flying Wonder". This consisted of flights from one end of the hall to the other over the audience using a trapeze but without a net or other protection underneath:

> The performances were so daring that there were cries from the audience of 'Enough!' His last movement, according to his customary programme, was to spring from a flying trapeze to a stationary one fixed over the stage. He made the spring, and succeeded in catching the trapeze both with his hands and feet; but his hold does not appear to have been firm enough, for, after swinging once or twice, he suddenly loosed his grasp and fell to the ground on his back and neck. One of the attendants came out and looked at the motionless body, and the drop curtain was immediately lowered.[250]

One French conductor and composer of light music found that Dublin audiences could be too appreciative of his efforts to bring classical music to the general public. According to the *Dublin Evening Post* for 10 April 1847, a disturbance arose between the audience and the

Bohemian opera singer Johann Baptist Pischek, whose friend Adolphe Jullien, a noted music critic, would not allow him to answer calls for an encore:

> On last evening, a scene of very great noise and confusion occurred in the Music Hall during the Concert. Owing to M. Jullien not allowing Herr Pischek to answer to a general encore, the audience in the promenade became very excited, which M. Jullien still further added to saying that it was all owing to letting in a sixpenny mob. All the remainder of the concert passed off in dumb show; and the audience retired amidst general crash of music-stands, benches, seats; in fact, whatever could be laid hands on suffered.[251]

Occasionally a celebrity would make their way to Ireland. No one provoked greater excitement than Charles Dickens, who was a noted performer of his own works:

> Last night Mr. Charles Dickens gave the last of his series of readings before an audience that occupied every available inch of space in the Round Room of the Rotundo. Many persons were unable to obtain admission, and it is much to be desired that the success which has attended the short series just concluded may induce Mr. Dickens at no remote period again to afford the citizens of Dublin a treat at once intellectual and so enjoyable.[252]

Dickens also gave a series of readings in Belfast's Victoria Hall in 1858 that proved memorable for his audience in unexpected ways. During his reading of *A Christmas Carol*:

> the audience responded to every touch of humour with peals of laughter, which rang again and from every corner

of the Hall. Two rather singular occurrences interrupted the reading. Just before the close of the first part, a large piece of molding from the ceiling over the orchestra fell with a crash amongst a detachment of the audience, who were accommodated with seats in that place. Most fortunately, no person was touched by the fallen mass, but it came quite close to some ladies, and, for a moment, startled everyone in the room. Later in the evening, an amusing catastrophe happened. A row of gas-lights, which are placed over and in front of Mr. Dickens, were fed by a flexible tube, which partly lay upon the orchestra. Just as the reader was describing the game of blind man's buff at Scrooge's nephew's, some person stood upon the tube, and for a moment all was in comparative darkness. The reading was therefore interrupted until ladders were procured, and the range of lights again set in order.[253]

Paschal Grousset visited Dublin's Gaiety Theatre during his tour of Ireland in the 1880s. At this time it specialised in musical burlesques that came straight from London. Grousset commented that, 'they are acted by Irishmen and Irishwomen, with all the dash, the brilliancy, the wit of the Celt. The comic actor of the company neglects nothing to amuse his audience; extravagant costumes, insane grimaces, jigs danced in brogues, impromptu verses on the events of the day, – he has any number of tricks at his command.' With perhaps his tongue firmly in his cheek he commented, 'The accomplished and fascinating corps de ballet exhibit tights of such indiscretion as the Lord Chamberlain would assuredly not tolerate in London. Is it that his jurisdiction does not extend to the sister isle; or does the thing which would imperil the virtue of club-loungers in Pall Mall appear to him without danger for those of Kildare Street?' The audiences were generally of the lower middle and working classes. Grousset noted that 'officers, in plain clothes as they are always when out of duty, are nevertheless easy to recognize and seem about the only swells visible in the boxes'.

By the 1890s a new phenomenon was attracting audiences across the country to musical halls, one that would eventually eclipse live theatre for many – the moving picture. According to the *Larne Times* for September 1899:

> We had occasion on Saturday to praise very highly the cinematographe entertainment and concert given on the preceding evening in the Ulster Hall. The display was so successful and the audience so warmly enthusiastic in demanding encores that the promoters were more than justified in repeating the performance on Saturday evening. The views are wonderfully clear and distinct, and embrace all kinds of subjects, humorous and serious, not to mention the picturesque sketches of Alpine scenery. But what predominates above everything else is the representation of the last Orange Procession in Belfast. It was a work of no ordinary magnitude in taking the movements of such a tremendous procession as what Belfast people are accustomed to every Twelfth of July. The views, which were taken from a point in Clifton Street, came out with remarkable clearness, and when the Grand Master was observed passing in his carriage a tremendous out-burst of enthusiasm was sent up.[254]

One of the attractions of this new invention was that it could be set up in any village hall or tent. As part of the entertainment organised by the Portstewart Total Abstinence Association, H.S. Morton of Belfast held an exhibition of a cinematograph and another recent invention, the gramophone, at the Cromie Institute Hall in Portstewart but with such poor results that the *Coleraine Chronicle* predicted a limited future for both inventions:

> The gramophone ... was ... introduced, and the only item recognisable to the audience was an imitation of 'The Soldiers

of the Queen,' played as a march by a military band, but it was reproduced at hornpipe tempo. The cinematograph was then put into action, and among the views were soldiers marching, arrival and departure of a train, a bathing scene. The vibration caused by the machine produced the pictures in such a flickering manner that they were painful to look at, and it was an evident relief when the cylinder had ran its course. Without exception it was the most unsatisfactory exhibition of the kind ever given here, and it is feared the hand of doom will be legibly written on similar entertainments here in future.[255]

Entertainment for the poor in the towns and cities took place on the streets. William Makepeace Thackeray observed street entertainment for himself during the early 1840s, considering it rather quaint by his cosmopolitan tastes:

One night I paid twopence to see a puppet-show – such an entertainment as may have been popular a hundred and thirty years ago, and is described in the Spectator. But the company here assembled were not, it scarcely need be said, of the genteel sort. There were a score of boys, however, and a dozen of labouring men, who were quite happy and contented with the piece performed, and loudly applauded. Then in passing homewards of a night, you hear, at the humble public-houses, the sound of many a fiddle, and the stamp of feet dancing the good old jig, which is still maintaining a struggle with teetotalism, and, though vanquished now, may rally some day and overcome the enemy. At Kingstown, especially, the old 'fire-worshippers' yet seem to muster pretty strongly; loud is the music to be heard in the taverns there, and the cries of encouragement to the dancers.

The Irish love for music was noted by a number of travellers including Johann Kohl, who was intrigued by the popularity of street balladeers:

On these and similar occasions of popular excitement in Ireland, the most remarkable objects are the ballad-singers, who are in no country so numerous as here. In Kilkenny there were literally twice as many ballad-singers as lampposts standing in the street. Their usual stand is in the gutter which separates the footpath on which the foot-passengers walk from the carriageway; and to this kennel they are perpetually strolling up and down. They are generally provided with a number of printed copies of the ballads which they sing, and their principal employment consists in the sale of these songs, which they are continually waving in the air, with a peculiar and stereotyped motion of the hand.

Kohl was amused by the rapt attention of the audience, who particularly enjoyed a melancholy ballad:

in Ireland the ballad-singers have not such an easy life: crowds of poor people, beggars and rabble, perseveringly swarm around them, follow them step by step, and listen to them with a degree of eagerness, which may partly be attributed to the fact that the singers proclaim their own misfortunes, which they have turned into verse, but still more to the great delight which the Irish take in music and singing, and in everything new that passes in the streets.[256]

The arrival of the circus caused considerable excitement as it paraded through the town. This did not always end happily. According to the *Cork Examiner* for 18 July 1862:

As Bell's troupe of equestrians were proceeding through George's-street, Kingstown, on Tuesday, previous to the mid-day performance, a man named Kelly, a shoemaker, incautiously got too near the van containing the lions, for the purpose of teasing them, when one of the beasts caught his arm in her talons and dragged it into the cage, lacerating it in a fearful manner – literally tearing all the flesh away from the shoulder downwards. The lion also clutched at his face. The crowd stood around bewildered until Mr Batty the lion tamer rushed bravely into the cage and subdued the beast with his whip forcing the animal to release the unfortunate man. To save the man's life it was deemed necessary to amputate the arm. The operation was skilfully performed by Dr. Plant who had gained considerable experience in amputating during the Crimean war.

Minstrel troops were also popular, although one can trace a defensive element in some of the reports about the suitability of this form of entertainment. The Christy Minstrels were a blackface group formed by Edwin Pearce Christy, a well-known ballad singer, in 1843, in Buffalo, New York. The *Cork Examiner* of 14 January 1862 announced that:

The Christy's Minstrels are returning to Cork, and have announced three performances, to be given towards the end of next week. The various claims of this troupe of performers on public support and admiration are well enough known already in Cork, and we are sure the attendance at each of the concerts will prove that the merits of their entertainment are sufficiently recognised. The Christy's stand first on the list of the innumerable bands of negro melodists who have for some years back visited these countries, and are amongst the very few whose entertainment is perfectly unobjectionable.

Sport and gambling were twin passions that infected the Irish at all levels of society. Horse racing was always popular in attracting crowds from the surrounding countryside. Johann Kohl noted in the 1840s:

We arrived at Kilkenny in the evening, and after having dined I had a sight of life in an Irish town, on the eve of a great horserace. Kilkenny has now about 25,000 inhabitants, and is, with respect to size, about the eighth town in Ireland; but as half the population of the surrounding country had streamed in on account of the races, the number was increased to about 40,000 during the three days they lasted. This great crowd of people wandered about I know not why, – standing, sauntering, singing, and performing music in the streets; so that the place seemed like a great mercantile town in Germany during the annual fair.[257]

Nearly fifty years later Marie Anne de Bovet commented:

They have an annual feast which is as serious a matter to the people of Dublin as the 'Functions' of Holy Week are to the people of Rome – I mean the races, which take place at the end of August. Chance took me to Dublin unintentionally on my return from a tour in the interior, while they were going on, and it might have been very unpleasant for me. There was not a bed to be had in the hotel, so I was almost reduced to sleeping out of doors. Kitchens were blazing from morning to night, there was a general jingle of forks and glasses, a continual popping of champagne corks, and the waiters, if not brutish or stupid, were generally drunk. In the streets were collected together, from all parts of the country, types of every variety, horse-dealers and well-to-do farmers, country gentlemen with the typical face; old men, fat and blooming, with red nose and long beard, in tight white waistcoats and black coats; young men, with, pink and white faces like girls, in large breeches and leather gaiters, mustard-coloured tweed jackets, and light blue or scarlet ties. The town echoed with their exuberant shouts of glee. The women came out in their best dresses, which though in deplorable taste do not diminish their beauty.[258]

Fishing and hunting continued largely unchanged during the Victorian period. Details of hunting appointments and activities appeared in the sporting section of the local press. Sometimes it ended happily for the fox:

> **THE CLARE HOUNDS.** Our county hounds were out for the first day of the season on Tuesday last, when there was a large attendance of gentlemen and a good sprinkle of the fair sex. The place of meeting was at Moyriesk House, the picturesque residence of J. F. V. Fitzgerald, Esq., the front of which several cars and carriages were drawn up, filled with ladies who came to witness the cheering national sport of a fox hunt. Shortly after eleven o'clock the hounds arrived, accompanied by their owner, Captain Butler, Ballyline, whose love of field sports tends so much to animate the sporting character of our county. The hounds appeared to be in good condition, and immediately on their arrival they were led to cover at the rear of Moyriesk lawn. Here after some delay Reynard made an appearance, and took to flight on towards Cloona, the residence of Mr. Hall, the hounds following him in full cry. When midway between Moyriesk and Cloona he gave his pursuers the slip by a clever double, and earthed himself safely in a bog that was convenient.[259]

A favourite eighteenth-century sport, bare-knuckle prizefighting, remained popular in Ireland until well into the nineteenth century despite attempts by the authorities to stamp out the practice. According to the *Dublin Morning Register* for Monday, 3 January 1842:

> On Saturday morning a large concourse of the fancy assembled to witness a prize fight between two men named Hayden and Byrne – the latter the brother of Simon Byrne, the well-known pugilist, who lost his life some time ago in an encounter with Deaf Burke. The 'mill' took place at Peamount, near Lucan,

and continued, with no decided advantage on either side, up to the nineteenth round, when the arrival of the police put an end to the exhibition.

During the first week of June 1859, a prize fight took place at a secluded spot between Randalstown and Ballymena, in Co. Antrim. Rumours had been circulating for some time of the forthcoming event and one of the combatants was reported to be under training in the neighbourhood of Comber. A special train was engaged to convey spectators from Belfast to the scene of the fight but an embarrassed Mr Cotton, manager of the Belfast and Ballymena railway, told a reporter from the *Banner of Ulster* that he had been led to believe that the train was to convey spectators to a foot race, several of which had already taken place along the line of railway. The spectators departed as early as 3.30 a.m., having fairly hoodwinked the police. The *Banner of Ulster* informed shocked readers that the two pugilists 'two disreputable fellows, named "Hussey" McVeigh and Peter McCann', fought each other for nearly an hour:

> At the end of that time, the former, having been battered, blinded and bruised into a state of stupor, relinquished the contest, and was led away and conveyed back to town in a condition from which it is doubtful whether he will recover. The stakes are said to have been £25 a side, and it is reported that 'a great amount of money changed hands' in bets. We deeply regret to hear that many of the inhabitants of the neighbourhood, including females, were spectators of the disgusting combat.[260]

As the nineteenth century progressed the Victorians sought to impose on sport rules and regulations, changing the focus from physical competition to one of discipline with a strong sense of fair play. Two important influences on the development of sport in Ireland during the nineteenth century were the army and educational institutions. Games such as cricket, golf and hockey depended on the existence of garrison towns throughout the county and a particularly large military presence in Dublin. The first recorded cricket match in Ireland took place in Dublin's Phoenix Park in 1792 between an 'All-Ireland' selection and a team representing the military garrison. Similarly, Ireland's second-oldest golf club was formed at the Curragh in 1883 by soldiers of the Highland Light Infantry. The enthusiasm with which the military embraced sports did not always go down well with those who preached Sunday observance. Someone out for a walk was appalled to see members of the armed services setting a bad example to locals: 'On way to Borough Cemetery Sunday last I was disagreeably surprised to see various groups of members of the Rifle Brigade busily engaged at cricket, football, and quoit throwing in full view of passers-by. Those Sunday pastimes, disagreeable in the eyes of Belfast Protestants, should be put a stop to by the local military authorities, as it had undoubtedly a damaging effect on the rising generation.'[261]

Universities such as Oxford, Cambridge, and above all Trinity College in Dublin, also had an important role in spreading sport in Ireland. A rugby club was established at Trinity College in 1854 and members of the College were also largely responsible for resurrecting the northern form of hurling which, like its southern counterpart, had declined in popularity particularly during the famine years of the late 1840s. However, they quickly merged it with the game of hockey codified by the Hockey Association in England in 1886. Cricket too was played enthusiastically by Trinity students and the university cricket club is thought to date from 1835. It had a strong following in the north, where from the 1830s onwards cricket clubs were formed, usually by former pupils of English public schools, and often these clubs were instrumental in the development of rugby. Charles Stewart Parnell was an avid cricketer and was captain of the Wicklow eleven. He was noted for enforcing the three-minute rule that permitted an incoming batsman three minutes in which to take the pads from his exiting teammate. This was considered bad form by his contemporaries, but the *Irish Press* later noted that 'in the House of Commons, he was to show the same ability at enforcing the rules to make his opponents uncomfortable'.

Football as a sport had been around a long time before it was codified by the Football Association. In Roscommon Assizes in March 1850, Edward Brennan was indicted for stabbing James Leyden:

> In this case it appeared an argument arose between the prisoner and the prosecutor relative to a game of football; words became so high that blows were resorted to, and the prosecutor, having been separated from the prisoner, took up a shoemaker's last, which he was about to fling at the prisoner, when the latter stabbed him with a knife in the side.[262]

In its modern form football had originated in public schools and English universities but it was the working classes that embraced it and ensured its success. In Belfast, the most industrialised part of Ireland, which had close ties with the west of Scotland and a large military presence, football quickly established itself as the most popular sport. The Irish Football Association was formed in Belfast in 1880 and at first teams representing British army regiments enjoyed conspicuous success in the early competitions. The inaugural meeting of the Irish Football League was held on 14 March 1890 in the Belfast Estate Office of the Marquess of Dufferin and Ava. Eight clubs agreed to participate: Cliftonville, Clarence, Milford, Oldpark, Distillery, Glentoran, Ulster and Linfield, making it essentially a Belfast affair. As the *Belfast News-Letter* pointed out on 17 March 1890:

> Irish football will have to make great strides before it can hope to contend with England, Scotland or Wales on anything like equal terms; but, with a genuine desire to benefit by

experience, and to remedy defects, we are not without hope
that victory may in the most remote future be found on the
side of the Shamrock. With regard to the association code,
we labour under the very great disadvantage that we have,
comparatively speaking, a very limited area to work in, for
the game has not taken a strong hold except in the north-
eastern corner of Ireland, and the teams which do battle for
us are merely representative of Belfast, having very little of a
national or representative character.

It lamented the fact that the forthcoming international match against
England would have only one possible outcome: 'Not even the most
enthusiastic supporter of Ireland anticipated a win on Saturday for the
home team – in fact, the only question seemed to be as to how many
the English would beat us by; but, at the same time it was hoped that
Ireland would cut a less humiliating figure than she has done in the
past.' This hope was doomed to disappointment – Ireland lost 9-1 on
a very wet afternoon in front of a damp and dispirited crowd of 5,000.

For much of its early history in Belfast, football appeared to serve
only as another outlet for sectarian conflict. According to the *Irish
News* for September 1899:

The exhibition of ruffianism and brutality witnessed on
Saturday at Cliftonville are calculated to destroy the hope that
Belfast will ever get beyond the stage of school development in
which prowess in the art of paving-stone warfare is regarded
as an ideal desirable of attainment … the only explanation
which can account for what took place is that it has been made
the settled policy of a section of the community to try by any
and every means to prevent those of the Catholic minority
who follow football taking part in the public competitions in
connection with that sport.

The match was between Belfast Celtic, 'identified with the Falls Road' and Cliftonville, whose supporters indulged in Orange party songs. According to the paper 'very soon the game of football was eclipsed in interest by the more fascinating sport of bear-baiting the "Papishes". There were too few policemen to stop the outbreak of fighting among the supporters.' The *Irish News* warned that, 'Football clubs who invite the public to their grounds have a serious responsibility, and it is to be trusted that, for the honour of the sport, some method will be devised to prevent the recurrence of such scenes.'[263]

Sport for girls and young women was an altogether gentler affair. Walking, calisthenics, archery and croquet were all socially acceptable among the upper echelons of society. None of these sports required too much movement of the body nor a woman to wear clothing that was too unbecoming. Lawn tennis developed in the mid-1870s and by the end of the century a tennis court in the garden became a symbol of respectability and wealth, supplanting the more stately game of croquet. 'Croquet is coming in again! So an English advertiser says. I don't believe him. Croquet is too slow nowadays. Tennis has taken its place, and requires in its play as much science and the exercise of infinitely more energy than croquet. For this reason, at all events, tennis will remain the pastime of ladies, while with gentlemen golf will be popular.'[264] The *Irish Society* noted the increasing popularity of tennis tournaments at private residences, 'A second private tennis tournament was held in the Co. Roscommon a few weeks since. The tournament was played as before on the grounds of Rookwood, Thornfield, Rocksavage, and Castlecoote. The prize, a tennis racquet, offered by H. d'Esterre Stevens, Esq, J.P., was hotly contested, being finally awarded to Miss Chute.'[265]

The popularity of lawn tennis played a major role in making sporting activity respectable for girls. 'But it is to the "safety" bicycle that our sisters and daughters who love healthful exercise are most indebted,' opined an article entitled 'Some Sports in Which Women Excel' in the *Irish Independent* in May 1899. Initially the majority of women's cycling accidents were caused by their long skirts becoming caught in the chain or spokes. Towards the end of the century they began to wear leggings and baggy knickerbockers, which caused much hilarity for a time. 'Once the first daring few had braved the passing curiosity and at times vulgar chaff the sight of a girl on a "bike" produced the fascination of the cycle spread like wildfire through the sex.' The article urged caution when it came to long-distance cycling, which although bad for men 'is a thousand times worse for practically all women. There are physiological reasons which are not suitable for explanation why prolonged exertion, especially cycling exertion is to be particularly avoided by girls and their elders of the same sex.'[266]

The popularity of British sports in Ireland caused a great deal of alarm in nationalist circles. Ireland, they pointed out, had its own sporting traditions. Various forms of football, including the game of Cad, were played in Ireland for centuries. A game resembling the modern sport of hurling was certainly indigenous to Ireland for centuries and by the beginning of the nineteenth century two versions of the game had become established; the caman (anglicised to 'commons') was similar to field hockey, or shinty, in that it did not allow handling of the ball and was played with a hard wooden ball (the crag). This was confined to the north of the country. The second (iomán or baire) was found in the south and in this form of the game the ball could be handled and carried on the hurl. It could be found only in three pockets: around Cork city, in south-east Galway and in the area north of Wexford town. The decline had been hastened by the Great Famine and the hostility of many clergy and magistrates, who condemned it because of the violence with which it was associated.

A major step forward occurred when Co. Clare teacher Michael Cusack set about reviving hurling. He codified a new version, principally modelled on the southern 'iomán' version that he had known as a child in Clare. Not surprisingly, this new game never caught on in the old 'commons' area, with the Glens of Antrim being the only major exception. During the second half of the nineteenth century Irish nationalists became increasing worried that the popularity of British sports would result in the lessening of a sense of Irish identity and believed that there was an urgent need to revitalise Irish sports and pastimes. This was most evident in the formation of the Gaelic Athletic Association for the Preservation and Cultivation of National Pastimes (GAA) in 1884. The GAA spread quickly across the country and organised competitions on a county basis that revived a sense of pride in place. From the beginning the GAA also developed an anti-British outlook. In a letter to the editor of the *Wexford People*, one supporter 'A Quiet Old Stager' declared:

> The GAA comes in the nick of time to save and upraise our Celtic manhood. No matter how men may differ as to the course best suited to serve our country politically, there can be but one opinion as to the utility of manly out-door exercises for producing a muscular, virile race.

In language curiously reminiscent of the Victorian public school, he declared that these sports would be a boon to 'our sleepy provincial towns or dull country villages, giving an aim to the aimless young men who now drift into public houses from sheer inanity, or lounge at crossroads or street corners'. He concluded that 'when drilling and the use of arms is forbidden them, cultivate the next best thing – Athletic Training ...'[267]

Between 1886 and 1891 the Association was almost completely taken over by the Irish Republican Brotherhood. The Association's opposition to British sports was expressed through its banning policy formalised in 1887. This not only banned members of the Crown forces from participating in Gaelic games (which in addition to hurling came to include Gaelic football, camogie and handball), but also prohibited GAA members from watching or taking part in 'foreign' games, a term that its first patron, Archbishop Croke of Cashel, defined as including 'such foreign and fantastic field-sports as lawn tennis, polo, croquet, cricket and the like'.

Gaelic sports were regarded with suspicion by Unionists and some members of the Catholic hierarchy alike. In February 1889 a number of newspapers reported an account by the local correspondent of the *Belfast News-Letter* of a game between the Gaels of the cathedral city and the John Dillons of Keady that was held in Armagh. At eight o'clock mass that morning the Roman Catholic Primate referred to the Gaels in his sermon and condemned the Gaelic Association. Although he had no objection to young men engaging in football or hurling for a few hours on Sunday morning, 'he was decidedly opposed to them going into remote parts to play where they would be exposing themselves to the danger of being enrolled as members of secret societies. Many of them he had no doubt, were in the pay of the Government, who would do all they could to entrap them.' He also condemned 'the system of going from one parish to another and from one county to another', on a Sunday which 'was a heavy drain on the slender resources of the small farmers and others in the country whose sons are members of the association'. In a moment of wishful thinking the Armagh correspondent declared that the GAA had 'received its death-blow'. The article went on to report that nearly 1,000 had witnessed the game that afternoon.[268]

Gaelic football nevertheless saw a rapid rise in popularity during the last two decades of the nineteenth century. The *Kildare Observer and Eastern Counties Advertiser*, of 10 November 1888 reported:

> Favoured with a fine day and the attendance of upwards of 2,000 spectators, the first day of the Athy tournament was in every way a complete success. The first team to arrive was Kellyville, accompanied by a crowd of admirers, and next Carlow-Graigue. The field was decorated by numerous flags with the Athy colours. The presence of the Athy Gaelic Brass Band added considerably to the days' enjoyment.

About half-past one o'clock the first match was got off, that between Kellyville and Carlow-Graigue. Kellyville had the best of the play throughout, and won rather easily by a goal and seven point to nil.

The games did not always go smoothly. According to the *Donegal Independent* for 1 September 1893, reporting on a game between Doon and Cappamore, there had apparently been ill feeling between the two teams for some time.

Murdered while Playing Gaelic Football

Terrible affair is reported from New Pallas, Co. Limerick. During the Gaelic Football Tournament Sunday, William O'Connell, aged 21, one of the players, was assaulted by some members of the opposing team, and knocked down. A man then stabbed him through the heart with a knife, causing instant death. No one has been arrested, but the police are searching for the assailant from whom O'Connell is alleged to have received the fatal wound.

Postscript

One Last Visit

Encouraged by the loyalty of close to 30,000 of her Irish troops during the South African War, which had been ongoing since October 1899, Queen Victoria visited Ireland for the last time between 4 and 25 April 1900. The Royal yacht arrived at Kingstown to the thunder of heavy guns and the cheering multitudes who had been making their way to the decorated barriers that surrounded the wharf. As the Queen made her way to the waiting carriage the combined bands of the *Majestic* and *Magnificent*, at that time the largest battleships ever built, played the national anthem and the waiting crowds waved thousands of miniature Union Jacks. Thousands made their way to Dublin where, according to the *Dublin Daily Nation*, 'not within the memory of any of the existing officials have the railway resources of this country been so severely taxed as they were yesterday to provide accommodation and the means of conveyance for the thousands of visitors who travelled into the city from the most distant parts of Ireland'.

The Second African War, more popularly known as the Boer War had, however, brought about a change in mood in Ireland: the pro-Boer Transvaal Committee, formed to discourage Irishmen from joining up to fight on the British side, would within six years become a new radical political party, Sinn Fein. The tone in the newspapers in 1900 was notably more subdued that it had been for Victoria's first visit more than fifty years earlier. With the Queen not expected to travel north, thousands travelled by the Great Northern Railway and according to the press, 'There is much rejoicing here in Orange circles at the extensive nature of the reception accorded to the Queen in Dublin', while Belfast had to make do with displays of the Union flag on its public buildings and miniature Royal Standards fitted to the tram-cars.[269] The *Sligo Champion* contrasted this with the actions of nationalists in the city:

... the people of Dublin city – the three hundred thousand nationalists who are yet uncontaminated – had no more part in the demonstration of servility than if they happened to spend Wednesday in Afghanistan. The workers who got a holiday came out and looked on. Many Dubliners left the city for the day, and the electric tramcars to Dollymount found hundreds of patrons at Nelson's Pillar even while brainless young bloods and Unionist dons of Trinity College were howling with joy at the sight of a poor old lady who should never have been subjected to such an ordeal.[270]

The Queen remained in Dublin for three weeks, performing official functions and visiting schools and hospitals. 'I felt quite sorry that all was over,' she wrote on 26 April, at the end of her trip. 'I can never forget the really wild enthusiasm and affectionate loyalty displayed by all in Ireland and shall ever retain a most grateful remembrance of this warm-hearted sympathetic people.' On her departure from Ireland on 26 April she thanked the Irish people for their greeting in a public letter addressed to the lord-lieutenant. Less than nine months later she died.

New of the Queen's death provided a chance for her Irish subjects to consider her legacy. The *Weekly Irish Times* for 26 January 1901 focused on the emotion of the occasion:

Flags flying at half-mast were to be seen in all quarters of the city and suburbs, while the windows of the business houses and the private residences of the citizens were to a very large extent either wholly or partially covered with blinds or shutters. These tokens of national morning were not confined to any one class or creed. No one could walk through Grafton Street, for instance, without being particularly struck with the intensity of the feeling which has been occasioned. Instead of the brightly dressed windows, and gaily attired throngs of shoppers which are under ordinary circumstances to be seen in this fashionable thoroughfare, there was an all-prevailing hue of the most sombre description. Crape and various other kinds of dark coloured material were profusely displayed in the windows of the many large drapery establishments in the street and amongst the pedestrians, of whom there were a goodly number during the day, bright colours were conspicuous by their absence.[271]

There was a similar mood in Belfast. The *News-Letter* reported, 'there were unmistakable manifestations of sorrow on the part of the citizens of Belfast at the death of the Queen. Flags floated at half-mast on the Town Hall, the Harbour Office, the Water Office, the Custom House, the Free Public Library, the Albert Memorial, and many business establishments, clubs, and public offices, while in a large number of cases blinds were drawn, shutters put up, and shop windows draped in black.' It continued, ' It was noticeable that a great many of the citizens had donned complete or partial mourning attire as a mark of respect to the memory of their beloved Sovereign ...'[272]

The *Freeman's Journal* was more circumspect. It recognised the historic significance of the event:

> Never, perhaps, in the history of the world has the death of a woman so deeply moved nations. However far aloof a people may stand from the attractive influence of the British Throne and Monarch, however its history may have been affected by the dead Queen, the deep significance and enthralling interest of the event must be recognised. For it is one of those events by which history is reckoned and the onward progress of men measured.

The newspaper recalled the optimism that had greeted Victoria's accession to the throne, and compared it with attitudes at the end of her reign. It contrasted Daniel O'Connell's optimism in 1838, declaring that in the end 'those hopes had been disappointed "generations ago" when they learned that Queen Victoria was never to make them her debtors, or to stand to them in dear relation which made her the most beloved of English monarchs among the British people'. The *Irish Daily Independent* concurred:

> Regarded merely as the Sovereign of England, Queen Victoria admirably fulfilled all the duties which belonged to her exalted position. Viewed as the Sovereign of Ireland, it can only be recorded of her late Majesty that she was imminently forgetful of her obligations towards this kingdom.

It acknowledged her domestic virtues but insisted that 'so far as Ireland was concerned, a reign more destructive for our people or more ruinous for their national prosperity has never been witnessed, since the time of the Tudor Queen, than was hers.'[273]

The *Dublin Telegraph* was also forthright in its comments:

> Amongst the great mass of the people there is decent grief and reverence in the presence of death. There is reverence for the pure life and domestic virtues of the Queen who has departed. But it would be mere folly to suggest that there is in Ireland that deep personal loyalty, that deep grief, that sense of loss, personal and political, that in England unquestionably prevails. For the great English Sovereign who has departed was no friend of the Irish people, or of liberty or justice in Ireland.

The Victorian era had witnessed significant political and social changes in Ireland that saw the end of landlord dominance, the conduct of county affairs into local hands, the rise of an increasingly confident Catholic middle class and an education and health system far in advance of that found in Britain. The *Cork Examiner* published the musings of the Dublin correspondent of the *Pall Mall Gazette*, 'A quarter of century ago the "educated" man in a country parish in most parts of Ireland was the priest, the rector (if there was one), and the Protestant doctor. Now you have in all directions Catholic doctors and Catholic solicitors, and often, too, businessmen and shopkeepers equally well trained. Similarly, in the Four Courts the proportion of sons of the people and Catholics are steadily increasing, though the Bench is still overwhelmingly Protestant. The Irish Bar to-day, it may be mentioned, is not any means as independent or as patriotic a Bar as was that a hundred years ago.'[274]

However, Ireland's population had plummeted by more than 3½ million since the Famine and was still in decline. An Irish Parliament had not been delivered and the divisions in religion, which had been so evident at the start of the Victorian era, were more firmly entrenched than ever as northern Unionists became more fervent in their support for the British connection. W.B. Yeats described the strong sense he had at the turn of the last century 'that Ireland was to be like soft wax for years to come'. A new brand of nationalism, pioneered by the Gaelic League, was beginning to challenge the old political order as the twentieth century dawned. On the death of the Queen the *Dublin Telegraph* declared, 'Undoubtedly expectation is in the air that with the opening of the new reign there will come a change, and the policy of plunder, disaster, and disgrace which broke the heart and shortened the life of the aged Queen will be reversed.'[275] It was not to be: within twenty years the First World War and the Easter Rising would change the political and social landscape of Ireland beyond all recognition.

Bibliography

Contemporary Sources

Ashworth, John Hervey, *The Saxon in Ireland*, 1851

Atkinson, A., *Ireland in the 19th c. & seventh of England's dominion*, 1844

Austin, Alfred, *Spring & Autumn in Ireland*, 1900

Bayne, Samuel Gamble, *On an Irish Jaunting-car through Donegal & Connemara*, 1902

Balch, William S., *Ireland as I Saw it: the witnessed in 1849*, 1850

Barry, William Whittaker, *A Walking Tour Round Ireland in 1865, by an Englishman*, 1867

Becker, Bernard H., *Disturbed Ireland: Being the letters written during the Winter of 1880–81*, 1881

Bennet, Arthur, *John Bull and his other Island*, 1890

Bennett, William, *Narrative of a Recent Journey of Six Weeks in Ireland*, 1847

Binns, Jonathan, *Miseries and Beauties of Ireland*, 1837

Burke, Oliver Joseph, *The South Isles of Aran (County Galway)* 1887

Caldwell, J.M., *Old Irish Life*, 1912

Cobbett, William (ed.) GDH & Margaret Col *Rural rides*

Cooke, Thomas L. 'Autumnal Rambles about New Quay, County Clare', *Galway Vindicator*, 1842–43

Coulter, Henry, *The West of Ireland: its existing conditions and prospects*, 1862

Croker, Thomas Crofton, *Researches in the South of Ireland*, 1824

Curwen, John Christian, *Observations on the state of Ireland*, 1818

de Bovet, Marie Anne, *Three Months' Tour in Ireland*, 1891

East, John, *Glimpses of Ireland in 1847*, 1847

Forbes, John, *Memorandums made in Ireland in the autumn of 1852*, 1853

Foster, Thomas Campbell, *Letters on the condition of the people of Ireland*, 1846

Grant, J., *Impressions of Ireland and the Irish*, 1844

Grousset, Paschal, *Ireland's Disease: notes and impressions*, 1888

Gwynn, Stephen Lucius, *Highways & Byways in Donegal & Antrim*, 1899

Haight, Canniff, *Here & there in the Home Land: England, Scotland & Ireland, as seen by a Canadian*, 1895

Hall, James, *Tour Through Ireland*, 1813

Hall, Samuel Carter, *Ireland, Its Scenery, Character & History*, 1846

Hall, Spencer T., *Life and Death in Ireland, as witnessed in 1849*, 1850

Holiday, H.B.H., *Haunts on the West Coast of Clare*, 1891

Hurlbert, William Henry, *Ireland Under Coercion: The Diary of an American*, 1888

Inglis, Henry D., *A Journey Through Ireland*, 1834

Johnson, Clifton, *The Isle of the Shamrock*, 1901

Johnson, James, *A Tour of Ireland with meditations and reflections*, 1844

Johnston, Charles, *Ireland, Historic & Picturesque*, c.1901

Khol, J.G., *Travels in Ireland*, 1843

East, John, *Glimpses of Ireland in 1847*, 1847

Lovett, Richard, *Ireland Illustrated with pen & pencil*, c.1891

Lynd, Robert, *Rambles in Ireland*, 1912

M'Manus, Henry, *Sketches of the Irish Highlands: description, social & religious, w/special ref. to Irish missions in West Con*, 1863

Macaulay, James, *Ireland in 1872; a tour of observation.*

McDougall, Margaret Dixon, *The Letters of 'Norah' on her Tour Through Ireland*, 1882

Martineau, Harriet, *Letters from Ireland*, 1851

Nicholson, Asenath (Hatch), *The Bible in Ireland; Ireland's welcome to the stranger, or Excursions through Ireland in 1844–5*, 1847

Osborne, Sidney Godolphin, *Gleanings from the West of Ireland*, 1850

Otway, Caesar, *A tour in Connaught: comprising sketches of Clonmacnoise, Joyce*, 1839

Ritchie, Leitch, *Ireland Picturesque and Romantic*, 1837

Russell, Thomas O'Neill, *Beauties & Antiquities of Ireland: a tourist's guide to its most beautiful scenery & an archaeologist's manual*, 1897

Thackeray, William Makepeace, *The Irish Sketch Book*, 1843

Tonna, Charlotte Elizabeth, *Letters from Ireland*, 1837

Tuke, James Hack, *A Visit to Connaught in the Autumn of 1847*, 1847

Walker, William Wesley, *An Itinerant in the British Isles*, 1896

West Cornwallis, Theresa, *A Summer Visit to Ireland in 1846*, 1847

Selected Secondary Sources

Akenson, Donald Harman, *The Irish Diaspora: A Primer* (Belfast, 1995)

Bardon, Jonathan, *A History of Ulster* (Belfast, 1992)

Bartlett, Tom and Jeffrey, Keith (eds), *A Military History of Ireland* (Cambridge, 1996)

Beckett, J.C., *The Making of Modern Ireland, 1603–1923* (London, 1966)

J.C. Beckett and R.E. Glasscock (eds.), *Belfast: The Origin and Growth of an Industrial City* (London, 1967)

Bourke, Angela, *The Burning of Bridget Cleary* (London, 1999)

Bew, Paul, *Land and the National Question in Ireland, 1858–82* (Humanities Press, 1979)

Bourke, Joanna, *From Husbandry to Housewifery: Women, Economic Change and Housework in Ireland 1890–1914* (Oxford, 1993)

Boyce, D.G., *Nineteenth-century Ireland: The Search for Stability* (Dublin, 1990)

Boyce, D. George, *Nationalism in Ireland* (Routledge, 1996)

Brown, Terence *Ireland: A Social and Cultural History* (New York, 1985)

Brynn, Edward, *Crown & Castle: British Rule in Ireland, 1800–1830* (Dublin, 1978)

Collins, B., (1993), 'The Irish in Britain, 1780–1921' in B.J. Graham and L.J. Connolly, S.J., (ed.) *The Oxford Companion to Irish History* (Oxford, 1998)

Coogan, Tim Pat, *Wherever Green is Worn: the story of the Irish Diaspora* (London, 2000)

Connell, K.H., *The Population of Ireland, 1750–1845* (Clarendon Press, 1950)

Connolly, S., (1987), *Religion and Society in Nineteenth Century Ireland*, Dundalk

Crawford, W.H., and Trainor, B. *Aspects of Irish Social History, 1750–1800* (Belfast 1969)

Cronin, Denis A., Jim Gilligan, and Karina Holton (eds.), *Irish Fairs and Markets* (Four Courts Press, 2001)

Crossman, Virginia, *Politics, Pauperism and Power in Nineteenth-Century Ireland* (Manchester, 2006)

Crossman, Virginia, *The Poor Law in Ireland, 1838–1948* (Dundalk, 2006).

Cullen, L.M. (ed.), *Six Generations: Life and Work in Ireland from 1750* (Mercier Press, 1970)

Cunningham, Terence P., *The Church since Emancipation: Church Reorganization* (Gill and MacMillan, 1970)

Curtis, Jr., L. Perry, *Apes and Angles: The Irishman in Victorian Caricature* (Smithsonian Institution Press, 1997)

Daly, Mary E., *Social and Economic History of Ireland since 1800* (Educational Company of Ireland, 1981)

Evans, E.E., *Irish Folk Ways* (Routledge and Kegan Paul, 1957)

Fitzpatrick, D., *Irish Emigration 1801–1921* (Dundalk, 1985)

Fitzpatrick, D., *Oceans of Consolation: Personal Accounts of Irish Emigration to Australia* (Cork, 1995)

Foster, R.F., *Charles Stewart Parnell: The Man and His Family* (Harvester, 1979)

Green, E.R.R. (ed.), *Essays in Scotch-Irish History* (Belfast, 1969)

Hachey, Thomas E., *Britain and Irish Separatism: From the Fenians to the Free State, 1867–1922* (Rand McNally, 1977)

Hempton, C. & Hill, M., *Evangelical Protestantism in Ulster Society 1740–1890* (London, 1992)

Hooper, Glenn, (ed.), *The Tourist's Gaze: Travellers to Ireland, 1800–2000* (Cork, 2001)

Hoppen, K.T., *Ireland Since 1800: Conflict and Conformity* (London, 1989)

Horgan, Donal, *The Victorian Visitor in Ireland: Irish Tourism 1840–1910* (Imagimedia, 2002)

Jackson, A., *The Ulster Party: Irish Unionists in the House of Commons 1886–1911* (Oxford 1989)

Jackson, A., *Home Rule: An Irish History 1800–2000* (London, 2003)

Kevin C. Kearns, *Dublin Tenement Life: An Oral History* (Penguin, 1994)

Keenan, D., *The Catholic Church in Nineteenth Century Ireland: A Sociological Study* (Dublin, 1983)

Kinealy, C., *The Great Calamity: The Irish Famine 1845–52* (Dublin, 1994)

Emmet J. Larkin, *The Roman Catholic Church and the Home Rule Movement in Ireland, 1870–1874* (University of North Carolina Press, 2009)

Emmet J. Larkin, *The Roman Catholic Church in Ireland and the Fall of Parnell, 1888–1891* (University of North Carolina Press, 1979)

Lyons, F.S.L., *Ireland since the Famine* (Charles Scribner's Sons, 1971)

MacRaild, Donald M., *The Irish Diaspora in Britain, 1750–1939* (Social History in Perspective) (London, 2010)

Maxwell, Ian, *Everyday Life in Nineteenth Century Ireland* (Dublin, 2011) de Nie, Michael, *The Eternal Paddy: Irish Identity and the British Press, 1798–1882* (University of Wisconsin Press, 2004)

Murphy, James H. (ed.), *Evangelicals and Catholics in Nineteenth-Century Ireland* (Four Courts Press, 2005)

Ó Gráda, C., *Ireland: A New Economic History 1780–1939* (Oxford, 1994)

Ó Gráda, *Ireland Before and After the Famine* (Manchester, 1988)

Ó Gráda, C., *The Great Irish Famine* (London, 1989)

O'Shea, J., *Priests, Politics and Society in Post-Famine Ireland* (Dublin, 1983)

O'Tuathaigh, M.A.G., 'The Irish in nineteenth century Britain. Problems of integration', *Transactions of the Royal Historical Society,* 21, 1981

Robbins, Joseph, *The Lost Children: A Study of Charity Children in Ireland 1700–1900* (Institute of Public Administration, 1980)

Scally, Robert James, *The End of Hidden Ireland: Rebellion, Famine, and Emigration* (Oxford University Press, 1995)

Townshend, Charles, *Political Violence in Ireland* (Oxford University Press, 1985)

Vaughan, W.E., *Landlords and Tenants in Victorian Ireland* (Oxford 1994)

Whelan, B. (ed.), *Women and Work in Ireland* (Dublin 2000), pp.51–62

White Harry, *Keeper's Recital – Music and Cultural History in Ireland, 1770–1970*, 1998

Notes

1. *Freeman's Journal*, 29 June 1838.
2. *Southern Reporter and Cork Commercial Courier*, 28 June 1838.
3. *Drogheda Journal*, 30 June 1838.
4. *Waterford Chronicle*, 30 June 1838.
5. *Belfast Commercial Chronicle*, 30 June 1838.
6. *Belfast News-Letter*, 25 July 1837.
7. *Daniel O'Connell* (1900), Robert Dunlop, *The Great Dan*, Charles Chenevix (1983).
8. James Macaulay, *Ireland in 1872: A Tour of Observation* (1873), p.6.
9. The Dublin pillar was finished thirty-four years before the statue of the admiral was hoisted into place on Nelson's Column in Trafalgar Square in 1843.
10. Known as Dunleary until 1821, when it was remained Kingstown in honour of George IV, who landed at its harbour. In 1920 it was renamed Dun Laoghaire, the Irish form of Dunleary.
11. William Makepeace Thackeray, The *Irish Sketchbook* (1844), p.2. His observations are witty and insightful but demonstrate much of the prejudice and sense of superiority of the time.
12. The statue sat on College Green from 1701 and was frequently attacked before it was removed in 1929 following an explosion in the early hours of Armistice Day that year. It was placed in storage in Corporation Yard, Hanover Street, where the King's head was removed from the statue.
13. Johann Kohl, *Travels in Ireland*, 1843, p.292.
14. Johann Kohl pp.14–15. In 1966 Nelson's Pillar was severely damaged by explosives planted by Irish Republicans. Its remnants were later destroyed by the Irish Army.
15. Paschal Grousset, *Ireland's Disease* (1888). Grousset was a French radical politician, journalist and science fiction writer who had

been imprisoned and exiled because of his membership of the Paris Commune.

16. *Derby Daily Telegraph*, 10 August 1880.

17. Elizabeth A. Muenger, *The British Military Dilemma in Ireland* (Kansas, 1991).

18. Henry Inglis, *Ireland in 1834: A Journey throughout Ireland, during the spring, summer and autumn of 1834* (1835).

19. Justin McCarthy, *Irish Recollections* (1912), p.156.

20. *Dublin Evening Telegraph*, 28 April 1894.

21. *The Irish Society*, 14 September 1889.

22. Thackeray, p.158.

23. *Irish Society*, 20 December 1890.

24. *Irish Society*, 14 September 1889.

25. Lewis *Topographical Dictionary* (1837) and *Dublin Daily Express*, 8 July 1899.

26. *Dublin Evening Mail*, 4 February 1857.

27. *Dublin Evening Packet and Correspondent*, 27 September 1851.

28. *Ireland Picturesque and Romantic* (1838), p.11: Leitch Ritchie.

29. Charlotte Elizabeth Tonna, *Letters From Ireland* (1852), p.89.

30. One consequence of the abandonment of these once grand Dublin houses was the healthy sale in portable items. The author of *Ireland Under Coercion* (1888) recalled that Edward Gibson, 1st Lord Ashbourne, at that time the Lord Chancellor of Ireland, 'went off early to look up some fine old wooden mantelpieces and wainscotings in the "slums" of Dublin. A brisk trade it seems has for some time been driven in such relics of the departed splendour of the Irish capital.'

31. *Dublin Daily Express*, 8 July 1899.

32. Lewis *Topographical Dictionary*, and Jonathan Binns (1785–1871), *The Miseries and Beauties of Ireland*, (1837), pp.3–5 Liverpool-born Binns was an assistant commissioner to the Royal Commission established in 1865 to enquire into the condition of the poorer classes in Ireland.

33. Mr and Mrs C. Hall, *Hall's Ireland: Mr and Mrs Hall's Tour of 1840*, ed. Michael Scott, p.288.

34. Grousset, p.41.

35. *Freeman's Journal*, 26 September 1884.

36. *Freeman's Journal*, 4 October 1884.

37. Sir Charles Cameron, p.169.

38. Grousset, p.43.
39. Tricia Cusack, '"This pernicious tea drinking habit": Women, Tea, and Respectability in Nineteenth-Century Ireland', *The Canadian Journal of Irish Studies*, vol. 41.
40. Sir Charles Cameron, *Reminiscences* (1913), p.166.
41. *Dublin Daily Express*, 14 August 1888.
42. *Irish Times*, 6 May 1865.
43. *Freeman's Journal*, 24 February 1879.
44. *Freeman's Journal*, 21 September 1898.
45. *Freeman's Journal*, 22 August 1860.
46. *Irish Society (Dublin)*, Saturday, 5 April 1890. Captain Paul Boyton is remembered for his water stunts, which included crossing the English Channel in a novel inflatable rubber suit that he designed himself.
47. Richard Lalor Sheil (1791–1851), *Sketches Legal and Political* (1855). Sheil was an Irish politician, lawyer and writer from Co. Kilkenny who was a supporter of Daniel O'Connell and the Catholic Association.
48. Grousset, pp.52–53.
49. Josephine Martin Callwell (1856–1935). A member of the Martin family, Co. Galway.
50. Edith Somerville, *Irish Memories* (1917). Somerville is best remembered for the books she wrote in collaboration with Violet Florence Martin, the latter using the pseudonym Martin Ross. Most popular was Some *Experiences of an Irish R.M.* (1899).
51. *Irish Society* (Dublin), 1 December 1894.
52. Mark Bence-Jones, *Twilight of the Ascendancy* (1987).
53. Martineau, *Letters from Ireland* (1852), p.7.
54. *Dublin Daily Express*, 14 October 1893.
55. *Cork Constitution*, 26 January 1884.
56. Mark Bence-Jones, *Twilight of the Ascendancy* (1987).
57. Grousset, p.171; Hussey p.39.
58. W.E. Vaughan, Farmer, Grazier and Gentleman: Edward Delany of Woodtown, 1851–99, *Irish Economic and Social History*, vol. 9 (1982).
59. Gerald Fitzgibbon, *Ireland in 1868* (London, 1868), pp.9–10.
60. According to Mr Horsley's report, 'Iron gates are like "Angels' visits – few and far between" and are rarely seen, except upon farms in the occupation of owners in fee, or upon large farms of tenants having leases, or upon holdings in the immediate vicinity of considerable towns.'

61. Martineau, p.69.
62. Inglis, p.30.
63. Now Daingean, Philipstown was named after King Philip II of Spain. Jonathan Binns, *The Miseries and Beauties of Ireland*, p.42.
64. Charlotte Elizabeth Tonna, p.332.
65. Kohl, p.34.
66. *The Illustrated London News*, 12 August 1843.
67. John Forbes, p.99.
68. Mr and Mrs Hall, *Handbook for Ireland* (1853), p.80.
69. Asenath Nicholson (1792–1855) *The Bible in Ireland: Ireland's Welcome to the Stranger* (1847) p.45. Nicholson was an American social reformer and philanthropist. She travelled through Ireland during the Great Famine distributing Bibles, food and clothing.
70. Kohl, p.225.
71. *King's County Chronicle*, 12 April 1854.
72. Samuel Carter Hall, *Ireland: Its scenery character and history* (1841).
73. Ian Maxwell, *Everyday Life in Nineteenth Century Ireland* (2011); Robbins, Joseph, *The Lost Children: A Study of Charity Children in Ireland 1700–1900*.
74. Kohl, p.278.
75. Thomas Campbell Foster, *Letters on the condition of the people of Ireland* (1846).
76. Sir Francis Head (1793–1875), *A Fortnight in Ireland* (1852), p.179. Known as 'Galloping Head', he was Lieutenant-Governor of Upper Canada during the rebellion of 1837 before becoming a Poor Law Commissioner in Kent.
77. Sidney Godolphin Osborne, *Gleanings from the West of Ireland*, (1850), p.107.
78. Theresa Cornwallis West, *A Summer Visit to Ireland in 1846* (1847), p.43.
79. *Freeman's Journal*, 11 September 1840.
80. Letter dated 17 December 1846 Mr N.M. Cummins, a justice of the peace, to the Duke of Wellington, *The Great Famine: Studies in Irish History 1845–52*, ed. T. Desmond and T. Desmond Williams.
81. Asenath Nicholson, *Annals of the Famine in Ireland* in 1847, 1848, 1849, p.43.
82. Osborne, p.79.
83. John East, *Glimpses of Ireland in 1847*, pp.17–19.

84. Osborne, p.6.
85. T. Martin, Life of the Prince Consort, vols 1–5 (London, 1875–79), vol. 11, p.192.
86. Sir Arthur Helps, Leaves from the Journal of Our Life in the Highlands, (1868), p.227.
87. *Belfast News-Letter*, 6 August 1849.
88. S.J. Conolly, 'Like an old cathedral city: Belfast welcomes Queen Victoria', August 1849, *Urban History*, vol. 29, no. 4 (2012).
89. Helps, p.241.
90. *Belfast News-Letter*, 14 August 1849.
91. James Loughlin, 'Allegiance and Illusion: Queen Victoria's Irish Visit of 1849', *History* vol. 87, no. 288 (October 2002).
92. William Stevens Balch, *Ireland as I saw it: the character, condition and prospects of its people* (1850), p.247.
93. Sidney Godolphin Osborne, *Gleanings in the West of Ireland*, p.29.
94. James Hack Tuke, 'A Visit to Connaught in the Autumn of 1847', pp.24–26, in Christine Kinealy, *A Death-Dealing Famine: The Great Hunger in Ireland* (1997).
95. *Anglo-Celt*, 15 April 1852.
96. Coulter, p.56.
97. James Macaulay, p.39.
98. John Forbes, p.202.
99. Donald Harman Akenson, *The Irish Diaspora* (1996).
100. Jules de Lasteyrie, *Ireland in 1862* (1863).
101. William Stevens Balch, *Ireland, as I saw it: the character, condition, and prospects of the people* (1850), p.166.
102. D. George Boyce, *Nationalism in Ireland* (1982).
103. Macaulay, pp.308–309.
104. Grousset, p.130.
105. Marie Anne de Bovet, *Three Months' Tour in Ireland* (1891), p.164.
106. Bernard H. Becker, *Disturbed Ireland: Being the Letters written during the Winter of 1880–81* (1881), p.18.
107. McDougall, p.83.
108. *Irish Times*, 20 June 1859 quoted from the *Edinburgh Review*.
109. Kohl, p.334.
110. James Macaulay, p.30.
111. Thackeray, p.64.
112. Kohl, p.344.

113. Colin Rynne, *Industrial Ireland 1750–1930: An Archaeology* (2006), pp.424–425.
114. Colum McCabe, 'History of the Town Gas Industry in Ireland, 1823–1980', *Dublin Historical Record*, vol. 45, no. 1 (Spring 1992).
115. Thackeray, p.21.
116. Ritchie, p.172.
117. *Ireland Picturesque and Romantic*, pp.172–173.
118. Coulter, p.58.
119. Grousset, p.19.
120. Margaret Dixon McDougall, *Letters of Norah on Her Tour Through Ireland* (1882), p.18.
121. Sir Charles Cameron, p.170.
122. Coulter, p.135.
123. Dr John Forbes, p.66.
124. Inglis, p.294.
125. *Mr and Mrs Hall's Ireland*, p.12.
126. Nicholson, p.182.
127. There was short-term growth immediately after the famine in most towns (evident in the 1851 census) reflecting short-distance migration, but this left little legacy in an age of high emigration.
128. Samuel Smiles, *Men of Invention and Industry*, 1884.
129. *Ireland Picturesque and Romantic* (1838): p.55, Leitch Ritchie.
130. *Mr and Mrs Hall's Ireland*, p.343.
131. *Letters from Ireland* (1886).
132. Reverend William Murphy O'Hanlon's in his *Walks Among the Poor of Belfast* (1853), p.1.
133. O'Hanlon, p.22.
134. *Cork Constitution*, 30 March 1865.
135. *Freeman's Journal*, 14 February 1878.
136. James Johnson, *A Tour in Ireland: With Meditations and Reflections*, p.352.
137. *The Southern Patriot*, 28 February 1844.
138. *Mr and Mrs Hall's Ireland*, pp.432–535.
139. John Morphy, *Recollections of a Visit to Great Britain and Ireland in the Summer of 1862*, p.11.
140. Mrs S.C. Hall, *Ireland: Its Scenery, Character*, &c, vol. 3, p.63.
141. *Freeman's Journal*, 15 July 1871.

142. *Belfast Telegraph*, 13 October 1877.

143. Jonathan Bardon, pp.332–333.

144. *Newry Telegraph*, 25 September 1855.

145. Joseph Lee, *Railway Labour in Ireland, 1833–1856*, Saothar, vol. 5 (May 1979).

146. *Leinster Report*, 22 October 1898.

147. Anthony Trollope, *An Autobiography* (1883), p.86.

148. William Stevens Balch, *Ireland, as I saw it: the character, condition, and prospects of the people* (1850), p.245.

149. *Carlow Sentinel*, 19 November 1870.

150. *Belfast News-Letter, Monday* 9 August 1852.

151. Thackeray, p.96.

152. *Kings County Chronicle*, 26 March 1851.

153. *Belfast Telegraph*, Saturday, 24 June 1882.

154. *Southern Reporter and Cork Commercial Courier*, Thursday, 13 February 1862.

155. *Northern Whig*, Friday, 3 March 1876.

156. *Mr and Mrs Hall's Ireland*, p.9.

157. Kohl, p.171.

158. Beverly A. Smith, 'The Irish General Prisons Board, 1877–1885', in the *Irish Jurist*, vol. 14 (1980).

159. Ibid.

160. Maria Luddy, 'Women of the Pave: Prostitution in Ireland', *History Ireland*, vol. 16, no. 3 (2008) and *Prostitution and Irish Society, 1800–1940* (Cambridge, 2007).

161. *Kilkenny Journal and Leinster Commercial and Literary Advertiser*, 23 October 1872.

162. *Dublin Weekly News*, 24 October 1874.

163. *Irish Times*, 26 January 1882.

164. William Stevens Balch, p.70.

165. Sir Charles Cameron, p.171.

166. Charlotte Elizabeth, pp.251–254.

167. S.M. Hussey, *The Reminiscences of an Irish Land Agent* (1904), pp.102–103.

168. Kohl, p.94.

169. Colm Kerrigan, The Social Impact of the Irish Temperance Movement, 1838–45, *Irish Economic and Social History*, vol. 14 (1987).

170. James Johnson, *A Tour in Ireland: With Meditations and Reflections*, p.15.
171. De Bovet, p.179.
172. Tricia Cusack, '"This pernicious tea drinking habit": Women, Tea, and Respectability in Nineteenth-Century Ireland', *The Canadian Journal of Irish Studies*, vol. 41.
173. S.M. Hussey, p.102.
174. *Cork Examiner*, 10 April 1844. Mr and Mrs Hall Ireland: Its Scenery, Character and History (1843)
175. *Dublin Evening* Post, 20 April 1843.
176. Dr John Forbes, *Memorandums of a Tour in Ireland*, p.173.
177. *Limerick and Clare Examiner*, Monday, 23 August 1852.
178. *Carlow Post*, Saturday, 6 April 1867.
179. Margaret Dixon McDougall, p.196; De Tocqueville, p.48.
180. Ibid., p.11.
181. *Belfast Weekly News*, 29 July 1876.
182. O'Brien, Richard Barry, *The Life of Lord Russell of Killowen*, (1902) p.23.
183. De Bovet, p.302.
184. Rev. W.M. O'Hanlon, *Walks Among the Poor of Belfast* (1853), p.3.
185. Charlotte Elizabeth, pp.39–40.
186. *Ireland Picturesque and Romantic*, pp.70–71.
187. De Bovet, *Three Months' Tour in Ireland* (1891), p.236.
188. *Wicklow People*, 21 July 1894.
189. *Mr and Mrs Hall*, p.426.
190. *Banner of Ulster*, 7 November 1848; Robbins, Joseph, *The Lost Children: A Study of Charity Children in Ireland 1700–1900*.
191. *Newry Telegraph*, 23 July 1840.
192. Second Report of the Irish Education Commissioners, June 1835.
193. A.M. Sullivan, pp.28-29 *Ireland: Political Sketches and Personal Reminiscences of thirty years of Irish public life*.
194. De Bovet, p.51.
195. Margret O hOgartaigh, 'A Quiet Revolution: Women and Second Level Education in Ireland, 1878–92', *New Hibernia Review*, vol. 13 (Summer 2009); Anne V. O'Connor, 'Influences Affecting Girls' Secondary Education in Ireland, 1860–1910', *Archivium Hibernicum*, vol. 41 (1986).
196. *Dublin Daily Nation*, Tuesday, 19 December 1899.
197. James Macaulay, p.386.

198. New Ireland, (1877) Alexander Martin Sullivan (1829–1884) was an Irish nationalist politician, lawyer and journalist.
199. Under the Intermediate Act of 1878 Irish was assigned 600 marks compared with 1,000 marks for Greek, Latin and English. French and German merited 700 marks.
200. It was not until 1904 that permission was granted for the implantation of bilingual programmes in Irish-speaking areas.
201. Correspondence between the Irish Executive and the Commission of Education in Ireland with respect to the teaching of Irish in the Irish National Schools (1884).
202. Gearoid O Tuathaigh, Language and Identities in the *Cambridge Social History of Modern Ireland*.
203. *Evening Herald*, 4 July 1896.
204. *Drogheda Independent*, 9 December 1899.
205. *Cork Daily Herald*, 11 April 1899.
206. Thomas E. Jordon, 'The Quality of Life in Victorian Ireland, 1831–1901', *New Hibernia Review*, vol. 4 no. 1 (Spring 2000).
207. *Derry Journal*, 5 October 1900.
208. *Dublin Medical Press*, 3 May 1865.
209. *Charter and Bye Laws of the Coombe Lying-in Hospital* (Dublin, 1867).
210. *Belfast News-Letter*, 6 November 1846.
211. *Cork Constitution*, 24 June 1862.
212. *Lewis Topographical Dictionary*.
213. Kohl, p.173.
214. This was not fully understood until 1909 when Charles Nicolle, director of the Institut Pasteur in Tunis, made the connection.
215. This role was gradually subsumed into the poor law unions and eventually local government.
216. *Freeman's Journal*, 20 September 1848.
217. D.A. Chart, *The Public Health of Ireland 1801–1911*.
218. The *Carrickfergus Advertiser*, Friday, 16 September 1892.
219. *Irish Times*, 8 June 1859.
220. *Irish News and Belfast Morning News*, Tuesday, 6 July 1897.
221. *Belfast News-Letter*, Monday, 13 October 1851.
222. *Belfast News-Letter*, Saturday, 15 October 1898.
223. Thackeray, The Roundabout Papers, *The Cornhill Magazine*, vol. 2, p.501.

224. Joseph Lee, 'Railway Labour in Ireland, 1833–1856', *Saothar*, vol. 5 (May 1979).

225. Thackeray, *Irish Sketchbook*, p.12; Khol, p.143.

226. Born Carlo Bianconi in Costa Masnaga, Italy, in 1786, moved to Ireland in 1802.

227. Macaulay, pp.63–76.

228. J.G. Kohl, p.17.

229. Sir Francis Head, p.169.

230. Kohl, p.325.

231. Grousset, p.13.

232. Becker, p.33.

233. Kohl, p.59.

234. Teresa Cornwallis West, *A Summer Visit to Ireland in 1846* (London 1847), p.5.

235. Jonathan Bardon, *History of Ulster*, pp.263–264.

236. Jonathan Bardon, p.263.

237. *Freeman's Journal*, 28 January 1848.

238. *Northern Standard*, 23 July 1842.

239. William Le Fanu, *Seventy Years of Irish Life* (1893).

240. *Cork Examiner*, 28 March 1845 [Carlow Sentinel].

241. Joseph Lee, *Railway Labour in Ireland, 1833–1856*, Saothar, vol. 5 (May 1979).

242. *Dublin Evening Packet and Correspondent*, Thursday, 12 October 1848.

243. Joseph Lee, *Railway Labour in Ireland, 1833–1856*, Saothar, vol. 5 (May 1979).

244. J. Morphy, *Recollections of a visit to Great Britain and Ireland in the summer of 1862*, p.76.

245. *The Dublin Penny Journal*, 26 December 1835.

246. W.H. Richardson, *Notes of A Tour in the North and North-West of Ireland* (Leicester, August 1880), p.28.

247. Margaret Dixon McDougall, *The Letters of 'Norah' on her Tour Through Ireland*, 1882, p.56.

248. In 1911 Dublin was still twenty-five minutes behind London, and it was only on 1 October 1916 that Greenwich Mean Time was extended to Ireland under the Time (Ireland) Act.

249. *Northern Standard*, 5 June 1852.

250. *Enniskillen Chronicle and Erne Packet*, 27 March 1882.

251. *Dublin Evening Post*, 10 April 1847.

252. *Dublin Daily Express*, Friday, 27 August 1858.

253. *Downshire Protestant*, Friday, 3 September 1858.

254. Paschal Grousset 20-21, *Larne Times*, 23 September 1899.

255. *Coleraine Chronicle*, 16 December 1899.

256. Kohl, pp.195–196.

257. Kohl, p.96.

258. De Bovet, p.62.

259. *Dublin Evening Mail*, Monday, 13 November 1865.

260. *The Banner of Ulster*, 4 June, 1859.

261. 'Observer', *Belfast Telegraph*, 14 April 1891.

262. *Dublin Weekly News*, 9 March 1850.

263. *Irish News and Belfast Morning News*, 4 September 1899.

264. *Irish Society*, 17 May 1890.

265. *Irish Society*, 14 October 1893.

266. *Irish Independent*, 29 May 1899, from an article in the *Morning Herald*.

267. *Wexford People*, 17 January 1885.

268. *The Londonderry Sentinel*, 29 January 1889.

269. *Dublin Daily Nation*, 5 April 1900.

270. *Sligo Champion*, 7 April 1900.

271. *Weekly Irish Times*, 26 January 1901.

272. *Belfast News-Letter*, 24 January 1901.

273. *Irish News and Belfast Morning News*, Thursday, 24 January 1901.

274. *Cork Examiner*, 4 January 1901.

275. *Irish News and Belfast Morning News*, 24 January 1901.

Index